ECON.   ~~1765~~
         1195

D1261607

THE FED

**INSIDE THE FEDERAL RESERVE,
THE SECRET POWER CENTER THAT
CONTROLS THE AMERICAN ECONOMY**

MAXWELL NEWTON

**Times
BOOKS**

Acknowledgment is made to the following:

The excerpt from "Monetary Policy: Theory and Practice" by Milton Friedman from *Journal of Money, Credit, and Banking,* vol. 14 (February 1982), pp. 98–118 is reprinted by permission. Copyright © 1982 by the Ohio State University Press.

The excerpt from "The Agony of the Federal Reserve" by Sanford Rose from his July 1974 article in *Fortune* is reprinted by permission. Copyright © 1974 by *Fortune.*

The excerpt from "A New Chairman at the Fed" by Milton Friedman is from his February 2, 1970, article in *Newsweek.* Copyright © 1970 by Newsweek, Inc. All Rights Reserved. Reprinted by permission.

Published by TIMES BOOKS, a division of
The New York Times Book Co., Inc.
Three Park Avenue, New York, N.Y. 10016

Published simultaneously in Canada by
Fitzhenry & Whiteside, Ltd., Toronto

Copyright © 1983 by Maxwell Newton

All rights reserved. No part of this book may be
reproduced in any form or by any electronic
or mechanical means, including information storage
and retrieval systems, without permission in writing
from the publisher, except by a reviewer who may
quote brief passages in a review.

Library of Congress Cataloging in Publication Data

Newton, Maxwell.
  The Fed: inside the Federal Reserve, the secret
power center that controls the American economy.

  Includes index.
  1. Board of Governors of the Federal Reserve System
(U.S.) 2. Monetary policy—United States. 3. United
States—Economic conditions—1971-   . I. Title.
HG2565.N44   1982   332.1'1'0973   81–84900
ISBN 0–8129–1012–5

Designed by Doris Borowsky

Manufactured in the United States of America

83 84 85 86 5 4 3 2 1

To Olivia
It Happened—One Day at a Time

ACKNOWLEDGMENTS

Although I have been a financial and political journalist for twenty-five years, it was a frightful shock to me when I realized what an appalling job it is to sit down and write, revise, and actually complete a book.

Certainly I would never have completed it had I not had to help me the constant encouragement, nagging, criticism, and honest professionalism of Edward T. Chase, Senior Vice-President of The New York Times Book Company.

Nor would I have had the opportunity to be asked to do this job had it not been for the invitation extended to me by Rupert Murdoch, chairman of News America Corporation, to come to work for him in the United States. He generously allowed me to go ahead with the composition of this book once the offer to do it had been made.

A quarter of a century of dealing with politicians and government officials has induced in me a scepticism about their professed motives and a disregard for their sly tactics. So I thank a generation of bureaucrats whom I have known for showing me through their actions just how dangerous they are.

In the United States I found a number of independent economists whom I have been able to know and respect. These men and women have discovered that the theories and practices of what is loosely called "monetarism" give the free world its best chance of holding on to the fragments of freedom still left. Among those whom I have been privileged to know in America are David Meiselman, professor of economics and dean of the Graduate School of Business Administration, Virginia Polytechnic Institute, Blacksburg; Karl Brunner, director of the Center for Research in Government Policy and Business, Graduate School of Management, University of Rochester, New York; Allan Meltzer, professor of economics at the Graduate School of Industrial Administration, Carnegie Mellon University, Pittsburgh, Pennsylvania; Dr. Beryl Sprinkel, under secretary for monetary affairs, United States Treasury; Leif Olsen, chief economist, Citibank; James Lothian of the Citibank economics department; and Harvey Seigal of Citibank, who first alerted me to Arthur Burns.

The work of Milton Friedman and Anna Schwartz pervades all such thinking, and no one who works in this field will come anywhere near understanding without being very closely touched by their ideas.

The Fed, alas, by its very nature, is a tyrannical and secretive, self-perpetuating bureaucracy. In its history it has all too often served as an enemy of freedom in America. There is much more at stake in the theories of "monetarism" than a mere method of analysis of economic fluctuations. That is why the Fed has been so antagonistic to the ideas of the economists whose names are on this page. I leave it to the reader to judge the truth and pertinency of my analysis. It bears directly on the well-being of us all.

CONTENTS

Note to the Reader

I have tried to minimize the use of technical terminology, but certain terms that recur deserve a definition at the outset. Some of the key words and terms are listed below:

1. *The monetary base* consists of (1) the reserve accounts of financial institutions (banks, savings banks, savings and loan associations, credit unions, etc.) with the Federal Reserve banks; and (2) currency in circulation. The major source of the monetary base is Federal Reserve credit.

2. *Federal Reserve credit* is the other side of the Federal Reserve's balance sheet from the monetary base. It consists of the Fed's investments in securities and in loans to financial institutions. It is "what the Fed does with the banks' reserve money."

Simplified Fed Balance Sheet

The following simplified version of the Federal Reserve's balance sheet was published by Anatole Balbach in the April 1981 issue of the St. Louis Fed *Review.*

Assets	*Liabilities*
	As of November 5, 1980
Gold Certificates: $11.2 billion	Monetary Base:
Foreign Currencies: $3.2 billion	(a) Deposits of
Federal Reserve Credit:	Financial Institutions:
(a) Security Holdings:	$33.2 billion
$130.7 billion	(b) Federal Reserve Notes:
(b) Loans to Financial	$119.4 billion
Institutions: $3.4 billion	Treasury Deposits: $3.1 billion
(c) Float: $5.2 billion	Foreign Central Bank
Other Assets: $7.2 billion	Deposits: $0.2 billion
	Other Liabilities
	and Capital: $4.9 billion

3. *The Fed can manipulate the size of the monetary base* very easily by engaging in open market operations, which involve buying or selling securities (bonds, bills, etc.) that are included in Federal Reserve credit.

4. *Money M1* is the stock of assets that people generally accept in payment for goods and services. It includes currency held by the nonbank public, demand deposits at commercial banks, and other checkable deposits of all depository institutions (such as the thrifts and credit unions) plus traveler's checks.

5. *Money M2* consists of M1 *plus* overnight repurchase agreements (whereby a bank sells an asset to a customer and agrees to buy it back next day—a means of evading Federal Reserve controls as well as of making use of otherwise idle overnight cash balances); *plus* Eurodollars, held by the banks (bank deposits of dollars, lodged in banks outside the United States); *plus* money market mutual fund shares *plus* savings deposits and small-time deposits at commercial banks and thrift institutions.

6. *M3* consists of M2 plus large time deposits and term repurchase agreements at commercial banks and thrift institutions.

7. *L* consists of M3 plus other liquid assets.

The table on page viii shows the measures for M1, M2, M3, and L for recent years.

8. *Velocity of money* is the relationship between the money stock (M1) and the gross national product—the sum of all the goods and services produced in the course of a year. The velocity of money has been very stable over time, tending to rise by about 3½ percent a year. The tables of the velocity of money are shown on page 267.

9. *The money multiplier* is the relationship between the monetary base and the money stock (usually expressed as the relationship of the monetary base to M1). This is also a very constant relationship, indicating that the Federal Reserve, by manipulating the level of the monetary base (through buying or selling securities from its holdings of cash and securities), can directly influence the level of the money stock.

The average level of the M1 money multiplier is set out on page xiv. It is taken from the article written by Anatole Balbach in the St. Louis Fed *Review* of April 1981.

[Averages of daily figures; billions of dollars, seasonally adjusted]

	Period	1974: Dec.	1975: Dec.	1976: Dec.	1977: Dec.	1978: Dec.	1979: Dec.	1980: Dec.	1981: Dec.
M1	Sum of currency, demand deposits, travelers' checks, and other checkable deposits (OCD) at banks and thrift institutions	278.0	291.8	311.1	336.4	364.2	390.5	415.6	441.9
M2	M1 plus overnight RPs and Eurodollars, MMMF shares, and small time deposits at commercial banks and thrift institutions.	908.0	1,024.4	1,169.4	1,296.4	1,404.2	1,525.2	1,669.4	1,842.0
M3	M2 plus large time deposits and term RPs at commercial banks and thrift institutions	1,060.4	1,163.0	1,302.3	1,462.5	1,625.9	1,775.6	1,965.1	2,187.4
L	M3 plus other liquid assets	1,246.0	1,373.5	1,528.9	1,722.7	1,936.8	2,151.7	2,378.4	
Percent change from year or 6 months earlier	M1	4.4	5.0	6.6	8.1	8.3	7.2	6.4	6.3
	M2	5.6	12.8	14.2	10.9	8.3	8.6	9.5	10.3
	M3	8.4	9.7	12.0	12.3	11.2	9.2	10.7	11.3

10. *The Desk* is the shorthand description of the New York Federal Reserve Bank's Open Market Operations Department, which conducts the hundreds of billions of transactions in selling and buying bonds, bills, etc., during the course of the year. Milton Friedman estimates the Desk buys and sells about $1,600 billion in securities each year, or about $32 billion a week, of total sales and purchases. This massive amount of buying and selling traffic is known as churning.

11. *The federal funds rate* is the rate of interest banks charge each

Year	Average Level of M1-B (M1) Multiplier
1970	2.913
1971	2.881
1972	2.875
1973	2.852
1974	2.763
1975	2.685
1976	2.636
1977	2.622
1978	2.596
1979	2.583
1980	2.543

1970–79 average annual decline 0.9%

other for overnight money that can be used to satisfy reserve requirements with the Fed. It has come to be an important rate of interest because for the whole period up to October 1979, the Fed formally tried to limit the variations of the federal funds rate as a key element in its monetary policy. In modified form, this practice continues to be an important element in the Fed's operations.

12. *The discount rate* is the rate at which the Federal Reserve will lend money to banks and other financial institutions, usually for the purpose of helping them meet their reserve requirements with the Fed.

1 The Fed—The Unique Source of America's Financial Crisis

Within four weeks of the 1982 mid-term elections the Federal Reserve, America's central bank, announced a series of major policy moves that injected a new element into the campaign. Interest rates, which had been collapsing since the end of June, fell even more quickly. Money supply growth, which had been slow for most of 1982 after a boomlet in January, accelerated. The stock markets boomed and the Dow Jones Industrial Average burst through 1000. The prime rate fell from 13½ percent to 12 percent. Mortgage rates tumbled by as much as one and a half percentage points in a single move. Rates on auto loans were cut by three percentage points by the Bank of New York on a single day. America's "independent" central bank proved yet again how deeply it was involved in the political process.

Paul Volcker, chairman of the Federal Reserve, thus came galloping to the rescue of Ronald Reagan and of a Republican administration increasingly desperate in the closing weeks of the 1982 campaign for some powerful signal that "Reaganomics" would work for the benefit of America.

Volcker had been appointed by the Carter administration, as had three others of the seven members of the Federal Reserve Board. Volcker had given Carter an explosive growth of money in the run up to the 1980 presidential elections. Now he was giving a worried Ronald Reagan an accelerated money growth, not so extreme as that for Carter, but sufficient to contribute significantly to a stock market boom and a precipitous fall in interest rates. The whole affair was brilliantly managed, a study in successful propaganda and administrative dexterity that would be a lesson for any student of politics.

3

On Tuesday, October 5, 1982, the Federal Open Market Committee, the supreme policy-making body of the Federal Reserve System, met in Washington. For the preceding two months, the Federal Reserve had managed to keep the federal funds interest rate (the rate on overnight loans made between banks and a crucial indicator of the cost of credit throughout the nation) at 10 percent. On Wednesday, October 6, the federal funds rate dropped sharply and was almost immediately stabilized at 9½ percent.

At the same time, prodigious leaks from Washington to the Dow Jones News Service, to the *Wall Street Journal,* and to *The Washington Post* stated that the Federal Reserve had decided at its Tuesday meeting to ignore a prospective rise in the money supply above its own accepted and publicly announced "targets." This news, leaked to these privileged media in contravention of the Federal Reserve's own established principles of releasing details of FOMC meetings a month afterward, came as a tremendous relief to the financial markets.

Long before the Fed stepped in to save Ronald Reagan on October 5, worried officials in the U.S. Treasury and concerned analysts in the banks and in the financial markets knew that there was most likely going to be a very big rise in the money supply announced Friday October 15. That big rise would put the money supply M1 way over the Fed's own target levels and in normal circumstances would have had the effect of depressing the financial markets (because of their fear of subsequent inflation) and of thus tending to depress the prices of financial securities—and hence to raise interest rates. The big expected rise in money supply of October 15 was the result of a "bunching" of social security payments that was not capable of being "smoothed out" by the Fed's own statistical procedures.

Knowledge of the big October 15 "money bulge" was widely disseminated in the financial markets and in the media. What was not known was how the Federal Reserve would handle the problem. Certainly, within the administration in Washington, facing bad election prospects after two tumultuous years, the prospect of a fall in financial securities' prices was horrible.

Miraculously, the Fed found the answer. First, the federal funds

4

rate was allowed to collapse on Wednesday, October 6. It briefly went down to 8½ percent, sending a signal to the financial markets that something big was about to happen. On Thursday, October 7, the federal funds rate was allowed to stay down around 9½ percent. Secondly, the Fed leaked to a joyous U.S. financial community that it would disregard the prospective October 15 money bulge announcement and would in fact disregard money stock as any sort of policy guide for the time being. The specious explanation was offered —and greedily accepted by a credulous financial community—that "financial innovations" had made money M1 less relevant as a guide for money policy. The Fed thus signaled that it would not take any action to offset the inflationary effects of above-target money growth "for the time being." Finally, the Fed announced on Friday, October 8, that it would reduce the discount rate (at which banks are allowed to borrow from the Federal Reserve) from 10 percent to 9½ percent. To no one's surprise, interest rates fell sharply on the news of these remarkable actions and statements; stock prices boomed; there was a rash of pronouncements from economists that "monetarism is dead."

Thus was it possible for a tiny group of appointed officials, the "independent" Fed, a majority of them economists and the prevailing group former Fed officials steeped in the traditions and practices of the central bank, nearly seventy years old at the time, to make major policy changes. No one knows whether these changes were made after consultation with President Reagan. They were certainly not made after any consultation with his advisers in the U.S. Treasury. Quite likely, the changes were in response to pressures felt by the Fed officials themselves.

What could such pressures be? Paul Volcker, the chairman of the Fed since August 1979, was to face the end of his first term in August 1983. It would hardly do his cause any harm to do a really big favor for the president in October 1982.

Ever since the Congress—the legal master of the Federal Reserve —had imposed statutory targets for money growth on the central bank in 1975, the Fed had fought, twisted, and turned to be free of the need to adjust its policy lines so as to meet these targets. "Targeting" removed too much discretionary power from Fed officials. What is more, there had recently been an increasingly raucous series of demands from within the Reagan administration for measures to cut down still further on the discretion of Fed officials.

The *Economic Report of the President, February 1982,* written by the Council of Economic Advisers in Washington, had called for the implementation of a constitutional amendment under which the Federal Reserve would be bound by the Constitution to permit a preset, more or less constant, expansion of money.

Another threat to the discretionary power of Fed officials had emerged during 1982, with a series of announcements from the U.S. Treasury of a study being conducted within that department on the future conduct of monetary policy. Leaks and statements from the Treasury indicated a desire by officials in that department to reduce the freedom of discretion of Fed officials. There were even suggestions that the Federal Reserve should be downgraded to a lower status, indeed a sub-department of the Treasury Department itself, subject to the direct power of the president.

Against this background, there was much to be gained from an attempt by Fed officials to short-circuit this criticism and to show how valuable the Fed could be to the administration in its existing form and with its existing powers.

But the Fed did not only give. It also received. As part of the propaganda program aimed at defusing the possible impact of the October 15 money supply announcement, as I said above, the Fed took unto itself the right to announce that money M1 was no longer a relevant guide for monetary policy. "Financial innovations" had rendered this particular measure of money irrelevant, so we were told. The advent of new forms of bank deposit instruments (to compete with money market funds) and the timely maturity of about $50 billion in All-Savers certificates were cited as reasons for ignoring movements in M1 as a guide to policy "for the time being."

For at least a year before October 5, senior Fed officials—notably the governor of the New York Fed, Mr. Anthony Solomon—had been criticizing the relevance of money M1 as a guide to monetary policy. With a delicious sense of timing and of maximizing political impact, the Fed's actions on Tuesday, October 5 and in the subsequent days drove a coach and four through money M1 and indeed through the whole apparatus of "targeting," built up so laboriously by Congress and by friends of Congress in the preceding decade. There could have been no more brilliant example of the ability of Fed officials to survive, to maintain their own discretionary power, and to defeat the intentions of reformers.

What Is Important—Fed "Independence" or Sound Policy-Making?

In a tradition alien to the fundamentals of American democracy, the officials of the nation's central bank have succeeded more than once in placing their own priorities of survival and discretionary power over and above the long-term interests of America.

In truth, the Federal Reserve, unlike the Supreme Court, to which some of its officials attempt to compare it, operates under no rule of law. While the Federal Reserve is legally answerable to Congress, my story shows that over time Fed officials have exerted tremendous efforts to evade the laws passed by Congress in relation to the Fed. Nor does the Federal Reserve have any "adjudicatory" responsibilities, as one of its most ambitious chairmen, Arthur Burns, tried to argue. The Fed does not sit in judgment; it does not stand apart from the process of administration.

As the example of October 5, 1982, shows, the Federal Reserve is part and parcel of the political process of America. It is a group of nonelected officials who have been granted virtually permanent job security. The members of the Federal Reserve Board are appointed for fourteen years at a time. Fed officials effectively have permanent jobs. The greatest threat to an aspiring young official in America's central banks is to speak out of turn, to cast a critical eye on past Fed actions and current Fed policies. Indeed, America has reached the point where the president of the United States can send men to war and can rain bombs on nations—but he cannot send a message to the Federal Reserve demanding that what he wants done be done. The officials of the Federal Reserve have achieved the prerogative of the harlot through the ages—power without responsibility—to use the phraseology so frequently charged against the press.

7

Not surprisingly, the Federal Reserve has proven a highly destructive force in the economic and financial affairs of America. It has been the unique source of America's financial crisis today.

Since 1978 the United States has been passing through a major financial convulsion as the nation has struggled to overcome the effects of runaway inflation, stagnating production, rising unemployment, declining investment, and unprecedented interest rates. In the process there has been a massive loss of production.

In terms of 1982 prices, the loss of the production America might otherwise have expected to enjoy is running at some $350 billion a year. If America had not lost that huge volume of output, there would have been little talk of balancing budgets, of decaying industries. There would have been far less concern about "my fair share" of the nation's wealth and far more joy in the ever-expanding material possibilities America has always offered its people.

Between 1970 and 1974 the real gross national product of the United States rose 15 percent, between 1974 and 1978 it rose another 15 percent; but between 1978 and 1982 the real gross national product will have grown a meager 3 percent.

The difference, 12 percent of the current value of the U.S. gross national product, is worth $350 billion a year. Out of that, every employed American could have expected an additional $1,500 a year in average earnings. The federal government could have expected an additional $70 billion in revenues; corporations could have made an additional $25 billion in profits.

Why has this enormous loss of output occurred? It has occurred because America in 1978 ran into a major inflationary crisis. Between 1976 and 1978 the rise in consumer prices jumped from 4.8 percent to 9 percent. By 1979 the nation was well into double-digit inflation, with consumer prices rising 13.3 percent.

And what was the source of this crisis, which showed itself in fantastic interest rates, collapsing investment, rising unemployment, and a pervasive fear of a looming financial collapse reminiscent of the ghastly failure of the 1930's?

Ultimately America's financial crisis of 1978–82 had its origins in the failure of the nation's central bank—the Federal Reserve. The institution uniquely charged with special privileges to safeguard the nation's money proved to be an engine of inflation, a profligate generator of excessive money. The Fed debased America's money. As a result, the integrity of the nation's financial system was put at risk and the stability of the nation's economy endangered.

The Nation Has No Faith in Its Central Bank

By now the Fed is no longer seen as the ultimate repository of the stability of America's money. Rather, it is feared for the destruction it can wreak.

During 1981 the disintegration of confidence by the financial markets in the future value of the dollar was expressed in stark terms. On two occasions, from February through April and from October through January 1982, the money supply rose at a very high rate. The reaction of the financial markets was speedy and unmistakable. On each occasion, within about three weeks of the beginning of the uptrend in money growth, interest rates rose sharply and continued to rise until it was clear the boom in money growth had been arrested. There could be no clearer indication of the decline of confidence among the financial markets.

In the past, when inflation was not so deeply ingrained into the thinking of all those associated with financial markets in America, a rise in the supply of money would have led to a *decline* in interest rates because of confidence that any substantial increase in money growth would be reversed. This confidence was in turn the tangible expression of a widespread belief that a dollar tomorrow would be worth as much as a dollar today. It was the expression of a deep-seated conviction, bred in a long period of peacetime price stability in America, that any movements away from the long-term trend in money and prices would be moderate and of short duration.

Once the immediate postwar adjustments following World War II were complete, a long period of price stability set in. Although there was some acceleration of price increases during the late 1960's, the whole period between 1950 and 1970 saw consumer prices in America rise by just over 60 percent—well under 3 percent a year. Since 1970, price increases have rapidly accelerated, and in the eleven years ended 1981, consumer prices rose 132 percent, about 8 percent a year, or some *three times* as fast as in the previous twenty years.

The inflation was gradually reflected in a complete change in the level of interest rates. From 1910 to 1968 the interest yield on a Treasury bond in the United States did not exceed 5 percent, with the exception of one year, 1920. The yield on a Treasury bill exceeded 5 percent only twice over that period, in 1920 and in 1929.

After 1968 the yield on a long-term U.S. Treasury bond never went *below* 5 percent. It rose progressively, breaking 7 percent in 1973, 8 percent in 1974, 9 percent in 1979, 11 percent in 1980, and 14 percent in 1981.

"Inflationary expectations" became a dominant factor, indeed *the* dominant factor, in American financial markets. The markets themselves began to acquire the characteristics of what by the standards of the previous half century looked like perverse neurotic behavior. When the supply of money rose, interest rates rose, defying the experience of the past; when money supply fell or ceased to grow (indicating the prospect of lower inflation), interest rates fell. Between April and October 1981, money supply remained stable for six months. Between May and December, in response, the three-month Treasury bill yield dropped from 16.3 to 10.9 percent—a decline of *one third* in seven months. As markets have become more and more unsettled, fluctuations in interest rates have become more violent, surpassing anything in the peacetime experience of the nation.

In America one institution, more than any other, controls the movement of money, prices, and the economy. That institution is America's central bank, the Federal Reserve. The role of the Fed in the financial catastrophe that has overtaken America is the dominant one. Without its active leadership in providing excessive supplies of money, inflation in America could never have begun. Without the continued provision of excess supplies of money, it could never have continued. And inflation has reached unprecedented heights in the last ten years.

Since 1979 we have had increasing instability in the financial markets. Interest rates and the rate of growth of money have fluctuated ever more widely. This extreme variability of major elements in the nation's finances has further unsettled planning, exaggerating the already dangerously excessive dependence on short-term financing and encouraging a myopia in all corporate and individual financial plans.

The New York brokerage firm of Drexel Burnham Lambert pointed out in March 1982 that over the last ten years, the average annual variability of the interest rate on commercial paper was just over 28 percent. This means that during the course of an average year over the last ten years, the commercial paper interest rate varied plus or minus 28 percent from its average. In the last two years the variability of the commercial paper rate has been 42 percent.

This increased variability of interest rates could be deemed acceptable had it been accompanied by greater stability in the growth path of the money supply—the driving force behind the growth of America's economy. But money supply growth has also fluctuated wildly, indicating a failure of management so deep as to cast doubt on the possibility of improvement without a major upheaval in the whole administrative structure of the Federal Reserve.

By now confidence has been so reduced that the financial markets will not believe that any increase in the money supply is of benefit to them. They have had their faith in the credibility of the central bank crushed. Hence, management of the nation's economic affairs has become excruciatingly difficult. Because a rise in the money supply causes an almost immediate reaction in higher interest rates, the Federal Reserve can reduce interest rates only by holding down the rate of growth of money. But holding down the rate of growth of money means that the nation's economy is confined in a financial straitjacket until inflation is eradicated.

Meanwhile, ever higher rates of inflation—the so-called inflation ratchet—have led to higher and higher interest rates. In turn, this meant less and less money available for long-term investment. Potential lenders were scared away from lending for long periods.

Corporations' profitability was eroded by their inability to find credit needed for modernization of their plants. Their profits were overstated for taxation purposes by the inadequate allowances for plant write-off. They were unable to finance themselves with new stock issues and had to rely more and more on debt financing. As a result, their financial structure became more and more fragile.

Government spending leaped ahead, fueled by buoyant revenues that have been an "inflationary bonus" for the big spenders in Washington. The diversion of resources to government meant less efficient use of resources. The explosive growth of social services handouts of all kinds added another element to the prevailing attitude that "it doesn't pay to work."

Thus, the very process of inflation undermined the willingness and the ability of American individuals and corporations to work and invest for the future. Gimmicky investments in art works, gold, and antiques replaced the solid investments in plant and modern machinery which were so important in bringing America to its preeminent wealth and economic power.

None of this undermining of America's economic growth would have been possible without the active intervention and cooperation of the Federal Reserve System. The central bank of America was the leading force, the principal participant, in the process of generating and fueling the Great Inflation of the last decade and a half. It has not even succeeded in protecting and strengthening the very financial system of America which it was established to improve and stabilize.

Instability in the financial markets has weakened the competitive stance of the institutions the Federal Reserve was set up to protect —the banks and traditional depository institutions of America. Major new financial services companies have grown voluptuously in the hothouse environment of inflation. Just one of these new institutions, the money market mutual funds, now counts in its assets nearly $200 billion of funds, a sum approaching the total of *all the demand deposits in all the banks of America.* This has been accomplished in the period since 1978. These new financial services companies and institutions may be financially stable. They have not yet been tested in the fires of major crises.

What we do know is that the Federal Reserve has failed in a major aspect of its stewardship—that of ensuring the strength and stability of the nation's banks and depository institutions. Inflation has brought the whole of the savings bank and savings and loan industry in America to its greatest crisis—a crisis that grew out of the very rapid rise of interest rates spawned by the Great Inflation.

On the face of it, therefore, the Federal Reserve has a lot to answer for. It was the central bank of the United States during a time of major financial breakdown.

Endowed with the great responsibility of caring for America's money and of caring for America's banks, the Federal Reserve has evidently failed. America's money was debased; its financial markets were demoralized and became perverse; its economy was disrupted, and its corporations were enfeebled; its government was overexpanded, and the private enterprise system on which its strength was built was gravely weakened. In the world at large, the U.S. dollar was persistently and heavily depreciated.

Certainly some special factors have been at work. The price of energy has increased greatly since the first "oil shock" of 1973. But other countries have felt the same shock and have dealt with it better. West Germany and Japan, both much more dependent than the United States on imported oil and gas, have responded to the price shocks by positive measures of monetary control which have prevented the agony of inflation suffered by America. Switzerland, which has virtually no energy resources at all, has shamed the United States by its record of price stability, despite OPEC.

From 1974 to 1981 inflation in West Germany averaged only 4 percent a year and in Switzerland only 2 percent, while in America it averaged over 7 percent a year. In Japan consumer prices have risen 61 percent since the aftermath of the first oil shock in 1973. In the United States consumer prices have risen 90 percent over the same period. America cannot blame OPEC for its relatively inferior performance in the control of inflation in the last decade.

No, the distinguishing feature of America's experience in the last decade has been a persistent failure to control an unprecedented inflation. Why did America fail so badly, compared with its own past and with other advanced nations, some of which are far poorer in resources and in accumulated wealth than the United States?

The answer must be found in the failure of the Federal Reserve to bring about a stable, slow, and steady growth of money. That was the one outstanding failure. Other countries have had big budget deficits; others have suffered from the depredations of OPEC; others have had to support big military expenditures; others have suffered from the spread of the ideas behind the welfare state, what Lyndon Johnson called the Great Society.

What marked the United States was its lack of success in meeting the challenges posed by the philosophical and political currents of the times. The United States did not control the growth of its money. From that cardinal failure followed the failure to control the surge of prices, the unprecedented rise in interest rates and the violence of their movement.

Between 1947 and 1970 the stock of money in America rose by 88 percent, or by less than 3 percent a year. In the eleven years to 1981 the stock of money rose by 104 percent, or by 6.7 percent a year. The rate of growth of money in the last eleven years has more than *doubled.*

That is the reason for the inflation—and the reason *perceived by the financial markets.* These markets "know" that more money growth means more inflation, and this in turn means higher interest rates. So more money is instantly translated into higher interest rates.

Fortunately for America, financial markets are not static institutions, incapable of change. They are dynamic and susceptible to changing policies. Thus, it was possible to change the pattern of disillusion and despair that had engulfed the financial markets of America by the end of 1980.

A new administration was elected in November 1980 and began to implement radical new policies of monetary control, under the general description of monetarism.

A Ray of Hope—The Reagan Monetary Policy

By the middle of 1982 it was apparent that the crisis of inflation and exploding interest rates *could* be brought under control. The cost, in terms of lost production, was enormous—$350 billion a year in 1982 prices.

But the persistent efforts, demanded by the president and by his senior advisers in the Department of the Treasury, to restrict the growth of money had begun to yield results. These efforts meant that the Federal Reserve had to abandon practices and habits of the previous fifteen years. Money growth had to be controlled. Interest rates had to be decontrolled. Intervention in the foreign exchange markets to support the dollar had to be abandoned. Such fundamental changes in the policies and practices of the Federal Reserve yielded drastic changes in the financial markets and in the financial stability of the United States economy.

President Reagan's administration inherited an exploding money supply. Between June and December 1980, the months leading up to the national election, the money stock (M1-B) rose at the very high rate of 10.8 percent a year. After a brief interruption in December the frantic pace of money growth continued, so that between December 1980 and April 1981 money stock (M1-B) rose at an annual rate of 13.6 percent.

There was absolutely no possibility of defeating inflation if this was to be allowed to continue. The president called Paul Volcker, chairman of the Fed, to the White House in April 1981 and asked him: "Do you intend to control the money of America?"

Almost immediately money growth ceased. There was no growth in money at all between April and October 1981. So severe was the restriction on money growth that a recession, largely unexpected by the majority of economists, began in the fourth quarter of 1981 and still had command of the American economy in the middle of 1982.

Fortunately for America, indeed for the whole of the free world economies, the president and his advisers in the U.S. Treasury never flinched from the need to maintain strict control over money growth in the first two years of the Reagan administration.

During the course of the prolonged and extremely painful process of adjustment to a new world of "disinflation" there was bitter criticism of the policy of improved monetary control. Many economists of the liberal tradition tried to maintain the pain was unnecessary, failing to acknowledge the finite danger of a total financial collapse that existed in 1980, before the policy of monetary control was forced on the Fed by the president and his advisers in the U.S. Treasury.

Both within and without the United States (particularly in Europe) the policy of strict monetary control was assailed, for the high real rates of interest that accompanied its early stages. With the abandonment of official support for the U.S. dollar (involving the removal of all Federal Reserve manipulation of the dollar foreign exchange markets) and the implementation of a tight money policy inside America, the value of the U.S. dollar in terms of foreign currencies soared. This was an affront to Germany and Japan, which complained long and loud at the revival of the much-derided U.S. dollar. Nevertheless, the president and his Treasury team did not relent in their demand for a policy of monetary restraint, of liberalized foreign exchanges, and of decontrolled interest rates.

It is now clear by the middle of 1982 that these policies are beginning to bear fruit. Monetarism has given America some stunning successes and has laid the foundations for future noninflationary growth. Beginning in the crisis of April 1981, there has been a radical reduction in the rate of growth of money in America. Although by the middle of 1982 this policy had been in existence for only about fifteen months, it had yielded some extraordinary results.

Apart from a brief period of more vigorous growth of money between October 1981 and January 1982 (when money M1 rose at an annual rate of 15.3 percent) there was after April 1981 no other period of significant money growth evident by July 1982. Between January and July 1982 the money stock M1 remained stationary.

The watershed in the implementation and enforcement of the policy of tight monetary control under the Reagan administration occurred in April 1981.

The Collapse of Monetary Growth in 1981–82

Month	M1 or M1-B	Percent Increase*
December 1976	$310.4 billion	
December 1977	335.5	7.4%
December 1978	363.2	8.3
December 1979	389.0	7.1
December 1980	414.5	6.6
April 1981	433.3	
July 1982	451.4	4.2

*From preceding period

The annual rate of growth in money, from the period when the Reagan administration gained the agreement of the chairman of the Federal Reserve to the broad lines of the Reagan monetary (and monetarist) policy, slowed down drastically. In the fifteen months between April 1981 and July 1982, money stock M1 rose at an annual rate of only about 3 percent, less than half that of the four years ended December 1980.

This drastic reduction in the rate of growth of money was accompanied by a similarly drastic decline in the rate of price inflation.

The Collapse of Inflation

	Percent Increase in Consumer Prices
1977	6.8%
1978	9.0
1979	13.3
1980	12.4
1981	8.9
1982 (first 6 months)	6.5 (annual rate)

At the same time the sharp drop in the rate of growth of money since April 1981 has resulted in a strong decline in the level of interest rates. This reduction has been accompanied by unprecedented public concern about the level and persistence of high real interest rates. Considering the long period of years over which escalating inflation has taken hold of the U.S. economy and the psychology of Americans, it is remarkable that the back of high interest rates has been broken as quickly as it has.

Prime Rate

	Percent
1976	6.8%
1977	6.8
1978	9.1
1979	12.3
1980	15.3
1981	18.9

Prime Rate (continued)

1981

January	21½–20
April	17½–18
July	20–20½
October	19½–18

1982

January	15.75
April	16.5
July	15.5 (close)
September	13.5 (close)

Clearly the worst of the interest rate explosion had passed in the middle months of 1981, as the program of regaining control over the growth of money gradually took hold.

By the middle of 1982 the fall of interest rates had become very marked. This was shown more dramatically by the collapse of the rate on short Treasury bills.

90-Day T Bills

1981	*Rate*
January	14.7%
April	13.6
July	14.7
October	13.9
1982	
January	12.4
April	12.8
July	11.5
July (end month)	10.2
September (end month)	7.5

By September 1982 the level of Treasury bill rates had fallen back to below any point since July 1980, more than two years previously.

The decline in the level of interest rates, which began in the middle months of 1981 and gathered momentum as the policy of slow money growth was implemented, occurred against a background of *rising* federal budget deficits and a positive torrent of expressions of public concern about the likely effect of those deficits on the level of interest rates.

By the middle of 1982 it was clear that any relation between deficits and interest rates had been finally dispelled, as the collapse of rates occurred *at the very time* as the federal government's borrowing requirement began to gather its greatest momentum. What had also become clear by the middle of 1982 was the need for a policy of steady and stable monetary growth, in which the participants in the financial markets would have confidence.

The Struggle over Monetary Policy

Within the administration, the principal public proponent of tight control over money growth was the under secretary for monetary affairs in the U.S. Treasury, Beryl Sprinkel. The earlier, rather outspoken comments of this outstanding official on the subject of a needed reform of monetary policy administration were gradually moderated as it became apparent that the Federal Reserve, under its chairman, Paul Volcker, had become increasingly committed to the policy earlier expounded by Sprinkel, as fully rounded out in the *Economic Report of the President, February 1982.*

In many public statements during 1982 Volcker repeatedly asserted it was not the intention of the Federal Reserve to permit excessive growth of money. He asserted his intention to maintain slow, steady money growth. Gradually the pattern that evolved was one of jerky growth around a steadily declining trend path.

Substantial "bulges" occurred from time to time, as they did during January, April, and September 1982. But on each occasion, subsequent experience showed that the bulge in money growth did not lead to a permanent incorporation of the bulge in the money stock. This experience, repeated two or three times, slowly led to an increase in public confidence in the future of monetary policy. In the financial markets this confidence was expressed in a gradual reduction in the level of yields.

At the same time the effect of tighter monetary control in reducing the level of inflation led to an increasing disillusion with tangible assets as an outlet for savings. Housing and autos, to take two outstanding examples, lost a tremendous amount of their attraction. More and more of the money available for investment was directed into financial assets, which had been spurned during the previous decade and a half.

In a meeting of his Economic Policy Advisory Board in June 1982, President Reagan turned to Arthur Burns, a member of this select group, and said: "The trouble with you, Arthur, was that you juiced up the money supply too much in 1971–72. That is something we are not going to do this time around." We shall see.

At no time up to the end of September 1982 (the time of this edition) had the president indicated any desire to be diverted from the monetary policy course that was laid down in the early months of 1981. Despite tremendous pressure to abandon the tight money policy, it had been retained during the crucial first eighteen months of his presidency.

Thus, as far as monetary policy was concerned, the president held to a very steady course. This, in turn, provided the foundation for the success in defeating inflation and high interest rates. The steady implementation of this policy had the additional effect of vindicating the criticisms which had been leveled against the Fed during the preceding years by eminent monetarist economists, including Milton Friedman, Karl Brunner, Allan Meltzer, and Beryl Sprinkel.

The Fed took an additional step to meet the criticisms made by these economists when, during the middle of 1982, the Federal Reserve Board announced its agreement in principle to instituting a system of contemporaneous reserve accounting, one of the important procedural reforms demanded by monetarist critics of the Fed. Implementation of the reform, which was to take place sometime during 1983, would have the effect of removing from the banks much of their power to get around Fed policy intentions. Banks had enjoyed this discretion under the system of lagged reserve accounting, which permitted them two weeks' grace to find the reserves they owed the Fed. In effect, lagged reserve accounting meant that the Fed was obliged to provide the funds the banks needed to meet the bills they owed the Fed, thus effectively undermining much of the intended result of reserve control policy.

Two Swallows Do Not Make a Summer

While there has been progress in monetary policy and practice since April 1981, it is clear there has been no change in the fundamental policies and attitudes of the Federal Reserve. An inspection of Fed policies and practices and a study of the statements of senior Fed officials reveal no important change in the attitudes and beliefs that brought the nation to the brink of disaster in 1980–81.

The Fed still practices furtively the totally discredited system of interest rate targeting. It follows obscure, even mystical systems of market intervention. Its senior officials crave more power—the desire of every inept bureaucrat. The senior staff of the central bank has not been changed. The membership of the Federal Reserve Board is still firmly in the hands of Carter appointees. Monetary policy is still unpredictable and sometimes unnerving in its jerky patterns.

Indeed, the principal limitation on a return by the Fed to the disastrous policies of the fifteen years before 1981 is the fear and loathing of the central bank in the financial markets. The situation was summarized by Leif Olsen, chief economist at Citibank, in January 1982, when he said:

In October 1979, the Federal Reserve reinforced its intent of controlling the rate of growth of the monetary aggregates. It continued its earlier practice of announcing publicly its targets. People who make markets in short-term financial instruments —Treasury bills, certificates of deposit, and commercial paper —have concluded that whenever the rate of growth of the money supply, even for a few weeks, appears to be running along a track above the Fed's targets, they drop their bids, so that they do not take into inventory securities which may decline in value as the Fed imposes a squeeze in order to bring the rate of money back on track. In effect, these market participants engaged in price searching in an effort to determine what interest rate is appropriate for the forthcoming squeeze by the monetary authorities. The publicly announced targets for monetary aggregates convey an implicit anti-inflationary promise to the marketplace. The Federal Reserve apparently cannot engage in even a temporary deviation from this promise without inspiring a strong reaction in the financial markets.

It has taken a decade and a half of failure on the part of the Fed to achieve the deep skepticism about its words and deeds that one finds in the financial markets of America today. *It is important, therefore, that we know why the Federal Reserve failed. We must remedy the situation in a permanent way.* Never again should an untrammeled group of officials be allowed to continue the failure to control money that has been seen in the last fifteen years.

This book details the inside story of the loss of control over money by the Federal Reserve, especially in the last twelve decisive years. It explains how political conditions and the attitudes of the chairmen, particularly Arthur Burns (chairman from 1970 to 1978), have contributed to the failure of control. It goes on to describe the failure of the Federal Reserve to learn from experience and to adjust its thinking and procedures to prevent and ameliorate the persistent crisis of excessive money growth. It reveals how deep-seated attitudes in the Fed official apparatus have contributed to its failure to learn and adapt positively to the chaos the central bank created. And it shows how the Fed's policies have laid waste much of the traditional structure of America's financial institutions.

Credible Policy Is Needed

Allan Meltzer, professor of political economy and public policy at Carnegie Mellon University and co-chairman of the Shadow Open Market Committee (from whose deliberations I have received much stimulation and inspiration), wrote in the *Wall Street Journal* on July 29, 1982:

> The easiest way to reduce interest rates and encourage expansion with declining inflation is for the Fed to increase its credibility by sticking to an announced policy of disinflation and improving its procedures. As the credibility of monetary policy increases, risk premiums and interest rates will decline. Short-term bulges in money growth won't be expected to persist, so they'll have smaller effect. This is the experience of Switzerland, where money growth is variable but policy is credible. In Britain, despite a war and a current rate of inflation above ours, interest rates on long-term debt declined this year. The in-

creased credibility of British government policy statements is a main difference between this year and last.

The Fed has an unusual opportunity to break the current impasse by gradually lowering the growth of money—to reduce inflation—and lowering the variability of money growth to reduce the risk premium in interest rates and encourage recovery. The procedural steps are well known and can be adopted whenever the Fed decides to do so. One such step, the move to contemporaneous reserve accounting, has, at last, been proposed but not implemented.

The next step is to recognize the obvious. Current monetary procedures are unreliable and costly. They impose an excessive burden on the economy. These procedures should be abandoned. Instead of targets for M1 and M2 the Federal Reserve should announce a disinflationary path for its own assets and liabilities. It should remove the remaining self-imposed restrictions and faulty seasonal adjustments that make monetary control more difficult and less reliable. A growth path for Federal Reserve assets and liabilities means that the growth rate of either total reserves or the monetary base (total reserves plus currency) becomes the target. Either of these targets is difficult to miss, so control would improve, credibility would increase and risk premiums would gradually return to normal levels.

To reduce the cost of ending inflation, the Fed must match its procedures to its policies, its deeds to its words. Proper monetary control is not a panacea, but it can help lower interest rates in the difficult months ahead.

On September 30, 1978, nine months after he had been rejected as chairman of the Fed by Jimmy Carter, Arthur Burns said: "The Federal Reserve is a collegial body of great moral and intellectual distinction." That may be so. It is also the most powerful single force for economic and financial destruction this nation has seen, and over the last decade it has been the principal creator of waste, destroyer of wealth, disrupter of markets, discourager of investment, and underminer of corporations. Single-handedly it has brought economic growth in the United States to a halt.

This little understood institution, created in 1913 with such touching hope, has become over the last ten years the one crucial barrier to the defeat of inflation and the restoration of economic growth as we knew it in the 1950's and the 1960's.

Professor Karl Brunner, the outstanding Swiss-born professor of economics in the Graduate School of Management at the University of Rochester and one of the nation's leading analysts of the Fed, said in September 1980:

> Sisyphus was condemned by the Gods, for good reason apparently, to eternal and hopeless labor. He was supposed to push a huge rock uphill which, at the edge of success, would inexorably slide back to the valley. Sisyphus may still be at work, for all we know, but the Gods seem to have changed their ways. They have provided us with the Federal Reserve and the more subtle torture of attempting to change the behavior of an important institution, operated by an entrenched bureaucracy. We are of course not condemned by the Gods (or Fate, or Society) to push at the Fed rock. It remains our choice. But the Fed has condemned us to live under the economic conditions created by the increasingly inflationary policies, insistently pursued, over the past fifteen years. It has condemned us to hear a litany of excuses obfuscating the failure of policymaking.
>
> It also has condemned us to watch a series of false or broken promises.
>
> Something is fundamentally wrong with the Fed's policymaking, requiring at this stage some radical action.

Beryl Sprinkel said on February 1, 1982:

> We tend to think that children eat and that makes them grow. It does not work that way. What often seems obvious turns out not to be correct. The physical growth of a child is an innate drive within their biological makeup. As the body develops, it demands food to replace the expanded energy and perpetuate the *ongoing* growth. Growth *creates* the demand for food—*not* the other way around. Stuffing a kid with too much food doesn't make him grow faster; it makes him sick.
>
> Similarly, injecting a lot of money into an economy does not make it grow faster; it just makes it sick.
>
> As the economy grows according to its own inherent rhythm and dynamism, that creates a legitimate need for additional money. Economies, like people, have a natural tendency toward creative growth and toward self-correction. Money exists to *follow* and facilitate that activity, not to make it happen.

If we can understand these fundamentals—and hold true to them—we are in for a future of real and sustained non-inflationary economic growth.

Finally, President Ronald Reagan commented in January 1982: "The Fed is sending the wrong signals to the markets." The Fed has been doing so for at least ten years.

2 The Present Crisis—Weary Indifference to Failure

By 1982 the American economy seemed poised on the edge of another Great Depression. On all sides there was speculation about the imminent prospect of a series of major corporate crashes, as America waited with baited breath for "this recession's Penn Central."

There had been virtually no economic growth since 1978. Stagflation and even slumpflation described the sorry state of the nation's economy. Nor was there any real prospect of substantial economic growth before 1983. This would mean that the real gross national product of the United States in 1982 would be only about 3 percent greater than in 1978. By contrast, the 1978 real gross national product was 15 percent greater than the 1974 real GNP.

Since 1978 the United States has been in the grip of the Great Recession, the most prolonged period of economic stagnation since the 1930's. The effect has been to devastate the living standard of the ordinary working American—the one who is not on social security, welfare, or self-employed. The real take-home pay of the average wage earner in America, after inflation, after federal and social security taxes, has been nose-diving since the end of 1977 and by 1981 was down by 18 percent. The average wage earner could buy no more, in 1981, out of his wages, than he could in 1956, some twenty-five years earlier! Workers in America are not in a recession; they are in a depression, brought on by inflation and a progressive income tax structure.

Once-great American industries are dying, throttled to death by inflation, high interest rates, and a shortage of credit. Autos, housing, consumer durables—all are dying. In 1982 the American auto industry entered its fourth successive year of severely depressed sales. By

26

late 1981 the rate of sales of new one-family homes in America had reached its lowest rate for two decades. Interest rates had reached the point where installments on the median-priced home in America were estimated at $760 a month, so high as to disqualify 85 percent of American households from eligibility for a loan on a new home, according to Manufacturers Hanover Trust. Great American cities —Detroit, Chicago, Gary, New York—and great American states— New York, Michigan, New Jersey, Illinois, Indiana, Ohio, Pennsylvania—are struggling to maintain their existing populations.

Unemployment has risen to average levels that in earlier times might have been thought likely to provoke marching in the streets. The rate of unemployment was 4.4 percent in 1955, 4.5 percent in 1965, and 5.6 percent in 1974. Thereafter, it has ratcheted steadily upward in line with the inflation rate. There has been no "virtuous trade-off" between unemployment and inflation. They have risen together. By December 1981 unemployment in America had reached 8.8 percent, presaging a level of unemployment in 1982 higher than anything seen for more than forty years.

The United States is passing through a major economic convulsion. Compare the average experience of latter-day America, from 1974 to 1979, with the nation's average experience in the years 1960–65, before the Age of Inflation began.

Productivity—output per man-hour—rose 2.6 percent a year during the years 1960–65 and only 0.7 percent a year from 1974 to 1979.

Unemployment averaged 5.5 percent a year in the period 1960–65 against 6.8 percent from 1974 to 1979.

Interest rates (corporate bond Aaa yield) were 4.4 percent on average in the period 1960–65 and 8.7 percent from 1974 to 1979.

The federal government spending share of gross national product rose from 18.8 percent 1960–65 to 21.7 percent 1974–79.

Inflation was 1.6 percent a year 1960–65 and 7.5 percent a year 1974–79.

The last five years of American economic history have been a story of disaster and failure.

Behind the crumbling facade has been one corrosive force: the money supply has grown more than twice as fast. In the 1960–65 period money supply growth in America was 3.0 percent a year;

between 1974 and 1979 money grew 6.6 percent a year. Beginning in 1978 the vast productive machine of the U.S. economy has become more and more deeply snarled in a crisis characterized by a failure of production to grow, by fear and confusion in the financial markets of the nation, by an unwillingness to invest, and by a progressive reluctance of consumers, corporations, and the self-employed to commit themselves to future debts, to future loans, to investments for the future.

By 1982 the real value of the Dow Jones industrial average had receded to the level of the early 1950's. All the gains of the intervening period of almost thirty years in real stock prices had been lost. The price/earnings ratio of the Standard and Poors 500 Index, which had been as high as 20 in the early 1960's, was down to 8, a reflection of sky-high real interest rates and rock-bottom confidence in the future.

America today by force of circumstances must live for the present and in the present. It has become impossible to plan ahead with confidence. Brief forward steps in production are followed by steep backsliding, with the result that there has been virtually no economic growth since 1978.

One can finally call these the years of the Great Recession. They are the product of what I call the Great Age of Inflation, which began in the mid-1960's and reached a crescendo in the last half of the 1970's. Significantly, this epoch is without precedent in the peacetime history of the United States.

There Can Be No Improvement Until the Reason for Failure Is Faced

There has been one source of the failures which have overtaken America in recent years. That has been the failure to control the growth of money. That is the one element in the American experience which marks it from much more successful economies, such as those of Japan, West Germany, and Switzerland. The failure of monetary control, leading to excessive growth of money, has permitted and stimulated the growth of inflation, with all that has meant in terms of loss of economic growth, loss of economic efficiency, and the trivialization of the American economy.

At the center of the process of monetary control is the Federal Reserve Board, a group of six men and one woman who have the power to control the growth of money in America. They enjoy extraordinary latitude, based on an early belief, at the beginning of the century, that it was a "good idea" for the central bank to be kept free from the influence and greed of elected politicians.

Tragically, these great powers, delegated to a group of nonelected officials, have been abused. The Federal Reserve Board and the officials who serve it within the Federal Reserve System have been willing participants, even active leaders, in the corruption of America's money in the last fifteen years.

Enormous trust has been placed in the members of the Federal Reserve Board and that trust has turned out to have been misplaced. The Fed has turned out to be the great embezzler of America's money. Why has this been? Has the Fed allied itself with presidents, aiding them in sidestepping congressional control over the public purse? Has the Fed proved a compliant ally for presidents desperate for reelection? Does the Fed understand how to control the growth of money? Is it interested in the subject? Or does it have other, less obvious priorities? What are the secret priorities of the Fed?

We must know the answers to these questions. Without them, there is no possibility of reforming the grim record of failure in economic policy. By now the actions of the Federal Reserve over the years have caused a total lack of faith in the stated intentions of the central bank.

Today every action of the Fed is scrutinized clinically and cynically by a very large number of experts. For the mass of participants in the financial markets, the Fed is to be feared. It is seen as an engine of inflation, and by now any move interpreted as expansionary is greeted with alarm and despondency in the markets.

Let us look at what happened in 1981. At the beginning of the year the rate of interest on a ninety-day certificate of deposit with a typical bank in New York was about 17 percent, a quite fantastic rate by the past standards of America but nevertheless the sort of rate lenders were demanding when they knew that inflation was in double digits (as it had been during 1980).

What happened to our ninety-day certificate of deposit rate? *It collapsed.* Along with most other short-term interest rates, it fell sharply between January and March from 17 to 13 percent. Four percentage points represents a very radical decline. Money supply did not grow; money became progressively tighter and *interest rates fell.*

Now we look at the next phase of our money experience in 1981. Between February and late April a very rapid growth of money set in. Between early February and late April money supply (M1-B) rose at a rate of about 18 percent a year. This was a huge rate of growth —it compared with an annual average of about 7 percent during the ten years of the 1970's. What happened to our ninety-day certificate of deposit rate in the face of such a huge growth of money? *It boomed upward.* Between the middle of March (by which time lenders had begun to wake up to what was happening to money) and the middle of May the rate on the ninety-day certificate of deposit in New York had gone from 13½ to nearly 19 percent.

At about this point President Reagan intervened. In April 1981 fears were growing rapidly in the U.S. Treasury, Office of the Under Secretary for Monetary Affairs, that the Fed had lost control of the growth of money and that this could bring about a failure of the whole of President Reagan's program for controlling inflation. Beryl Sprinkel, the newly appointed under secretary for monetary affairs and a long-standing critic of Federal Reserve thinking and actions, in testimony before the Joint Economic Committee of Congress on April 8, called for reform of the Federal Reserve's procedures and for monetary restraint.

That month there was a meeting between the president and the chairman of the Fed, Paul Volcker. I have been told by Treasury officials that the president in effect asked Volcker, "Do you have any intention of controlling the growth of money in America?" After that meeting the Fed suddenly seemed to gain a new surge of strength, and for the whole period to the end of October money growth came to a halt.

Between late April and late October 1981, a period of six months, there was no growth in money (M1-B) to speak of at all. As a result, over this period money became progressively tighter. It became so apparent that there was no growth in money that senior officials in the U.S. government, including Secretary of the Treasury Donald Regan, in public, and assorted fuming and angry Treasury officials in private, began making public demands that the Federal Reserve do something about getting money growth going again. They were frightened, entirely correctly as it turned out, that a serious recession would result from the failure of money supply to grow for six months in an environment of inflation.

What happened to our ninety-day certificate of deposit rate during this six months of acute freeze on money growth? *It collapsed again.* Between the peak in May 1981 (when lenders were looking at the big February–April money growth boom and worrying more and more about inflation) and the bottom in November (when the same lenders were more and more relaxed about the prospect of inflation because money growth had been restrained), the rate on our ninety-day certificate of deposit fell like a stone from just under 19 to about 11½ percent.

During October 1981 the American economy itself collapsed, under the influence of money starvation. I don't want to give the impression at this stage that I think the Fed's action in freezing money growth for those important six months was necessarily wrong. At this stage I want you to realize only that the money freeze led to a recession and to *much lower interest rates.*

And this brings us to the last phase of our money roller coaster in 1981. In October all the main economic indicators of the American economy fell and fell and fell. At the same time the Federal Reserve began to realize what was happening. It was also well aware that it was undershooting its target growth rate for money in 1981. These targets will be discussed later, but for now, you only need to know that the Fed was way under its self-imposed target rate of growth for money (M1-B) by October.

Hence, for a variety of reasons—fear of not meeting targets, fear of the rapid development of recession as evidenced by the October indicators—the Fed suddenly stimulated money growth. Between the end of October and the beginning of December money growth once again jumped to the sky. There was an annual rate of increase of money (M1-B) of about 17 percent during this period.

And what happened to our ninety-day certificate of deposit rate in this time of booming money growth? You guessed it. The ninety-day CD rate *jumped upward again,* rising by 165 basis points (meaning 1.65 percent) between November 25 and December 25, from 11.51 percent to 13.16 percent.

Money Grows—Rates Rise; Money Slows—Rates Drop

There is a fundamental lesson in this. After fifteen years of progressively increasing inflation the American people have woken up to one thing. More money means more inflation; more inflation means lenders demand higher and higher interest rates, so that they will not be robbed by inflation. They were cruelly robbed during the early years of the Age of Inflation—before they woke up to the fact that something in American life had changed: the dollar was not something you could count on any longer.

Economists of all stripes and shades are still fighting about the issue of the importance of money as a cause of inflation. The theory first enunciated in its present form by Milton Friedman more than twenty years ago is still bitterly resisted by many economists. But the people of America have accepted monetarism. They know that more money means more inflation and act accordingly. Maybe I am overstating this. Perhaps I should say "the wise heads among the people of America, those wise heads who move the financial markets of the nation and of the world" have woken up to the fact that more money means more inflation and more inflation means higher interest rates.

Fear in the financial markets of America—the markets that move the world—has reached such a point that the reaction to news of higher money growth is almost instantaneous. As soon as it becomes apparent that money growth is accelerating, the prices of all fixed income securities (from Treasury bills through certificates of deposit, Treasury bonds, and municipal bonds to corporate bonds) drop. Inversely, the yields rise and interest rates rise.

Slow Money Growth Means Slow Economic Growth—While Inflation Lasts

As the representatives of the auto, housing, construction, machine tools, and steel industries troop off to Washington, they have one complaint: "Please get these high interest rates down—they're killing us."

In the olden days when there was faith in the value of the dollar, the president could have a quiet chat with the chairman of the Fed, and a little more money might possibly have led to a little lower interest rates. Those days are gone. Today a little more money means a little *higher* interest rates.

So what about making sure we have a little lower rate of money growth to achieve a little lower rate of interest? There is a snag. Many statistical studies have well established that there is an *average* lag of about eighteen months to two years between a lower rate of money growth and a lower rate of inflation. (See the figures below and on pages 34 and 35.)

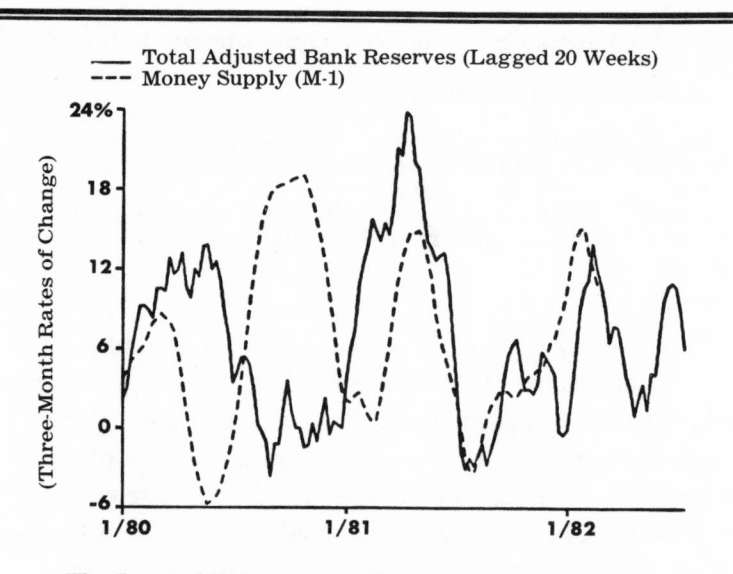

——— Total Adjusted Bank Reserves (Lagged 20 Weeks)
--- Money Supply (M-1)

**The Lagged Relationship Between Bank Reserves
and Monetary Expansion**

Data are four-week moving averages.

Sources: Econalyst Data Base; Morgan Stanley Research

The graph shows the relationship between bank reserves and the money supply. With an average time lag of about twenty weeks, adjusted bank reserves and the money supply move together, pointing to the "controllability" of money through manipulation of bank reserves.

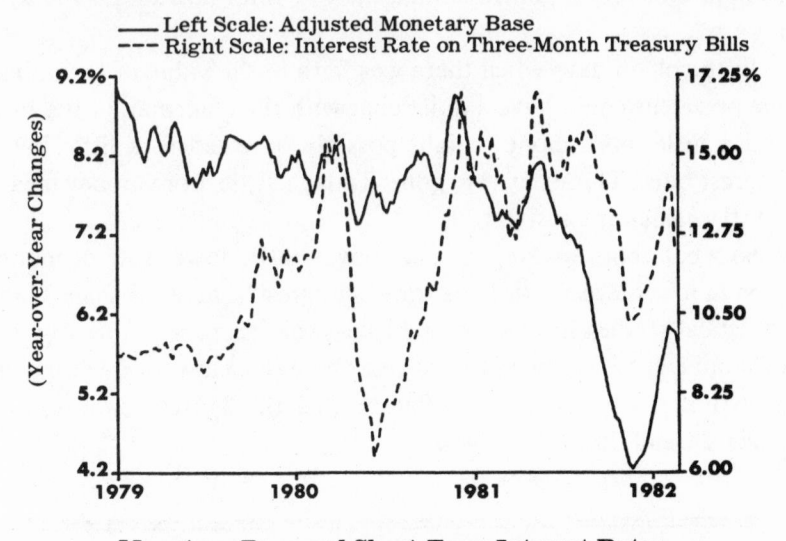

Monetary Base and Short-Term Interest Rates

Data are four-week moving averages.

Sources: Econalyst Data Base; Morgan Stanley Research

The graph shows the strong relationship between the adjusted monetary base and interest rates. They both move in the same direction. This is the result of years of inflation which have conditioned money market participants to expect more inflation from more money growth. More inflation means that lenders demand more interest on their money.

The *immediate* effect of lower money growth is to stifle the growth of *output* and hence the growth of employment. It is not hard to figure out why this is so. The growth of gross national product at current prices is made up of the growth of the *volume* of output and the growth of the *price* of that output. So, in the case of 1981, there was a growth of nominal gross national product (in current prices, that is) of 11 percent.

In 1981 the real value of the gross national product (that is, the *volume* of output) rose by only 1.7 percent. And the price of that volume of output rose by 9.1 percent. The result was a rise in the current value of GNP by 11 percent.

If this seems elementary, bear with me. The Federal Reserve hasn't figured this out yet, and that is why our economy is in

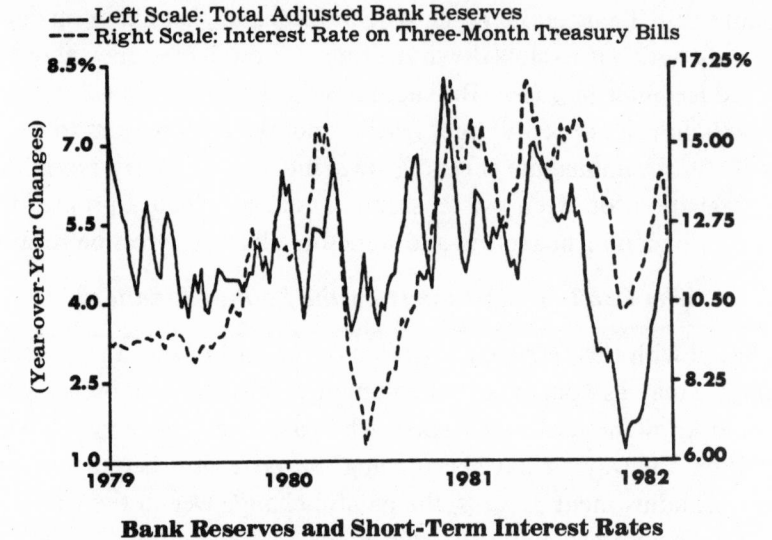

Left Scale: Total Adjusted Bank Reserves
Right Scale: Interest Rate on Three-Month Treasury Bills

Bank Reserves and Short-Term Interest Rates

Data are four-week moving averages.

Sources: Econalyst Data Base; Morgan Stanley Research

Here is yet another example of the direct relationship between changes in an important determinant of money growth -adjusted bank reserves -and interest rates. In today's world, movements in interest rates are dominated by movements in expected inflation. Movements in money provide the link. As money grows, so it is expected, Inflation will grow and interest rates rise as a result.

such terrible trouble and why the Age of Recession may go on for some more years until there is a complete change of crew at the Fed.

When money supply growth is slowed, prices do not slow down immediately. That is because current price growth is the result of *past* money growth—about two years into the past on the average. This means that if money supply growth is slowed down, there has to be a slowdown in the growth of nominal (current prices) gross national product. A slowdown in the growth of nominal GNP, with a *constant* or even *increasing* (in the case where past money growth has been accelerating) money growth can mean only one thing—a much slower growth of real gross national product (see the figure on page 36).

And therein lies the heart of the present crisis in America. Because of the lack of confidence in the value of money (by the people who count in the financial markets—the movers and shakers in money), the only option is to slow down the rate of growth of money in order to reduce interest rates. But because the effect of slower money growth on prices takes about eighteen months to two years to work itself out, the immediate effect of slower money growth is a recession, or stagflation, or, even worse, slumpflation, in which a progressive collapse of confidence sets in and something like a depression results.

Why Can't We Just Carry on the Path of Inflation?

Faced with this terrible realization of the cost of the Age of Inflation, we may ask ourselves (in common with many economists who should know better, may I add): why can't we just carry on with inflation, the way we have been going? Surely that is better than the horrible adjustment process, the painful changeover to the world of *dis*inflation we are going through now?

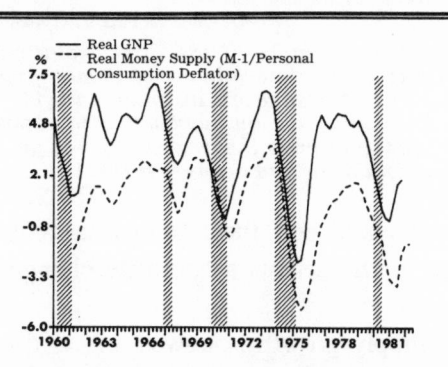

The Synchronous Movement of Money and the Economy

Data are trailing four-quarter moving averages.
Money supply has been lagged two quarters.

Sources: Econalyst Data Base; Morgan Stanley Research

Shaded areas, except for the mini-recession of 1966-1967, represent periods of recession as designated by the National Bureau of Economic Research.

We already know from our experience, during the Great Recession since 1978, that the process of ever-increasing inflation eventually causes a cessation in growth of output. The table below sets out some of the broad facts:

More Money Means More Inflation—Leading to Stagnation

(Average Annual Rate of Growth)

	Real GNP	*Money Supply (M1 or M1-B)*	*Consumer Prices*
1951–60	3½%	2%	2%
1960–70	4½	4	3
1970–78	4	6½	6½
1978–81	1.7	6½	11½

We know that during 1981 there was little or no economic growth in America, and similarly in 1982 there will be little or no growth, making four years of negligible economic growth, the Age of Recession. There are good reasons for the development of economic stagnation following years of progressive increases in inflation.

Firstly, inflation means that more and more banks, savings and loan associations, finance companies, and other lenders are less and less willing to lend for a long term. Hence, it becomes more and more difficult to raise money to finance long-term investments, such as houses, construction, new plant and equipment purchases, power utilities, gas pipelines, and the like. Uncertainty about the likely course of inflation was a critical deterrent to investment growth. Yet these long-term investments create the future wealth and greatness of nations. Among other factors, America was developed by huge investments in canals, railroads, roads, electric generating plants, gas and oil fields and their associated pipelines, ships, ports, and (perhaps most important of all) long-term expensive and very risky research and development expenditures.

Secondly, everyone is less willing (and less able) to afford to save. When inflation is increasing, families, corporations, and the self-employed know that the dollar they are holding is going down in value—so they had better get rid of it, fast. This leads to all sorts of short-term speculative activity: to investments in gold, precious metals, speculative real estate and land investments, antiques, carpets—in short, to the sort of nonproductive investments that have led to such a shortage of long-term investment capital in the so-called

37

developing nations where fear of inflation and of confiscation of publicly visible wealth is endemic.

Thirdly, ever-increasing inflation means ever-increasing effective rates of taxation—the so-called bracket creep that has been such a boon to the ambitions of politicians for the last fifteen years in America. Automatically an ever-increasing share of national income goes to governments levying progressive income taxes. This means that as governments are big consumers and highly inefficient producers, a bigger and bigger share of national income goes to the least efficient and least prudent recipient—the government.

Fourthly, corporations find that they cannot raise long-term loans and start to depend more and more on short-term loans. This leads to a severe deterioration in the financial stability of corporations. Their liquidity ratio—the ratio of debt to total assets—deteriorates. They come to depend more and more on debt to finance their expansion, insofar as they continue to expand their operations at all. They are forced into this because taxation takes an increasing share of profits (not only because of a progression in corporate income tax rates but also because profits are inflated by underprovision for the depreciation in fixed assets and by the taxation of the inflationary upvaluation of inventories). They also find they cannot make stock issues to keep their equity financing up with their debt financing. Stocks are not favored during periods of escalating inflation, as they fail to maintain increases in value, on average, like the rate of inflation (a result in turn of the failure of corporations to expand and to produce increasing after-tax dividends—a vicious circle effect).

Fifthly, inflation erodes the stability of basic financial institutions, as has happened with the savings and loan associations and the mutual savings banks in America, which in 1981 recorded their biggest net loss in their history, on the order of $5 billion. As financial collapse faces such institutions, they are unable to continue financing the long-term investments that was their role in the past.

Sixthly, more and more clever financiers invent more and more clever short-term financing arrangements that put more and more emphasis on the next few days, rather than on the next few years. In the last two years money market funds, which invest their depositors' money for a period of about thirty days on average, have risen

38

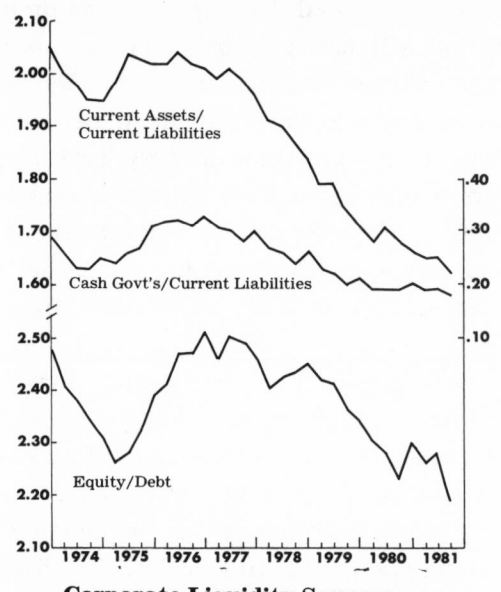

Corporate Liquidity Squeeze

Source: Federal Trade Commission

The graph, published by Henry Wojtyla and Nicocles Michas of the New York brokerage firm of Rosenkrantz, Ehrenkrantz, Lyon & Ross, shows the deterioration in the "liquidity" of American corporations. The ratio of current assets to current liabilities has plumeted, as has the ratio of equity (shareholders' funds) to debt. American corporations are awash in debt.

to a size about equal to one half the total money supply (M1-B)—getting on toward $200 billion.

Banks, which in past times, when the dollar was trusted, were able to finance their business by ordinary deposits that came in the door, are decreasingly able to do so. As more and more millions of Americans have awakened to the fact of inflation, they have been less and less willing to leave money on deposit with a bank. So the banks have had to go out and sell securities in the marketplace to finance their loans. As they have done this on a bigger and bigger scale, the whole cost of credit has been pushed up to a higher level.

There has resulted an extremely precarious situation, in which corporations and individuals are relying more and more on shorter-and-shorter-term loans to finance their activities. Great potential instability is imparted to the whole financial system. The prospect of

39

financial collapse is enhanced. Families that sign up for very short-term housing loans with near-term balloon payments give extraordinary hostages to fortune. More and more of American business, so it seems, is being financed on overnight money, or on thirty- or sixty-day money. Long-term loans are very hard to raise.

Another barrier to progress from inflation during the 1970's has been the decline in the international value of the dollar and the mounting invasion of American domestic markets by Japanese, West German, Taiwanese, Korean, and other products from these nations which for one reason or another have managed their affairs more prudently and with greater foresight than has been the case in the United States (see the graph on page 41).

All these forces lead to less and less concentration on *production* and less and less concentration on *long-term planning and investment.* More and more emphasis is put on short-term speculative activity, on consumption, on a struggle for a fair share of a static or even declining national output. Output stagnates, employment declines, and unemployment mounts. More and more effort is devoted to the gimmickry of financial planning; less to the planning of real improvements in productivity. This is necessarily so because of the nature of the forces unleashed by inflation.

There are various ways the process may end. In many countries, as those in Latin America, the social disorder produced by endemic inflation leads to such chaos that dictatorships are accepted by the people as a price to be paid. Controls of all sorts, including rationing of capital, imports, foreign currency, and even food and fuel, are imposed.

In other countries, such as France and Britain, either overt or covert socialization has been taking place, with the state coming in to take over private enterprises that are failing or that are judged, in the atmosphere of corrosive envy produced by inflation, to be exploiting their advantages. Gradually, in these countries, the power over the "commanding heights" of industrial production passes to the state as the last repository of financially exhausted enterprises.

The progress toward a socialist system in turn exaggerates the

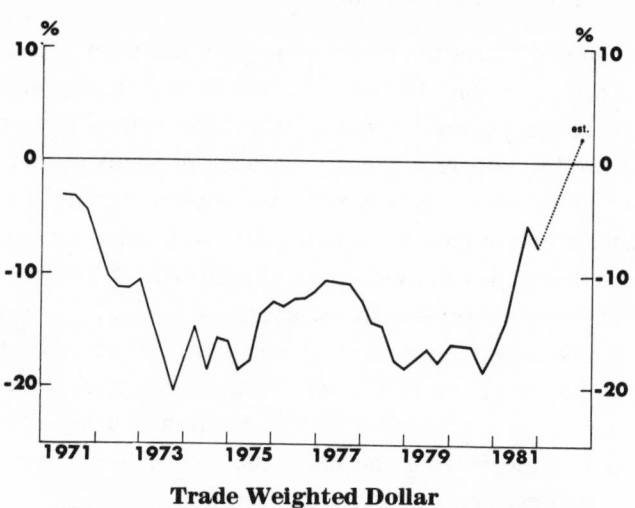

Trade Weighted Dollar
(Percent Change vs. Pre-June 1970 Parities)

Source: Morgan Guaranty; RELR Estimates

The chart shows the drastic decline in the value of the U.S. dollar during the Age of Inflation. By 1980, the dollar had dropped almost 20 percent below its pre-June 1970 average value, as compared with other currencies. During 1981 there was a rapid improvement in the value of the dollar, following the cessation of any official intervention to support the currency, on the instructions of the U.S. Treasury, Office of the Secretary for Monetary Affairs. Other factors contributing to the big improvement in the strength of the dollar were the rapid decline of inflation during 1981, the result of some improvement in the control over the growth of money; the deregulation of oil in America, which contributed to the worldwide collapse of oil prices during 1981; and the election of the Reagan administration with new financial and defense strategic goals.

inefficiency produced by inflation. Price controls are introduced; rationing of imports is advocated and eventually accepted; the stimulus to efficiency provided by international trade is diminished. Inflation of prices may be diminished, to be replaced by the more deeply corrupting so-called hidden (to use the terminology of economists) inflation through lines at shops, through the scramble for allocations or quotas of scarce raw materials and parts (which are other ways of expressing scarcity), as is typical in the communist system. This in turn deteriorates into breakdown, as in Poland.

A Little Inflation Makes a Politician Look Good

In the United States the inflationary path has been a most attractive one for politicians to take. As we know, the initial effect of accelerated money growth is to increase the growth of nominal gross national product (current prices). Because previous money growth was less than current money growth, this means that the initial effect of an acceleration in money growth is not to increase prices (because their growth rate is determined by the growth of money eighteen months or two years previously, on average). Rather, the initial effect of accelerated money growth is to accelerate the growth of output and employment. That is fine for politicians; it makes them look good. They are in the highly desirable position of being able to look good today while leaving the consequences of their actions to be faced by the next chap.

Hence, there is a strong political momentum in inflation. A president inheriting a certain rate of inflation will always know that if he confines his activities to pumping up the rate of growth of money a little above what it was before he came to office, then he will be sure to be able to get away with a *no worse* rate of inflation than the previous president passed on to him, while ensuring that output and employment continue growing, through the effects of *today's* higher rate of growth of money.

There is a great incentive for a president—or for any other politician—to *postpone* doing anything about money growth which is excessive. He can always gain some positive political results by stoking up the fires of money growth just a little more, putting off the evil day when the consequences of long-term accelerating inflation would have to be faced. Until Ronald Reagan, no president since Dwight D. Eisenhower was prepared to take a stand against excessive monetary growth. The only possible exception was Gerald Ford, whose brief period in power was marked by his determination, and by his actions, to "whip inflation first."

Lyndon Johnson's tenure was marked by the beginning of the progressive acceleration in money growth. Annual growth of money rose from about 3 percent at the time of the assassination of John Kennedy to about 7 percent by 1968. Richard Nixon made an early attempt to take a tough stand on money, and during his term money growth fell away sharply to about 4 percent in 1970. A rapid acceleration was soon set in train, however, as he abandoned a serious anti-inflationary policy and adopted the gimmickry of price-wage controls accompanied by a simply furious rate of growth of money up to 7 percent a year in time for his reelection in 1972. The growth of money reached about 9 percent by 1973, when the inflationary boom collapsed and the then biggest postwar recession (1974–75) set in. President Ford's time at the White House saw money growth drop back to about 4 percent by 1975, only to be pushed rapidly back up again in time for the 1976 election. Under Jimmy Carter, the beginning of the end was becoming apparent. Despite a very rapid growth in money—in the range of 6½ to 8 percent a year—it was clear that output was ceasing to respond to monetary stimulus. The underlying forces of stagflation were becoming so strong that the economy could no longer get a "high" out of more money growth. Monetary stimulus simply led to more fear, higher interest rates, less investment, failing production growth, and rising unemployment. For President Reagan this means that the *possibility* of using more monetary stimulus to overcome the grave problems of unemployment of labor and resources is very limited.

Britain and America—Two of the Worst Examples of Monetary Disorder

Of all the Reserve banks in America, the leader in the analysis of monetary disorder has been the St. Louis Federal Reserve Bank. This bank has undertaken major research into the relationship between money and inflation and for years benefited from the pioneering work of Homer Jones, its director of research. The bank still provides a substantial source of stimulating research and analysis of money, and its monthly *Review* has been the source of major articles supporting the theme of monetarist theory and practice in economic policy.

It was therefore not surprising that on October 7, 1981, the president of the St. Louis Fed, Lawrence K. Roos, in an address to the St. Louis Council of World Affairs (reprinted in the St. Louis Fed *Review*) pointed up the importance of monetary control in the control of inflation.

There are three basic propositions that I wish to stress:

First: that persistent inflation whenever it occurs is a monetary phenomenon; it results simply from excessive growth of the money supply.

Second: that central banks are the creators of money and, consequently, in spite of monetary control techniques that differ between nations, they are capable of reducing, even eliminating, inflation, *if they so choose.*

Third: that when central banks have chosen not to contain the growth of money and inflation, this choice has usually resulted from pressures exerted by social and political forces that do not especially desire price stability.

The first two propositions are most easily demonstrated by simply comparing the monetary expansions and inflation experiences of West Germany, Switzerland, the United Kingdom and the United States over the past 15 years.

As mature, developed and open economies, each of these nations has been similarly affected by a host of nonmonetary factors, such as the vagaries of the weather, OPEC and the general expansion of government activities. Yet, in spite of the commonality of these influences on their respective economies, there are discernibly *uncommon* differences between the four nations in the manner in which they have conducted monetary policy and in the associated inflation they have experienced.

During the early 1960's, Switzerland had the *highest* rate of money growth (over 9 percent per year) and, consequently, the *highest* rate of inflation (about 5 percent per year).

At that time, the United States, by contrast, had the *lowest* rate of money growth (about 3 percent per year) and again, not surprisingly, the *lowest* inflation rate (less than 2 percent per year).

Rates of money growth and inflation in the United Kingdom and West Germany fell somewhere between the United States and Switzerland (See table on page 45)

What a difference the past 15 years have made! Since the mid-1960's, money growth in the United States and the United Kingdom has steadily accelerated. Over the past five years, U.S. monetary expansion was more than *double* what it was in the early 1960's. Money growth in the United Kingdom more than *tripled* its pre-1965 growth rate.

The patterns of Swiss and West German money growth over the past 15 years stand in sharp contrast to those of the United States and the United Kingdom. The Swiss rate of monetary

Annual Rates of Money Stock Growth and Price Levels

	Period	*Growth in Money*	*Growth in Prices*
West Germany	1960–65	9.0%	3.6%
	1965–70	6.0	3.5
	1970–75	10.2	6.6
	1975–80	8.3	4.0
Switzerland	1960–65	9.4	4.9
	1965–70	7.5	4.9
	1970–75	6.3	8.2
	1975–80	5.2	2.0
United Kingdom	1960–65	3.1	3.6
	1965–70	3.6	4.9
	1970–75	12.4	13.1
	1975–80	13.1	14.5
United States	1960–65	3.1	1.6
	1965–70	5.0	4.2
	1970–75	6.1	6.5
	1975–80	7.1	7.2

increase has declined sharply since the mid-1960's. West German money growth has shown a mixed pattern—sometimes sharply decelerating, sometimes sharply accelerating. However, over the past five years it was less than its rate of growth in the early 1960's.

As a result of these divergent patterns, while inflation has averaged more than 13 percent per year in the United Kingdom and over 7 percent per year in the U.S. for the past five years, Germany has experienced only a 4 percent average annual inflation, and inflation in Switzerland averaged a minuscule 2 percent per year.

Of course, over short periods, nonmonetary factors can also affect the rate of inflation. For example, as a result of OPEC, rates of inflation increased dramatically in all four nations, from 1973 to 1975. After 1975, however, the fundamental relationship between changes in the growth of money and changes in the rate of inflation was reasserted. Inflation *declined* in West Germany and Switzerland, and *increased* in the United Kingdom and the United States, reflecting the different patterns of monetary expansion in these countries.

45

International Success of "Tight Money" Policies

Milton Friedman, senior research fellow at the Hoover Institution and the father of modern-day monetarist theory and policy prescription, outlined the meaning of a monetarist policy in the February 1982 issue of the *Journal of Money, Credit and Banking.*

A monetarist policy has five points. First, the target should be growth in some monetary aggregate—just which monetary aggregate is a separate question; second, monetary authorities should adopt long-run targets for monetary growth that are consistent with no inflation; third, present rates of growth of monetary aggregates should be modified to achieve the long-run target in a gradual, systematic, and pre-announced fashion; fourth, monetary authorities should avoid "fine tuning" [the attempt to influence very short-run movements in the economy by tinkering with the rate of growth of money on a very short-term basis]; fifth, the monetary authorities should avoid trying to manipulate with interest rates or exchange rates.

Almost every central banker in the world today agrees verbally to at least the first three of these five points, and most also to the fourth. The fifth is unquestionably the most controversial. However, in many cases, the profession of faith is simply lip service and does not carry over to actual practice.

Rhetoric is one thing. Performance is often a very different thing. The fascinating and challenging question, I believe, is how to explain the frequent wide discrepancy between rhetoric and practice.

Internationally, those countries that have broadly followed the five-point monetarist policy have succeeded in controlling inflation and have done so while achieving relatively satisfactory economic growth.

Among the advanced countries of the world, the outstanding example is Japan. In 1973, Japan's inflation rate was around 25 percent per year, following monetary growth at a similar rate. Japan brought the rate of monetary growth down drastically, to the neighborhood of 10 to 15 percent, and has continued to reduce it still further.

After an intervening recession—by Japanese standards, not necessarily ours—of about eighteen months, inflation started to come down. It came down gradually and steadily, reached a level below 5 percent, then temporarily went up again after the most recent oil shock. Since then, it is starting to come down again and clearly seems under control. And the reduction of inflation has been accompanied by a growing economy.

West Germany is another example, not quite as successful, not quite as dramatic but still, on the whole, successful with respect to both inflation and economic growth because it has followed a policy of controlling the quantity of money along monetarist lines.

Among the less developed countries, Chile provides an even more dramatic case. In 1975, Chile had an inflation rate of about 800 percent per year. It has brought that down to under 20 percent a year, has now pegged its exchange rate to the U.S. exchange rate, having decided that, bad as U.S. monetary policy is, it is likely to be more successful than their own.

In Chile, as in Japan, an initial period of about a year and a half of great difficulty was followed by highly satisfactory real growth along with declining inflation. Real growth in Chile has been in the neighborhood of something like 6 to 10 percent a year during the past three or four years.

In my experience, these countries are exceptions.

In most countries that I know about, lip service, not actual adherence, has been paid to monetarist policies. Essentially, every major country, and many a minor one, proclaims monetary growth targets annually and pronounces its determination to stick to them. However, any relation between the targets and actual monetary growth is purely coincidental.

The United States is a particularly egregious case.

Variability of Money Growth Demoralizes the Economy

Not only has the trend of money growth in the United States over the past twenty years been one of acceleration, but the actual movement in money rate around this trend has been highly variable. Such variability has greatly intensified the sense of uncertainty and fear engendered by the accelerating trend of money growth.

The last two years' experience is enough to show the state of affairs. During 1980 M1-B grew at an annual rate of 6½ percent in the first three months; declined sharply in April, then grew very rapidly, at an annual rate approaching 16 percent for the six months to October. Between November 1980 and January 1981 M1-B fell at an annual rate of about 12 percent; from February to April rapid expansion ensued at an annual rate of about 18 percent a year; the

47

six-month freeze then intervened until October, when growth resumed at an annual rate of about 17 percent until December.

The effect of these wild swings in the rate of money growth is profoundly demoralizing to the financial markets. Their nervousness, after fifteen years of accelerating inflation, is gravely increased. The result is to increase the average risk cost involved in all financial transactions and to drive up the average cost of money. Another effect is that corporations never know when they will be able to jump into the financial markets to float some long-term issues. The flotation of such issues tends to be concentrated in very short periods, when there is some evanescent appearance of stability in monetary growth, at a low rate. This was the case in the second quarter of 1980, when a torrent of corporate bond issues was released between May and September, in the aftermath of the acute monetary squeeze of April—the time of credit controls.

Another frantic burst of bond offerings occurred in November–December 1981, following the money growth freeze that ended in October. While the prospects of raising long-term debt by corporations are undermined by the roller coaster ride of money, as it affects the financial markets, the rise in short-term business borrowings continues strongly upward. In 1980 the cumulative increase in the issuance of short-term bank loans and commercial paper (which are in effect intercompany loans backed by some fallback arrangement with a bank) was just over $20 billion. In 1981 this increase was over $48 billion.

As corporations are driven to rely more and more on short-term debt, the stability of the whole financial system is increasingly endangered. By the end of 1981 the total of short-term business loans from banks and of total commercial paper outstanding had reached in excess of $360 billion. This was an increase of some $70 billion over the previous two years, a rise of nearly 25 percent. By comparison, M1-B rose by about 12 percent during the same period.

Inflation Accelerates Over Time—Interest Rates Rise Progressively

The last twenty years have seen interest rates in the United States rise progressively and sharply, reflecting the acceleration in the growth of money which has been our experience over that time. The uptrend in interest rates began in the middle 1960's—about the same time that money growth began to accelerate. Until 1968 the long-term bond yield in America was fairly stable around 4 percent. With the progressive acceleration of money growth from the middle 1960's, however, interest rates also began to climb steadily. Long-term bond yields peaked at about 7 percent in 1970, about the time President Nixon was beginning his first and only attempt to control money growth. After falling away to about 6 percent during 1971, they began to rise sharply in the second half of 1972 (which was also the time President Nixon and the chairman of the Federal Reserve at the time, Arthur Burns, joined to balloon the money supply with extraordinary speed as part of the plan to reelect the president).

From 1972 to the present, the level of long-term bond yields has hardly ever looked back. It has been a story of increasing rates for long-term bond yields. The money supply expansion of 1972 pushed yields to a new level of about 8 percent by the middle of 1974, where they stayed until the Carter money growth boom really got going, with G. William Miller at the head of the Federal Reserve. Beginning in the second half of 1979, long-term bond yields headed still higher, in response to the rising inflation of 1979 and 1980, when price increases went into the double digits. By the end of 1980 bond yields were up around 12 percent, and by the end of 1981, despite the advent of a very bad recession and a sharp reduction in the rate of price increases, they were still up around 14 percent.

Uncertainty and fear of the future have combined to make a reduction in long-term interest rates very difficult to achieve. Between 1980 and 1981 the rate of increase of both producer and consumer prices dropped sharply and there was a reduction in the rate of money growth between the two years. Yet long-term bond yields rose, indicating the extreme reluctance of lenders to commit themselves after a decade and a half of mounting inflation.

This deserves emphasis. Since 1965 long-term bond yields in the United States have risen progressively and relentlessly, with only two setbacks in the upward climb. During 1971 and 1972 yields retreated from their 1970 peak of 7 percent back down to about 6 percent— a rate 50 percent above the 4 percent yield typical of the first half

49

of the 1960's. That retreat in bond yields was in response to the temporary reduction in the rate of price inflation which followed Nixon's only attempt to impose a tight money policy to arrest inflation, during 1970. The delayed impact of Nixon's money squeeze on prices (which he soon abandoned as I have said) temporarily arrested the uptrend of long-term bond yields. The return to an expansionary money policy in 1971–72, as the buildup for the 1972 election, set off inflation again, and bond yields resumed their uptrend in the second half of 1972.

A second period of moderate decline in bond yields took place in 1976 and 1977 as a result of the price inflation decline that occurred in those two years. The reduction in the rate of price inflation was in turn the result of the sharp reduction in the rate of growth of money in 1974 and 1975, two years previously, when President Ford made an effort, following the resignation of President Nixon, to repair the damage caused by the monetary explosion of 1972 which had carried on into 1973. During 1976 and 1977 bond yields leveled off around 8 percent, trending down very gradually to about 7½ percent at their bottom in 1977.

But as inflation accelerated in 1978, 1979, and 1980, the level of bond yields continued to rise, from the 7½ to 8 percent of 1974 through 1977 up through 9 percent in 1979, on through 11 and 12 percent in 1980 to the 13 and 14 percent levels reached in 1981.

There is a very clear pattern here. Bond yields follow the course of inflation. As inflation increases, so does the level of bond yields. Inflation in turn was the result of previous increases in the supply of money, in the rate of money growth. Hence, over this long period of time, twenty years, bond yield movements have been dominated by the movements in inflation.

We may compare U.S. experience once again with that of West Germany, Switzerland, and the United Kingdom. Between 1960 and 1980 the level of long-term bond yields in West Germany rose from just under 7 percent to just under 9 percent. Only one really strong upward move in German bond yields occurred during that time— in 1973 and 1974, at the time of the first oil shock, when yields on German long-term bonds rose briefly toward 11 percent. There was another uptick in 1980, following the second oil shock. In the case of Switzerland, bond yields started about 3 percent in the early 1960's and ended under 5 percent. Once again, there was an uptick in 1974, to over 7 percent.

Neither country has experienced the steady, secular increase in bond yields which has been typical of U.S. experience in the last twenty years. We know there is a good reason for this. Neither country has experienced the strong secular uptrend in inflation as has the United States.

For a really pathological example of the effects of inflation on bond yields in an advanced industrialized country, let us look at the experience of the United Kingdom. During the early 1960's bond yields in Britain were around 6 percent. They rose to over 9 percent by 1969–71. In 1972, in response to the extraordinary explosion of inflation which set in during the 1970's, British bond yields (exacerbated in their rise by the added factor of the 1973–74 oil shock) started to rise to a peak of nearly 17 percent at the end of 1974. Thereafter, with the passage of the oil shock, bond yields retreated somewhat, but remained in the range of 11 to 15 percent from 1977 through 1980.

We therefore know:

1. During the last twenty years the rate of growth of money in both West Germany and Switzerland has been relatively stable.

2. During the same period money growth in the United Kingdom and the United States has been progressively increased.

3. Inflationary expectations in West Germany and Switzerland have been relatively stable, in line with the relatively stable growth of prices in these countries over the twenty years.

4. But in Britain and America inflationary expectations have progressively increased, in line with the acceleration of price increases that has been a feature of those two countries' experience in the last twenty years.

5. Bond yields have increased on average only 2 basis points (one hundredth of one percentage point) per quarter in the last twenty years in West Germany and Switzerland, while rising by 8 and 14 basis points per quarter in the United States and the United Kingdom.

Commenting on this issue in the October 1981 St. Louis Federal Reserve *Review*, Dallas S. Batten stated:

> The key to price stability is to prevent money growth from accelerating over the long run. Germany and Switzerland have not permitted money growth to accelerate over the last twenty years; as a result, the rates of inflation and inflationary expectations in these countries have remained relatively unchanged. On the other hand, the United States and the United Kingdom have allowed their rates of money growth to accelerate. Consequently, the rate of inflation and inflationary expectations in each country have also increased.

To get bond yields down, it is clear money growth has to be strictly controlled because only through control of money growth will inflation be controlled.

The Age of Inflation NOT Due to "Special Factors"

It is clear that the Age of Inflation has *not* been the result of special factors such as the OPEC oil crises of 1974 and 1979. Nor is the Age of Inflation due to some inherent weakness in the national character of the British or the Americans. As I have shown, both Britain and America in earlier periods succeeded in maintaining control over money growth and hence over inflation. In the 1950's the average annual rate of inflation in America was little more than 2 percent a year. Until the middle 1960's there was an enviable record of price and monetary stability.

Now all that has gone, and in the five years to 1980, we are talking about an annual average rise of 8 to 9 percent a year.

Deeply ingrained in the American psyche today is the fear of

**Increase in Consumer
Prices—United States**

1950–55	11.4%
1955–60	10.4
1960–65	6.5
1965–70	23.2
1970–75	33.0
1975–80	53.1

inflation and contempt for money as an asset worth holding. This belief is reflected in the growth of a mass of institutions and arrangements that expect continuing price rises. Most notably, a mountain of short-term debt has been accumulated as part of a huge debt load built up during the long period since 1965, when the rate of inflation generally was equal to or exceeded the rate of interest, thus making debt virtually free of interest, after inflation.

Lenders of Money Revolt at Last—High Real Interest Rates

As inflation progressively accelerated in America during the last twenty years, the real rate of interest which a borrower was required to pay declined. The thinking and understanding of lenders lagged. From 1960 to 1970, as inflation began to gather momentum, the real rate of interest (that is, the nominal rate of interest paid on debts divided by the rate of inflation) in America gradually declined from about 2 percent to zero. In the 1970's the real rate of interest continued to drop, falling to a low point of −4 percent (negative) in both 1973 and 1978.

In effect, these negative rates of interest permitted borrowers in America to get money for which they were paid a bonus by the lenders. Borrowers had a heyday; lenders suffered grievous losses after inflation. Yields on bonds and other debt instruments were rising, but they were not rising fast enough to keep pace with inflation.

Real Interest Rates Turn Positive

	Percent Increase per Annum Consumer Prices	*Three-Month Treasury Bill Rate of Interest*
1976	4.8%	5.0%
1977	6.8	5.3
1978	9.0	7.2
1979	13.3	10.0
1980	12.4	11.5
1981	8.9	14.1
Fourth Qr '81	5.2	11.9

As the table shows, not until 1981 was there a decisive change in the level of real interest rates. Until then the three-month Treasury bill rate had been either below the inflation rate or, as in 1976, only very slightly above it.

But in 1981 there was a major reversal of attitudes, and the rate of interest remained very high, by historical standards, while the inflation rate fell sharply. By the fourth quarter the rate of inflation had fallen to about 5 percent a year while interest rates remained in double digits. This was a reflection of a very profound change in attitudes on the part of lenders. Whereas in the 1970's lenders were slow to realize that they were being robbed by inflation, now the lag is working the other way. Lenders will not give up their money except in return for yields that by historical standards appear amazingly high. Lord Keynes once spoke about the coming of the "euthanasia of the rentier"—the merciful killing of lenders. That time came for a brief span in America during the 1970's, as rentiers—lenders—failed to wake up quickly enough to the losses they were suffering owing to inflation.

Between 1978 and 1981 the real rate of interest in America rose from a negative figure of more than 3 percent to a positive real interest rate of over 5 percent. There does not appear to be any other period in this *century* when the real rate of interest in the United States exceeded 3 percent, with the possible exception of the year 1937. Indeed, there have been only brief periods in American economic history in this century when real interest rates have been positive at all. Mostly, real interest rates have been zero or negative. The period between 1950 and 1970 was the longest continuous period during which there were positive real rates of interest in this century, and even then we are talking about an average of something like 1 to 1½ percent.

It is not hard to appreciate the importance of the change indicated by the emergence of high, positive, real interest rates. The financial services industry in America today is one of the top glamour industries, expanding at a hectic pace. Regulations imposed back in the 1920's and the 1930's, in an attempt to control bank profits and to insulate local banks from big city competition, have held back the development of banks in this new atmosphere of lush potential profits from moneylending. New institutions, like Sears, now the biggest financial services company in the United States, Shearson–American Express, Bache–Prudential, and Philipp Brothers–Salomon Brothers, have rushed in. Lenders are having a wonderful time, with the prospect of profitability likely unprecedented in the twentieth-century United States.

Today we are seeing not the "euthanasia of the rentier" but the "revolt of the rentier." Money in America today is real and hard. Its price, after taking inflation into account, is higher than at any time since 1900.

Bank shares will become glamour stocks. We are reminded that during the 1920's the value of bank shares rose over 400 percent, as declining inflation boosted the real value of bank earnings, even though nominal interest rates remained fairly stable.

These high real interest rates are being charged on a stupendous outstanding volume of debt, as it is converted. The total outstanding debt of all kinds in the United States, in terms of 1972 prices, was about $900 billion in 1950, about $1,300 billion in 1960, about $2,100 billion in 1970, and about $2,900 billion in 1980.

Between 1960 and 1980 total debt in relation to gross national product rose from about 1.7 times to about 2.1 times. Over the same twenty-year period the ratio of total debt to the money supply (a measure of the rate of increase of debt to the funds available for ordinary transactions) increased from six times to over fourteen times.

There is no doubt that this is a very precarious situation. In every direction, there appear to be blind alleys. We are, it seems, caught in a maze, built over the last fifteen years of inflationary and monetary excess.

Is There No Way Out—Short of a Major Financial Crash?

It is already clear that the United States is in a frightful bind. Years of inflationary excess have brought about a decline of long-term lending, a decline of long-term investment, a deeply ingrained fear of inflation among lenders, a catapult to unprecedented levels of real interest rates, a mountain of debt affecting corporations and indicating a deep-seated crisis of liquidity in America's corporate sector, a terribly dangerous dependence on short-term borrowing by American business, a decay of major sectors of American industry with less and less chance of their finding the resources to rebuild.

A continued resort to excessive monetary growth will simply bring about a return to even higher nominal interest rates. So easy money policies are no longer a practical route to take.

Do we have to just wait until, by a slow process of pain, confidence in money is restored, inflation subsides, and real interest rates come down to a level where once again long-term productive investment can resume? Or will there simply be a financial crash, wiping out much of the debt by the process of mass bankruptcy?

It is certainly not hard to imagine such a financial crash. The indebtedness of corporate America is so huge and the cost of servicing the debt so onerous, in relation to profitability, that it remains to be seen whether corporate America, saddled with huge debts at rising real rates of interest and facing stagnant markets (part and parcel of the Age of Recession) will be able to avoid major corporate collapses. There has been a very sharply rising tide of personal bankruptcies and many major American corporations are in the intensive care ward.

The whole savings and loan and mutual savings bank industry is struck down with grave illness, and in 1982 fully one quarter of all the S and L's in America were expected to fail. While lenders generally are having a wonderful time in America today, the S and L's have been stuck with a debt load based on previous low rates of interest. As a result, they have been in the invidious position of having to pay much more for their deposits monies while not being able to renegotiate their long-standing (cheap) mortgage loans. They are casualties of the Age of Inflation. They are also casualties of the wide-ranging Federal Reserve controls over interest rates, which in earlier years prevented the S and L's from being able to offer competitive rates of interest, with the result that they lost business to competing institutions, such as money market funds.

At the same time, the major industrial complexes of autos, steel, airlines, aerospace, housing, and construction have been gravely weakened by the Age of Recession and the consequences of progressive financial weakness which was the result of the Age of Inflation. The same has happened in Britain, where the process of dismantling the industrial base of that once great industrial power has gone much farther than anything we have yet seen in America. Yet we face the same sort of mixture of implacable forces that have brought the British into crisis.

There is a hope in this country that the election of President Reagan may have been a sufficient change to bring back order and to permit once again a revival of long-term investment and of production and economic expansion. But it could hardly be expected that the election of one man to power would be enough to arrest the powerful trends set in train over a period of fifteen years of failure. The world over, as governments grapple with the problems caused by the Age of Inflation and now by the Age of Recession, electors have shown themselves very fickle. They have not shown much patience. Governments have gone in and out as through a revolving door. In 1981 alone, governments changed in France, Greece, and Poland. In Holland and Belgium there was incessant political crisis. The same went for Italy. In West Germany there was rising unrest and crowd scenes. Canada is divided and filled with internal disputes. In Australia the government faces growing resentment and opposition.

If it is possible for the existing corporate and financial structure to survive in America during the necessary period of adjustment to a lower rate of inflation, then there would be a prospect of a new world of disinflation. *The crucial element in reaching this promised land is the persistent reduction in the rate of money growth.*

Many of the conditions for disinflation are already in place. The financial markets have shown their trenchant resistance to any evidence of excessive money growth. That is a powerful barrier. The rate of price inflation has already dropped sharply, in response to the moderation in the rate of money growth in 1980 and 1981, compared with earlier years. The painful adjustment process in the Age of Recession is changing attitudes among the people at large. The price of gold has dropped and is exceedingly reluctant to revive. Commodity prices remain low, as falling worldwide demand, the product of the Age of Recession, kicks out the underpinnings of prospective shortage on which commodity markets thrive. The energy crisis is a thing of the past. The world today has a massive surplus of available energy. Coal is superabundant; oil production outside OPEC continues to thrive; energy conservation is producing a static world energy demand, helped as always by the Age of Recession.

The foundations of traditional family finances, built on the notion of the inevitable escalation in the value of the family home, the family's biggest single asset, have been thrown into disarray. It is no longer possible to expect a continuous increase in the value of the family home. Nor will negative real interest rates make it such an easy process to borrow on the inflationary surplus in the family home's value. Today the family faces a double negative, compared with the double positive of the past, in relation to the family home. In the 1970's, before the Age of Recession, it was possible to experience the pleasant sensation of borrowing against the increase in the family home's value and at the same time to know that the cost of the money borrowed was either zero or (more likely) negative. Today the family home has ceased to escalate in value at anything like the rate which pertained in the Age of Inflation. Family homes are in fact a drug on the market. What is more, any loans secured against the family home carry a high real rate of interest.

Real estate markets languish; collectibles are very hard to sell; speculation in all real commodities is less and less profitable.

High real interest rates have produced a new world of investment opportunities in financial assets. During 1981 the best investment, excluding gold, collectibles, and commodities—which were a dead loss—was cash. Money invested in four-month commercial paper yielded the top return, higher than bonds and far higher than stocks. Taxation incentives such as the IRA and Keogh incentives have given the middle classes of America a chance to build up their own investments in financial assets. We are moving into a world where saving has become a far more profitable thing to do.

This process *could* become self-perpetuating. The expansion of savings and the growing commitment that the middle classes of America have made for the preservation of their newly won financial investments could gradually produce a constituency in favor of disinflation and of sweating it out, as prices come down and down. There could be a further bonus, in the shape of a wholesale switch of investment attention away from real assets to financial assets. This in turn could produce an overwhelming downward push in nominal interest rates.

A Sudden Collapse of Nominal Interest Rates—The Payoff

In recent years there has been a movement out of financial assets into real assets, such as gold, commodities, real estate, collectibles, and the like. People have been cashing in financial assets, such as stocks and bonds, to invest the money in what seemed to them like better hedges against inflation. This was logical. They were trying to protect the value of their assets.

The total value of assets, financial and real, held in the United States runs into trillions of dollars. There is a stupendous *stock* of assets. A change in the manner in which those assets are distributed between financial and real assets will affect the relative prices of financial and real assets.

In recent years the value of debt instruments such as bonds, bills, and mortgages—that is, financial assets—has fallen. That is the other side of the rise in interest rates which has occurred. The fall in the price of financial assets has meant a rise in the yield on those assets —and hence a rise in interest rates since their annual rate of interest is fixed at the time of the contract.

This process can be reversed. As inflation tends to come *down*, it becomes more attractive to buy financial rather than real assets. Financial assets give the investor an *annual return* and may also produce some *capital appreciation*. Real assets yield only capital appreciation. They actually cost money to hold on to, because the money invested in something real like gold is money that could have been invested elsewhere, to earn a rate of interest.

In recent years, of course, inflation has been so bad, and the real return on financial assets so low, that investors could do much better by buying real assets for their capital appreciation, despite the fact that these assets did not earn any interest or dividends, as financial assets, like bonds or stocks, would have done.

In 1980 and 1981 inflation started to subside. A degree of monetary restraint and the Age of Recession have combined to make a dent in the seemingly unstoppable uptrend of prices. If this process continued, we could expect a continuing movement by people back into financial assets.

The size of the stock of assets held by Americans is huge in relation to the annual increment to that stock, which is the total of savings made each year. As more and more Americans became convinced that inflation was going to recede, then more and more of them switched their assets into financial investments. This is what most of the farsighted brokerage advisers in New York have been telling their clients to do since 1980. They have been saying that we should think about investing in a new sort of world—a world of *dis*inflation. Since the middle of 1981, when interest rates started to collapse, this seemed a better and better idea.

The movement toward lower interest rates has a much longer distance to travel before we can expect to get back to the sort of rates we enjoyed in the 1960's and even better, the 1950's (when Americans enjoyed a decade of strong economic growth based on a growth rate of money about 2 percent and a bond yield of under 3 percent. The long-term bond yield did not get above 4 percent until after 1965).

There is hope that in the future we will get the big payoff in sharply lower interest rates as a result of persisting with a policy of steadily reducing the rate of growth of money. In such an environment, where people are switching more and more of their *stock* of assets into financial assets and out of real assets, the movement of funds will be so great as to overwhelm any *incremental* imbalance between the supply of savings generated each year and the demand for those savings.

We often hear it said that the American savings ratio is very low —as it appears to be. It is only about 5 or 6 percent of personal income, far lower than in other developed industrial countries such as West Germany, Japan, or even the United Kingdom. But a vast stock of assets has built up over a long period of time. Changes in the allocation of this stock can make possible major changes in interest rates. The motivating factor is the expectation of inflation. If more inflation is anticipated, there will be a movement out of financial assets—*and the reverse applies.* Such changes are so large that they can overwhelm the effect of incremental supplies of savings and demand for savings.

Many economic commentators become upset about the prospect of big federal government budget deficits. It is thought they will overwhelm the financial markets because the demand for savings on the part of the government appears to be so great in relation to *that year's* supply of savings out of *that year's* national income. In truth, as previously stated, the relative prices of real and financial assets are determined by the net results of millions of individual decisions about the size of the stock of assets—real or financial—to hold.

There is much more reason to hope that the stranglehold of high interest rates can be broken than is generally recognized. There is certainly far less reason to be concerned about the problem of bringing about a collapse of interest rates than one might assume from listening to the gloom and doom on Wall Street when the subject of prospective federal budget deficits and their effects on bond prices is raised.

It All Depends on the Success We Have in Controlling Money Growth

Success in defeating inflation, in reducing onerous interest rates, and in providing the foundations for a resumption of strong economic expansion is possible. There is no doubt about it. But such success depends on one vital element—there must be a radical and continuing reduction in the rate of growth of money. Just as excessive money growth brought us to the present crisis, so minimal money growth will provide the conditions for getting out of it.

We then ask ourselves: who controls money growth? In America money growth is controlled by the actions and policies of the Federal Reserve. We must ask ourselves: can we trust the fate of the nation to this frail and fallible institution? Can the Federal Reserve possibly give us a long period of stable money growth? Does it know how to do it? Is such a thing really possible—quite apart from the social and political upheaval involved in the process of adjustment? What possible confidence can we have that the Federal Reserve is even interested in controlling money growth?

Has the Fed Ever Been Seriously Interested in Controlling Money Growth?

America has suffered a major monetary disaster in the past fifteen years. The Age of Inflation has seen the growth of output slow down; productivity growth has fallen toward zero, unemployment has ratcheted to ever higher levels; effective tax rates have risen rapidly, reflecting bracket creep; corporate finances have been undermined; and financial instability has spread. The Age of Inflation has been followed by the Great Recession of 1978–83, the longest period of economic stagnation for fifty years.

Three presidents—Nixon, Ford, and Carter—failed to bring inflation under control. Three chairmen of the Federal Reserve Board—Burns, Miller, and Volcker—have failed to give America steady, slow monetary growth, the sine qua non of stability of prices and stable, strong economic growth.

Yet without stable money growth there will be no permanent return to the sort of negligible inflation the nation enjoyed for the first twenty years after 1945. Nor will there be a return to low interest rates.

Has the Federal Reserve demonstrated any real interest in achieving slow, stable money growth? The answer is that it has not demonstrated any such interest by its actions—as distinct from the utterances of chairmen of the Federal Reserve and other officials of the central bank.

In his article in the February 1982 *Journal of Money, Credit and Banking,* Milton Friedman wrote:

Ever since the establishment of the Federal Reserve System, every chairman of the Federal Reserve Board, indeed, I suspect, every member of the board, has proclaimed that the Federal Reserve will not be an engine of inflation. Yet the Federal Reserve System was an engine of inflation during both world wars and has been one in peacetime at least since 1960.

My examination of that experience impresses me with the unbelievable strength of bureaucratic inertia in preventing the system from learning from experience. The inertia has prevailed not only since 1960 but for the whole sixty-seven years of the Federal Reserve's existence. With perhaps a few minor exceptions, the system has repeatedly been unable or unwilling to change its methods of operation in order to benefit from its own experience.

As will become clear, Federal Reserve officials have fought tooth and nail against changing their procedures. They have fought against any change that would set objective, publicly visible (and checkable) criteria for the administration of monetary policy. The Fed has fought against "visible and checkable targets" for money growth. Fed officials have twisted and turned to evade externally imposed (and easily verifiable) targets. They have done everything in their power to retain their "discretionary" power over monetary policy, subject to no "bottom line" test of success.

Thus, the Fed does not have to meet a profitability test. It does not have to meet the sort of political test that imposes some sort of limit on the policies and practices of "normal" departments of government such as Defense, Interior, Agriculture—even Treasury and State. There is no political head of the Fed who can be deposed by the electorate. It is an institution that has managed to escape all objective tests, whether political or financial. The Fed has never demonstrated any persistent interest in modifying its actions to meet the demand for stable, steady money growth.

Open Market Operations

Federal Reserve officials exercise their influence over the financial system of the United States mostly through the medium of open market operations. These operations involve a massive program of buying and selling government securities, such as Treasury bonds and bills. Through these operations the Fed *could* bring about changes in the quantity of money by buying or selling (mainly government) securities.

When the Fed buys securities, it pays for them with a Federal Reserve bank check. This check is as good as cash, for the credit of the central bank is never in doubt. That check is deposited by the seller of the bond or bill into his bank account, thus increasing the cash reserves of that bank. This increase in its reserves of cash would allow the bank, other things being equal, to increase its rate of lending. In reverse, sales of securities by the Federal Reserve System require the dealer who buys the securities to give the Fed a check on his bank. This transfer of funds from the bank to the Fed reduces the bank's cash and would, other things being equal, lead to a reduction in the rate of lending by the bank concerned.

In mobilizing their cash, the banks make use of federal funds, which are overnight loans made in immediately usable funds. The market in federal funds is thus a market in immediately usable funds, and the federal funds rate of interest is an indicator of the supply and demand of such marginal funds. Because of its particular relevance to the operations of the major banks, the federal funds rate of interest has acquired a particular significance as an especially sensitive indicator of the balance of supply and demand for immediately available funds for the banks' use.

The federal funds rate is obviously influenced by the actions of the Federal Reserve System in buying and selling securities, as these actions influence the amount of cash available in the main money markets. The banks must maintain reserves with the Federal Reserve System. They are also permitted to borrow money from the Federal Reserve System, to meet reserve requirements that they would otherwise not be able to meet (lacking the immediately available cash or for other reasons). The rate of interest which the Federal Reserve charges on these loans to the member banks is called the discount rate.

Money Is Not Credit

Money—in the form of coins, currency, and checkable deposits— is an asset that people generally accept as payment for goods and services. By contrast, credit is one party's claim against another party, which is to be settled by a future payment of money. Confusion about the difference between money and credit arises because people can increase their spending either by reducing their money balances (spending coins or currency or writing a check) or by obtaining credit (getting a loan from a finance company to pay for a car).

The rate of interest is the price of credit. Changes in the supply of and demand for money influence the price of credit only indirectly, through changes in the purchasing power of money. Additional confusion arises because the Federal Reserve creates money primarily by purchasing credit market instruments, such as Treasury bills and bonds, which are simply contracts to repay debts by the U.S. government. As already noted, when the Federal Reserve purchases government securities and pays for them with a check, it increases the cash available to banks, thereby tending to give them more freedom to make loans or increase the available supply of bank credit. Thus, initially, we would expect increased purchases of government securities by the Fed to lead to lower interest rates.

However, over a longer period of time, the higher creation of money by the Fed (which follows from the rise in the banks' cash —money—upon the increased purchase of securities by the Fed) has important effects on economic activity which tend to raise interest rates. Monetary expansion leads to greater economic activity, to increased demand for credit (to finance more sales and production), and thus to a tendency for higher interest rates.

We have seen how this whole process has become vastly foreshortened by the inflation which has resulted, over the years, from the excessive creation of money by the Fed. This process has been summarized in the *Economic Report of the President*, written by the Council of Economic Advisers. In the February 1982 report, we are told:

> When interest rates are high, credit is often said to be "tight," meaning that it is expensive. This does not necessarily mean that money is tight in the sense that its quantity is restricted. Indeed, quite the opposite is likely to be the case. "Easy" money, in the sense of rapid growth in the stock of money, may

very well be the underlying reason for a tight credit market. Conversely, tight money, in the sense of slow growth in the stock of money, is likely to lead eventually to a fall in "nominal" (as quoted) interest rates as inflation expectations subside.

[This is what we have seen powerfully at work in the last couple of years in America.]

Conversely, tight money in the sense of slow growth in the stock of money is likely to lead eventually to a fall in nominal interest rates as inflation expectations subside. But it is credit, not money, that is easy.

The Fed Does Not Need to Create Much Money for Normal Economic Growth

The relation between the stock of money and the nominal (current prices) gross national product is called the velocity of money. In America the velocity of money (meaning the number of times the stock of money has to turn over each year to finance the gross national product) was about 6.8 in 1981. This meant that the stock of money (M1—which is the total of currency, demand deposits at commercial banks, and checkable deposits at all other depository institutions) turned over approximately 6.8 times to finance the gross national product in 1981.

The velocity of money is a very stable number. It has increased each year, over a long period of time, by about 3½ percent. The graph on page 68 shows the very stable relationship between the monetary base (which is the sum of currency and bank reserves with the Fed) and the gross national product. We also know from long experience that the relationship between the monetary base and the money stock (M1), called the money multiplier, is very stable and predictable. It has been plotted over a long period of time by, among others, Professor Robert Rasche of the University of Michigan and by the Federal Reserve itself.

It is obvious that there is no need for the Federal Reserve to create much additional money each year at all.

We know from long experience that in America the real increase in gross national product has averaged about 3 to 4 percent. It has not averaged that high in recent years because the progress of the

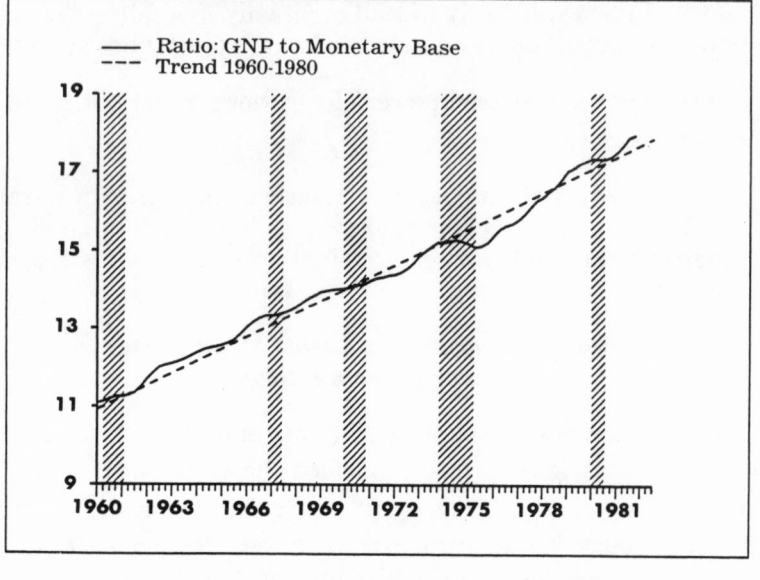

The Trend of Velocity Has Been Stable

Data are trailing four-quarter moving averages.
Monetary base has been lagged two quarters.
Shaded areas, except for the mini-recession of 1966-1967, represent
periods of recession as designated by the National Bureau of Economic Research.

Sources: Econalyst Data Base; Morgan Stanley Research

The graph shows that the relationship between the monetary base (currency plus the banks' reserves with the Fed) and the gross national product has been very stable over a long period of time. As we also know there is a very stable relationship between the monetary base and the money stock (M1) — known as the "money multiplier." We can readily forecast what the gross national product will be from our knowledge of the size of changes in the monetary base. The "velocity of money" (the ratio between the money stock and the gross national product) increases about 3½ percent a year very regularly over long periods of time.

economy has been frustrated by the consequences of the Age of Inflation. But assuming we did eventually get back to more normal conditions, we could expect a rise of 3 to 4 percent, on average, in the real gross national product.

We know from long experience that the average increase in the velocity of money is about 3½ percent a year. So if the money stock were held constant, there would be enough money, simply as a result

68

of the increase in the velocity of the stock of money, to finance that rate of increase of the real gross national product *without any rises in prices* on average. But we also know that in recent years the rate of growth of the stock of money has been more in the range of 7 to 8 percent a year.

It is immediately obvious that the increase in the stock of money in recent years has been *grossly excessive* when measured against what would have been needed to finance, without inflation, the normally expectable 3 to 4 percent annual increase in the real gross national product of America. Some economists, looking at these numbers, would say there is no need for *any* increase in the money stock because the normal increase in the velocity of money is sufficient to finance the feasible growth of real gross national product.

Professor David Meiselman, professor of economics at Virginia Polytechnic Institute and an adviser to the U.S. Treasury, has suggested we should increase the money stock by *zero;* after the normal rise in the velocity of money had been taken into account, there would be plenty of money to finance the prospective likely feasible increase in the real (noninflationary) gross national product each year. Meiselman would simply call a halt to the increase in the stock of money and leave it at that.

Dr. Robert Weintraub, the staff economist at the Joint Economic Committee of Congress who has been a great innovator in thinking about the problems of monetary control in America, has strongly supported the stable growth of, and indeed has done much of the original work on, the velocity of money in America. He stands by the figure of about a 3½ percent a year increase in velocity and has himself recommended that the rate of growth of money should be reduced virtually to zero, arguing that such a rate of increase would be sufficient to finance normal noninflationary growth for the U.S. economy over the years.

Our historical experience also shows that very slow growth of money is entirely compatible with strong, steady economic growth. From 1951 to 1960 the average annual rate of growth of the money stock (M1) was 2.2 percent. Over that period the real gross national product of America rose by 3½ percent a year. And the level of prices increased on average by 2.2 percent a year (consumer price index). If we had had a little *less* money growth over that period, we might have had a little *less* inflation. As it was, the period from 1951 to 1960 was one of solid achievement in money, prices, and output. It certainly showed that we don't need big increases in money supply to achieve big increases in output.

The 1950's were for all practical purposes the Eisenhower years, and it has become fashionable to suggest they were years of very disappointing economic performance. Yet during most of the decade, output grew at a rate that we would envy today. And price stability was remarkable by today's standards. We will be fortunate if in the five years ending in the fourth quarter of 1983, America's real gross national product grows as much as 1½ percent a year and if America's rate of price inflation averages as little as 6 percent a year.

The monetary restraint of the Eisenhower decade continued into the early 1960's. The rate of growth of M1 (those days' equivalent of yesterday's M1-B—the sum of currency and demand and checking deposits in banks and thrift institutions) was 2.1 percent in 1961, 2.2 percent in 1962, and 2.9 percent in 1963. Monetary policy crossed the border between tight and easy during the presidency of Lyndon Johnson.

Early in his administration President Johnson made it clear he wanted the Federal Reserve to help him promote economic growth. In his January 1964 message to Congress, he said: "It would be self-defeating to cancel the stimulus of tax reduction by tightening money." In his 1965 economic report, President Johnson asked Congress to repeal the requirement that Federal Reserve banks maintain a gold certificate reserve behind their deposit liabilities, lest it prevent accommodative monetary expansion. (The gold restraint was removed entirely in 1968, when backing behind Federal Reserve notes was eliminated.) From that time, money growth in the United States has been clearly excessive, far in excess of what is needed to support a steady feasible rate of growth of total output, at 3 to 4 percent a year.

Now let us come to grips with the obvious question—namely, what the Federal Reserve thinks it is doing about money growth. Indeed, is the Federal Reserve, on the basis of what we know about its actions over the last fifteen years, at all interested in controlling the growth of the money supply?

The Fed Has Been Mostly Interested in Stabilizing Interest Rates, Not Money Growth Rates

Astounding as it may seem, the evidence clearly and starkly points to one conclusion about the Federal Reserve's policy actions in the last decade. The Fed has not been interested primarily in controlling the growth of the money supply at all. It has been concerned mainly with controlling the movement of interest rates. This conclusion is so amazing, as will be seen, that its factual basis and, above all, its implications must be understood.

There is no doubt that during the 1970's the Federal Reserve placed a far higher priority on achieving certain levels of interest rates than on achieving rates of growth of money. Interest rate stability was a prime, indeed the prime, aim of Federal Reserve policy during this decade. The Federal Reserve has always regarded interest rates as an indicator of the ease or the tightness of money. The price of money has been the indicator of its relative availability. That is fundamental in the Fed's way of thinking. Hence, when Federal Reserve officials looked at the money markets and saw that interest rates were rising, they assumed this meant that money was getting tighter. And when they looked at the money markets and saw that interest rates were falling, they assumed money was getting easier.

They are not alone in this belief. This general view is repeated over and over again in the *Wall Street Journal* and *The New York Times,* either in quotes from so-called money market experts or in the written opinion of the journalist attempting to explain what is happening in the money markets.

Federal Reserve officials, who report to the Federal Reserve Board and to the monetary policy committee of the Federal Reserve System —the Federal Open Market Committee—take the trend of interest rates as an indicator of the relative ease or tightness of money. They look at interest rates and conclude from a rise in interest rates that money is getting tighter. They conclude from a decline in interest rates that money is getting easier.

We know from the discussion earlier in this chapter that when interest rates are falling, *credit* is getting easier and that when interest rates are rising, *credit* is getting tighter. If credit is tight (as indicated by rising interest rates), we are unlikely to cure this problem by making *money* easier. If the Federal Reserve increases the supply of *money* by increasing its purchases of Treasury bills and Treasury bonds and paying for them with its own checks (which are the same as cash), the effect will be *initially* to reduce the rate of interest because banks will tend to increase the loans. But increasing the supply of *money* will tend to increase the demand for credit because it will stimulate more economic expansion. The whole process has become so short-circuited over the years of inflation that an increase in the supply of *money* almost immediately leads to an increase in the *price of credit*—which is the rate of interest.

Unfortunately, over the years the Federal Reserve has not understood this basic fact. Fed officials have thought if interest rates were going up, this meant money was getting more expensive and therefore less freely available. If interest rates were declining, this meant money was getting cheaper and therefore more freely available.

The Fed has got the point exactly backward.

When the Fed position is stated, it sounds perfectly reasonable, and one thinks one must be churlish for criticizing journalists, financial commentators, so-called money market experts—and the Federal Reserve itself—for holding such a view. Yet the very idea that high interest rates *mean* money is tight has had utterly disastrous consequences for the American economy and indeed for the whole industrialized world.

It would not be putting too fine a point on it to state that much of the battle over monetary policy in this country in the last twenty years has been over the attempt by outsiders to eradicate from the thinking of the Fed erroneous notions about interest rates.

Consider the consequences of the idea. Imagine you are sitting in the New York Federal Reserve, on the Open Market Desk, deciding, within the guidelines given to you by the Federal Reserve Board, whether you should take a certain line of action. You see that interest rates are rising. This means money is getting tight, as you see things. You have been told to keep interest rates in a certain range. So what do you do? You go out into the market, buy securities, and pay for them with Federal Reserve checks. The effect of your action is to increase the quantity of money because Federal Reserve checks, being as good as cash, may be used by the banks that receive them as the basis for expansion of their loans.

Or imagine that you are sitting in the Federal Reserve at the Open Market Desk and you observe that interest rates are tending to drop below the range you have been told to work within. You go out into the market and you sell securities—T-bills or T-bonds—this has the effect of draining cash out of the banks and putting pressure on them to restrict their lending activity.

From the point of view of the thinking process of the Federal Reserve, what you have done is perfectly reasonable and responsible. You have attempted to moderate the degree of tightness or ease of money by taking compensating action.

In the days of the Great Depression this attitude led the Fed to continue selling securities (pulling cash out of the banking system) while banks were collapsing all around it and unemployment was soaring. Between 1929 and 1932 the yield on Treasury bills fell from over 5 to under 1 percent and at the same time, the quantity of M2 —a broad definition of the money supply—*fell* by about 20 percent. This was a major financial disaster and a terrible example of how fallacious thinking at the Federal Reserve makes things much worse than they already are. Poor President Hoover remembered in his memoirs: "I concluded [the Reserve Board] was indeed a weak reed for a nation to lean on in time of trouble." By restricting money and in fact presiding over a huge reduction in the money supply between 1929 and 1932, the Fed made the depression much, much worse than it already was and much worse than it need have been.

The Fed's Money Policy Has Made Inflationary Booms Worse and Recessions Deeper

Why can I say that the Fed's method of thinking is wrong? Why do things not work out as the Fed has for at least two *generations* thought they worked? Let us go back to the idea that rising interest rates *mean* money is getting tighter and therefore the Fed should buy securities, increasing the banks' cash.

73

The essence of the Fed's *conceptual* failure has been in the inability of its officials, steeped in generations of traditional thinking, to work out the difference between money and credit. That is why you will find this essential difference spelled out in such detail in the work of modern monetarist economists, as in the *Economic Report of the President, February 1982* and in the speeches of Beryl Sprinkel, under secretary for monetary affairs in the U.S. Treasury.

(It is also most important to understand the difference between money and credit when one assesses the likely effect on interest rates of changes in the budget deficit. An expanding budget deficit, being in effect an increase in the demand for *credit*, will tend to raise interest rates. But if the supply of *money* is kept stable—the Fed does not monetize the deficit by buying the government bonds needed to finance that deficit—there will be no inflation and no rise in "the inflation premium" part of the rate of interest. The ultimate determinant of the rate of interest in America today is the rate of inflation, which is uniquely determined by movements in the supply of *money*.)

The failure of Fed officials over the years to understand the dominant role of *money* in the determination of the rate of interest has accounted for the perverse results of Fed policy.

Imagine that we are starting out on an upswing in economic activity. Demand for credit will tend to increase. This will tend to induce a rise in interest rates. The Fed observes the rise in interest rates, and in accordance with its procedures going back at least to the 1930's (fifty years ago, might I add for emphasis), the officer in charge of the Open Market Desk in New York buys securities, adding cash to the system. This tends to increase the available cash and to increase the money supply. The availability of money increases, meaning there is more money to *spend*. Increased money supply leads to more economic activity. More economic activity pushes once again up against the limits of available credit. Interest rates tend to rise once again. The Fed desk man sees rates starting once again to go over his limit. He buys more securities and puts out more cash. The process continues. In response to the rise in the money supply, economic activity increases again. Soon an inflationary boom develops. The man on the Fed desk in New York is still buying securities, trying to stop interest rates from rising. At some point there is a crisis. Interest rates rise so high that major industries cannot expand any longer. Inflationary expectations have come to dominate the movement in interest rates by this time. The boom bursts of its own accord or is helped by some panicky move by the government in Washington.

At that stage, demand for money starts to collapse. The man on the desk in New York, who by that time has been given a much revised (higher) operating target for interest rate control, starts selling securities in an attempt to moderate the collapse of interest rates, which has started with the bursting of the inflationary boom and the accompanying decline in the demand for credit. The more the desk man sells securities, the more he exaggerates the downturn in business. He is pulling money growth down by his actions at the very time when, in the aftermath of the boom, everyone is scrambling for cash.

That is not an imaginary scenario for a disastrous monetary policy. It is exactly how the Federal Reserve has operated in the United States over the past decade.

Before I go on to the actual figures and reports which show that my story is true, let us consider for a moment how the Federal Reserve could come to have gained such a tradition of thinking, one that is deeply ingrained in the thinking of the whole institution. It seems to come down to this: the Fed does not believe that money is for *spending*. Rather, it, like any other banker, thinks money is for *holding* or for *lending*. The Fed's ideas about the importance of interest rates go back to the thinking of the 1920's and indeed back to the thinking of the nineteenth century. The central bank, it was thought, would buy bills from the banks. There would be a discount rate at which the central bank would be prepared to buy bills from the banks. These bills would be trade bills, or commercial bills—in effect, promissory notes issued by traders to finance the movement of goods in trade from one part of the country to the other. If the discount rate tended to increase, this meant that the banks were short of cash. The central bank would discount the bills more readily at such times, knowing the banks were short. But none of this, in the thinking of the times, had anything to do with the movement of

75

production or with the trade cycle. At the time the Fed was first set up, in 1913, it was a tradition of financing which went back over a hundred years.

In his article in the February 1982 issue of the *Journal of Money, Credit and Banking,* Milton Friedman said of this traditional way of thinking:

> In our book on U.S. monetary history, Anna Schwartz and I found it possible to use one sentence to describe the central principle followed by the Federal Reserve System from the time it began operations in 1914 to 1952. That principle, to quote from our book, is: "If the 'money market' is properly managed, so as to avoid unproductive use of credit, and to assure the availability of credit for productive use, then the money stock will take care of itself." The principle is, of course, the Real Bills doctrine of the nineteenth century—so the continuity extends not only back to 1914 but even to the early nineteenth century when Henry Thornton had already given a correct theoretical analysis of the problem and had indicated the fallacy of this approach. It also, unfortunately, extends forward to the present —manifested most recently in the 1980 credit controls instituted by President Carter.

Today, as I previously stated, the Fed still has a discount rate at which it will make loans to the banks. But this rate has little policy significance because the Federal Reserve officials have generally kept this rate below the relevant *market* rate for money. As a result, the discount rate has become a preferred borrowing rate for the banks. It is not a penalty rate at all. Hence, the Fed has become for the banks, the lender of *first* resort, not the lender of *last* resort. The failure of the Fed to use the discount rate as a *penalty* rate is one of the reasons for its failure to achieve control over money growth, as explained in more detail later on.

Far more important today in routine monetary policy operations is the federal funds rate, or the rate at which banks are prepared to lend to each other overnight money. In the thinking of the Fed, the federal funds rate has come to assume a crucial importance in policy action. The federal funds rate is the central rate that the Federal Reserve used as its indicator of money tightness or ease through the

1970's. And in its single-minded attempt to stabilize the movements of the federal funds rate, the Federal Reserve laid the foundations for the excessive money growth we have experienced.

Professor Meiselman, whom I have already mentioned and who has worked with the Fed through the U.S. Treasury and before congressional committees, put the issue most adroitly as follows when he discussed it with me in December 1981:

"Bankers and the Federal Reserve in effect have a view that everyone who has money is a bank. If you have money, you lend it. If you spend it, you go to jail. You don't spend it, except for expenses. This idea is central to the thinking of all central bankers and is also central to much of the Keynesian theory of money. Money is to lend, not to spend.

"Under this theory, when you increase the quantity of money, what do you do with it? Well, you lend it, you buy bonds.

"On the contrary, the monetarist economists and the people in the tradition of Irving Fisher, the great American monetary economist, say that if you get money, you spend it. You buy goods.

"Without factual confirmation, we do not know which analytical fiction is the more powerful. But it seems to me that the Fisher tradition is the more powerful because there is in fact a relatively stable velocity of money—the relationship between nominal gross national product and the money supply is relatively stable over long periods of time. The money theory of Irving Fisher fits the facts. But that is something a banker cannot understand. If you just step back a little and look at it, it is clear that an increase in money will *cause* higher interest rates. And a restrictive money policy will make interest rates go down. I put it this way: *Tight money causes easy credit and easy money causes tight credit.*

"This is exactly the opposite to the way the Fed thinks and it is this failure to think this thing out correctly that is behind so many of its disastrous mistakes. The Fed has had this totally wrong ever since it started. Over the last fifteen years of increasing inflation, the Fed has made a lot of relatively small errors, mostly in the same direction. Just a little bit at a time, of wrong policy, repeated over and over."

The Fed Has Been Hypnotized by the Federal Funds Rate

In practice, the Federal Reserve has over a long period of time, certainly during the 1970's, tried to maintain a very tight rein on one crucial interest rate—the federal funds rate. In its publication *Statfacts* the Fed stated:

The Federal Funds rate is the cost of borrowing immediately available balances, primarily for one business day. Federal funds are used by many banks, large corporations and non-bank financial firms. For example, banks borrow balances of other banks when they want immediately available funds to meet reserve requirements, to meet unexpected loan demand, or to offset unexpected drains of reserves. Banks may borrow from each other for any period, but only one-day transactions are classified as federal funds transactions for the purpose of this rate.

The Federal Funds rate is sensitive to changes in the demand for, and supply of, reserves and lendable funds in the banking system.

The funds market has been used by many banks as a major, if not the prime, source of funds for adjusting reserve positions. For these and other reasons, such as Federal Reserve open market operations, conditions and rates in the Federal Funds market had been very closely watched by analysts as a key barometer of monetary policy.

In October 1979, the Federal Reserve announced a series of actions aimed at better controlling the expansion of money and bank credit, helping curtail speculative excesses in financial, foreign exchange and commodity markets and thus, serving to damp inflation.

Among the changes was the method used to conduct monetary policy. The action involved increasing emphasis in daily operations on the supply of bank reserves and reducing emphasis on confining short-term fluctuations in the Federal Funds rate.

For some time, the Federal Reserve had operated to keep fluctuations of the Federal Funds rate within a relatively narrow range.

To help achieve better control over the reserve base, the Federal Open Market Committee decided it was necessary, within broad limits, to permit wider fluctuations of the Federal Funds rate, if so determined by market forces.

This statement by the Federal Reserve in its own publication reveals that the Fed has admitted that over the years monetary policy operations have been directed toward moderating the fluctuations in the federal funds rate. We know that the federal funds rate is the rate at which banks lend to each other overnight money, and as a consequence, it is a sensitive indicator of the ebb and flow of demand and supply of *credit.*

Over the years, and certainly up to October 6, 1979, on the Fed's own admission, the Federal Reserve officials in New York bought and sold government Treasury bills, bonds, and other securities in the money markets with the aim of achieving a *very narrow* range of fluctuations in the federal funds rate. That is not very hard to do. The Fed has unlimited money at its disposal because its checks are as good as cash. Hence, it can engage in dominating purchases of securities, with the aim of driving their prices up (and of driving the rate of interest down—this latter aim being doomed to failure, as we shall see).

When the federal funds rate tended to rise, the Fed officials would buy securities, thus increasing the supply of *money.* And the reverse would apply. We have already seen how this process would make inflationary booms worse and deflationary recessions worse. The Fed officials were trying to stabilize the federal funds rate because they thought that in this way they could stabilize the demand and supply of loanable funds. But that is not how things worked out.

We may think of the same mistake in another way. If the Fed were trying to stabilize the growth of money (which in fact it was not trying to do, for reasons to be spelled out later), it could not possibly stabilize the growth of money while simultaneously freezing the price of credit, the rate of interest. By its attempt to hold down the rate of interest—the federal funds rate in most cases—it was *necessarily* put in the position where it had to sacrifice control over the growth of money. The Fed thought of the federal funds rate as *the indicator* of the balance of the demand and supply of money. But it was only the indicator of the price of credit.

Even if the Fed had been interested in maintaining control over the growth of money in the last fifteen years, its preoccupation with stabilizing the federal funds rate would necessarily have robbed it of success. It would have been very difficult, if not impossible, to maintain a stable federal funds rate *and* a stable rate of growth of money at the same time.

The Federal Reserve has been very unwilling to change its longstanding practice of trying to control the movements of the federal funds interest rate. It is a practice embedded in its bureaucratic traditions.

It cannot be argued that Fed officials were unaware that their aim of maintaining tight control over the federal funds rate and their *supposed* aim of achieving control over the growth rate of money were *irreconcilable*. The Fed officials have known for years that their federal funds rate policy aims were not compatible with any policy aim to control money growth.

On June 10, 1976, in a statement to the House Banking Committee, Governor Charles J. Partee of the Federal Reserve Board condemned any attempt by the Federal Reserve to operate interest rate targeting as a key part of its monetary policy. Born in Ohio in 1927, Governor Partee joined the Federal Reserve of Chicago in 1949 as an economist, specializing in consumer finance, mortgage markets, and savings. In 1962 he became a member of the staff of the Board of Governors, on which he served as chief of the Capital Markets Section, Division of Research (1962–63); adviser in charge of financial sections, Division of Research (1964–65); and associate director (1966–69) and then director of the Division of Research and Statistics and adviser to the Federal Reserve Board (1969–74). In November 1973 Partee was appointed managing director for research and economic policy of the board, which office he held until he became a member of the board. He was the second member of the board's staff to be appointed to the board.

In a crucially important statement to the House Banking Committee in June 1976 on the issue of interest rate targeting, he said:

> While it is theoretically possible to specify the course of monetary policy in terms of interest rate levels, as well as in terms of the monetary aggregates, it must be recognized that interest rates are particularly exposed to the influence of many variables, external to the scope of monetary policy and that there is thus a large risk of specification error. The announcement of

interest rate intentions or expectations could lead borrowers and lenders to believe that the Federal Reserve could—and in practice would—guarantee particular levels of interest rates.

But the system does not have the power to do so, for interest rates are influenced not only by the interaction of demands for credit with the available supply of funds, but also by the strength of the economy and the public's willingness to defer current consumption in order to save for the future. Interest rates are also importantly affected by the expectations of both borrowers and lenders about the rate of inflation.

If the Federal Reserve did nevertheless attempt to maintain selected interest rates at some predetermined level, the effort could well lead to inappropriate rates of growth in bank reserves and the money stock. If interest rates came under upward pressure, because of rising demands for funds, for example, System efforts to prevent interest rate increases would inevitably generate more rapid monetary expansion, thereby feeding new inflationary pressures.

If, on the other hand, interest rates came under downward pressure because of slackening business activity and declining demand for funds, System efforts to prevent the decline in rates would inevitably retard monetary growth rates, quite possibly exacerbating the recessionary problem.

Thus, any serious effort to specify monetary policy aims in terms of interest rate intentions or expectations could well prove inconsistent with stated objectives for growth rates in the monetary aggregates.

Of course, the Central Bank might attempt to hold to the interest rate objectives, regardless of the performance of the monetary aggregates.

But even in this extreme case, the result would very likely be self-defeating, as lenders and borrowers move to protect themselves against the prospect of accelerating inflation or deepening recession, foreshadowed by what might be very high or very low monetary growth rates. Needless to say, these effects would be quite perverse from the standpoint of economic stabilization.

Here is an astounding series of admissions by a very high official of the Federal Reserve. He admitted, *six years ago,* that a policy of interest rate targeting would be disastrous; it would make inflationary booms more violent and would make recessions deeper. He stated it would be deplorable of the Fed even to attempt such a policy. And he surely told the world, his position being what it is, that the Fed has not been pursuing such policies.

Yet we know from subsequent public statements of the Federal Reserve and from the record of its actions that it *always* gave top priority to holding the federal funds rate fluctuations in a very narrow band, and hence, all other considerations were secondary.

Among the key points made by Governor Partee in his statement were the following:

1. It is impossible for the Federal Reserve to control *both* the federal funds rate *and* the growth of money at the same time. If demand for loanable funds increased, the interest rate would tend to rise. In attempting to hold the interest rate down, the Fed would have to sacrifice control of money growth (because it would be feeding out fresh money to fight the rise in interest rates).

2. Even if the Fed did still try to hold down interest rates by feeding out huge amounts of new cash, this would also be self-defeating because inflation would result, and this would carry interest rates up with it.

3. That accounts for the implication in the final sentence of the statement that a policy of attempting to stabilize the federal funds rate would destabilize the economy by destabilizing money growth.

This is a crucial series of admissions by a very senior and experienced Fed official. It is all the more appalling, therefore, that the Fed has shown very little willingness to change its traditional practice of stabilizing the federal funds rate as the prime aim of policy.

The Tail Wags the Dog in Monetary Policymaking

In an important study in 1978, published in the *Journal of Monetary Economics,* James L. Pierce, professor of economics at the University of California at Berkeley and a former senior member of the staff of the Board of Governors of the Federal Reserve System (until he clashed with Arthur Burns, then chairman of the board), showed how the Fed had pursued very narrow ranges for the federal funds rate from 1974 through 1977.

The average (or mean) range for the federal funds rate in that period, as set each month by the Federal Open Market Committee of the Federal Reserve System, was 100 basis points (that is, one percentage point). For example, in February 1975 the FOMC specified that the range in which the federal funds rate would be allowed to fluctuate would be between 5 and 6 percent, a very narrow range. A similarly narrow range for the federal funds rate was laid down over the thirty-six months specified by Professor Pierce.

By contrast, as Pierce pointed out in 1978, the FOMC specified at each of its monthly meetings a two-month target for the growth of the monetary aggregates, the money supply. The mean target growth range for the two-month horizons for M1 money was 3.7 percent. This meant that in the two-month period the FOMC would be prepared to permit the annual growth rate of MI to vary between, say, 4 and 7.7 percent. That is a very big range, nearly four times the range permitted for the movements of the federal funds rate.

The relatively narrow federal funds rate range did not stop the Fed administrators from hitting those targets with great accuracy. Over the four years 1974 through 1977, the mean absolute change in the level of the federal funds rate from month to month was less than 40 basis points (0.4 percent), a very tight control. The very narrow band of permitted fluctuation in the federal funds rate and the very small changes in the actual federal funds rate from month to month are consistent with attempts by the Fed to stabilize the money markets by controlling the federal funds rate.

By contrast, even the much wider bands permitted for growth in M1 were very rarely achieved. M1 growth varied widely and wildly over the three years, indicating that money growth was being accorded a very low priority by the Fed. In 1978 Pierce could state that since the Fed had announced money target ranges for M1 and M2, it had kept both of these monetary aggregates within their (wide) ranges 50 percent of the time.

Subsequent to the work of Professor Pierce in 1978, the Subcommittee on Domestic Monetary Policy of the House Banking Committee in its 1980 report showed that the Federal Open Market Committee had continued right up to October 1979 with the policy of maintaining a very narrow permitted range of movement for the federal funds rate while permitting a very wide range for the growth of the M1 money supply. Thus, in September 1979 the permitted range for the federal funds rate was 50 basis points (one half of the already very narrow rate permitted from 1974 through 1977). And in the same month the permitted band for the growth rate of M1 money was 500 basis points (5 percent).

The policy of the Fed could thus be characterized as one of allowing the tail to wag the dog. Because the price of credit was fixed, the supply of money had to be allowed to fluctuate. What is more, those fluctuations in the supply of money were bound to exaggerate both upward and downward movements in economic activity.

Has the Fed Changed Its Spots?

By the middle of 1979 it was obvious that the jig was up. Inflation was roaring ahead in the double digits. Money supply was expanding out of hand. A crisis was in the making. In August Paul Volcker was appointed chairman of the Federal Reserve Board, and in October the Fed announced it was beginning a new approach to monetary policy: it would attempt to achieve better control of the growth of the monetary aggregates by "placing greater emphasis in day-to-day operations on the supply bank reserves and less emphasis on confining short-term fluctuations in the Federal Funds Rate." A reason for adopting such a strategy was to "assure better control over the expansion of money and credit."

Once the lid was taken off interest rates, they soared to the sky. Between the fourth quarter of 1979 and the first quarter of 1980, long-term bond yield in New York rose from 9 to 11½ percent—the biggest single rise in the previous twenty years.

The change in policy in October 1979 was largely forced on the Fed by the widespread recognition that it would require fantastic infusions of cash by the central bank to hold down the federal funds rate in 1979. Between the time of the announcement in October and the end of October the federal funds rate rose extremely sharply, from 12 to 16 percent. During 1980 the funds rate swung around violently, reflecting the cumulative outpouring of reaction to a decade and a half of closely controlled interest rate movements, during which time the Fed had as often as not been attempting to keep the inevitable explosion of interest rates bottled up by a process of force-feeding the financial markets with cash.

During 1980, the Federal Open Market Committee increased the permitted range of variation of the funds rate from 50 basis points in September to 200 basis points in October 1979 and to 300 basis points by October 1980. Even so, the Fed was still very unsuccessful during 1980 in meeting its own targets and the roller coaster progress of money growth was still very much in evidence.

By the end of 1981 there was very serious room for doubt whether the so-called new operating procedures were going to give America steadier and slower growth of money. In its December 23 issue of *U.S. Financial Data,* the Federal Reserve of St. Louis, the maverick among the various Federal Reserve banks and the home of much of the criticism of Federal Reserve Board procedures, drew attention to the fact that during the period November 27 to December 23, 1981, most short-term interest rates had risen but the federal funds rate had shown no change.

It is also clear that during 1980, the first year of operation of the "new" system, while the federal funds rate permitted range was greatly widened, compared with what had been going on previously, there was no question about the Fed officials' ensuring that the funds rate remain within those (admittedly wider) ranges. No such success accompanied the attempts by the Fed, either in 1980 or in 1981, to keep the growth rates of money within the predetermined ranges. Money growth in both years fluctuated wildly, indicating grave problems of control which remain. (A more detailed discussion of the post-1979 period is given in Chapter 7.)

Exaggerating Swings in Economic Activity

The sum total of the Federal Reserve's policy actions over the last fifteen years, given the basic operating priorities it has assumed, has been to make economic fluctuations in the American economy worse than they would otherwise have been. Not only has the trend of money growth been steadily upward, but money growth has expanded rapidly during periods of economic expansion and has fallen sharply during periods of recession.

- In the 1961 recession money growth fell from 3 to $-\frac{1}{2}$ percent.

- From 1961 to 1967 money growth rate increased steadily through 1 percent in 1962, 3 percent in 1965, to 5 percent in 1967.
- In the 1967–68 recession money growth fell from 5 to 3 percent.
- In the subsequent recovery, money growth rose from 3 to nearly 7½ percent in 1969. In the 1970–71 recession it dropped heavily back to just over 3½ percent.
- Between 1971 and 1974 money growth once again boomed, rising from just over 3½ to over 8 percent. In the 1974–75 recession money growth once again fell right away from over 8 percent prerecession to about 4½ percent at the end of the recession.

The same thing happened in the buildup to 1979. From the low point of 4½ percent annual money growth in 1974–75, money growth boomed up to a peak of about 8–8½ percent in 1979. In the subsequent Age of Recession, money growth has already fallen away to about 6 percent.

A Penchant for Stabilizing Interest Rates

I conclude this broad outline of the policy priorities of the Federal Reserve by quoting the 1976 report of the Subcommittee on Domestic Monetary Policy of the House Banking Committee in which the following statement by Professor James Pierce is reported:

Historically, the Federal Reserve, like other central banks, has exhibited a strong tendency to stabilize fluctuations in interest rates, particularly short-term fluctuations.

The Fed's penchant for stabilizing interest rates has among other things helped to produce a procyclical behavior in the growth of the money stock; that is, money grows rapidly during economic expansions and slowly during recessions. The reason for this is clear enough; when the economy is expanding rapidly, credit demands also expand, tending to put upward pressure on interest rates.

The Federal Reserve attempts to constrain these interest rate increases by providing more bank reserves through open market operations.

The increase in bank reserves in turn leads to expansion in the money stock and underwrites an expansion in economic activity. During recessions, credit demands decline and interest rates begin to fall; the Fed attempts to constrain the decline in interest rates by selling securities on the open market, therein reducing bank reserves and retarding growth in the money stock.

The retardation of money growth and constraint on interest rate declines tend to exacerbate the decline in economic activity.

It seems clear that attempts to stabilize interest rates can and have produced greater cyclical fluctuations in income, production, employment, and inflation than would have been the case had the Fed not been so concerned about interest rate fluctuations.

If the Federal Reserve adhered more closely to a target growth for the money stock, interest rates would tend to move more quickly; that is, fall more rapidly in recessions and rise more rapidly in expansions than has heretofore been the case.

These sharper interest-rate movements would tend to moderate the fluctuations in economic activity. If interest rates were allowed to move more quickly, aggregate demand would be affected more rapidly and hence would not probably fluctuate so widely.

As a result it is likely that interest rates themselves would actually fluctuate less widely.

None of what you have read to this point can be said to be a blinding revelation. Many people in and around the Congress of the United States and in the various administrations have tried to bring the Fed under control. Many attempts have been made to try to "discipline" the Fed. The story of the adroit maneuvers that the Fed has employed to defend itself from these would-be reformers is not only a story of massive and successful resistance to any change imposed from the outside but also an object lesson in the durability of bureaucracies.

4 Many Have Tried to Get the Fed to Control Money—All Have Failed

Many attempts have been made in the last ten years to *make* the Federal Reserve change from a system of interest rate targeting to a system of control of the so-called monetary aggregates. Behind this pressure, which came from a number of sources and was eventually embodied in legislation by Congress, was the idea that somehow an attempt should be made to control the growth of money in America. There was an idea that, inasmuch as it was clear that excessive growth of money was behind the Age of Inflation, it would be a big improvement if money growth could be controlled—reduced to a low rate. Some, as I have observed, would have the rate of growth of money reduced to *zero*, believing this would be entirely sufficient to meet the needs of feasible noninflationary growth in America.

The intellectual inspiration for these ideas came from the work of Irving Fisher, the great American monetary economist. His work was added to and enriched by the insights of Milton Friedman and Anna Schwartz. In turn, Professor Allan Meltzer of the Carnegie-Mellon Institute at the University of Pittsburgh and Professor Karl Brunner of the Graduate School of Management at the University of Rochester have devoted almost twenty years to the public exposition of ideas the outcome of which is the belief and the knowledge that movements in money are manageable within very narrow limits of tolerance.

Brunner and Meltzer's work began with the publication of their path-breaking study *The Federal Reserve's Attachment to the Free Reserve Concept,* which was written on behalf of the Subcommittee on Domestic Finance of the House Banking Committee in 1964. At that time Wright Patman was chairman of both the House Banking

88

Committee and the Domestic Finance Subcommittee. Brunner and Meltzer foreshadowed the problems that the Federal Reserve would have during the 1970's in controlling the growth of the money supply.

> If the Federal Reserve's conception of the monetary process, centered on the position of free reserves, were the only admissible view, we would have to concede that monetary policy is little more than a futile exercise.
>
> But alternative conceptions of the monetary mechanism have been formulated and it is essential to consider them before accepting such a negative conclusion. It should be noted, therefore, that our analysis does not suggest the futility of monetary policy, but only supports our contention about the failure of the Federal Reserve to develop a coherent, validated conception.
>
> The failure of the Federal Reserve to develop a useful conception of the monetary mechanism does not mean that one cannot be developed.

Brunner and Meltzer were writing at a time when the record of monetary control in America had not turned disastrously wrong. In 1964 America was still in the middle of a strong period of economic expansion which at that stage had been going on for more than twenty years with little or no serious inflationary or monetary control problems. The two authors stated, further, that:

1. "Our appraisal of the Federal Reserve's record indicates they have been alert and sensitive to a variety of indicators and they have made timely and appropriate judgments about the pace of economic activity."

2. But "the Federal Reserve has an extremely short-run policy focus and actions are taken in response to weekly, daily and even hourly events on the financial markets."

3. Hence, "concentration on short-run occurrences and the absence of systematic analysis leads to a substantial grant of authority to the Manager of the System Open Market Account" (the official known today as the main "Desk" officer who actually controls the process of buying and selling securities by which the Fed increases or decreases the amount of cash in the financial markets at any time).

4. "A comparison of decisions by the Federal Open Market Com-

mittee with the recorded movement of free reserves indicates that the level of the recorded movement of free reserves quite often moved decisively in advance of a decision by the Open Market Committee to 'ease' or 'restrain.' The observed pattern strongly supports our interpretation that the absence of a systematic framework and the concentration on the extremely short-run market events has resulted in a substantial grant of authority to the Manager. At major turning points, it has often been the Manager's action that reversed the direction of policy. This action was then ratified at a meeting of the Federal Open Market Committee. Contrary to published statements by officials of the System, the Manager appears to occupy a major policymaking role."

Evidently in 1964, almost twenty years ago, there were forebodings about the way in which the Federal Reserve might react when put under pressure. Those pressures were, of course, starting to build up at the very time Brunner and Meltzer indicated their fear that the Fed did not have a systematic plan or policy to guide its actions. They feared that the Fed, under pressure, would find it had no developed system for controlling bank credit or money. They said: "The evidence is quite clear. The modified free reserves mechanism bears almost no relation to changes in the stock of bank credit or money. Indeed, the relation is so poor that it raises questions about the usefulness of Federal Reserve policy as a means of controlling money or credit."

In December 1981 Professor David Meiselman, the noted monetarist economist and former official of the U.S. Treasury in the area of monetary policy, in referring to the question of the discretion available to the official on the Fed Open Market Desk in New York, said to me: "This person has had huge discretion. He often sets the tone of monetary policy which is then simply validated by the Federal Open Market Committee. And this person has been in the position, with his huge discretion, to blow the whole monetary policy because he is so worried on a day-to-day basis, about the fate of bond dealers.

"The people on the Desk then go and work for the dealers. So they can't afford to offend the dealers too much because they won't get jobs. It's the same fraternity, at somewhat different stages of the game. There is no doubt in my mind that these considerations are

very important and have an important role in the operating procedures of the Fed, which virtually every disinterested economist will
say is a source of added instability and the source of the lack of good
monetary control."

I would like to quote a statement made to me in November 1981
by a very senior official in the U.S. Treasury who, referring to the
Fed's myopia, commented on so long before by Brunner and
Meltzer, said: "The way I think about the Fed is like a hunter who
has gone a long way from home and is trying to get back home in
the dark. He can see the light of his house a long way off. So, in order
to get back home, he takes out his torch and concentrates it on the
ground a couple of feet in front of him. This torch eventually runs
out of power, and he looks up, to see that the house has disappeared
and he is lost."

The doubts expressed by Brunner and Meltzer back in 1964 were
not confined to a couple of brilliantly perceptive academics. They
were typical of an apprehension among significant figures in Congress and elsewhere in the government apparatus about the guidelines which influenced Fed policy and about the procedures used by
the Fed to carry out whatever policy guidelines it may have had.

Congress Tries to Put a Leash on the Fed

In his 1978 study *Congressional Supervision of Monetary Policy,*
Dr. Robert Weintraub, senior economist of the Joint Economic
Committee of Congress, outlined the steps taken over the years to
make the Federal Reserve answerable to Congress. Among the steps
outlined in his study are:

1. The Federal Reserve Act of 1913 included the famous dictum
exhorting the Fed to "furnish an elastic currency," without specify-
ing how this was to be done.

2. The Employment Act of 1946 established "maximum employment, production and purchasing power" as national goals and also
as the goals of monetary policy.

3. In 1964, during hearings before the House Banking Committee,
Representative Richard T. Hanna of California suggested that "perhaps Congress might think seriously about establishing more responsible directives from Congress to the Board of Governors, requesting

some form of responsive reporting so that we could know exactly how they are carrying out the directives."

4. In 1964 the House Banking Committee published studies, Brunner and Meltzer's, which argued persuasively that money growth could be controlled.

5. In August 1964 the chairman of the Banking Committee, Wright Patman, and other majority members of the Subcommittee on Domestic Monetary Policy issued a proposal to require that the president set forth guidelines for the growth of money supply in his periodic economic reports.

6. In 1967 the Joint Economic Committee recommended the policy of moderate and relatively steady increases in the money supply (M1), avoiding the disruptive effects of wide swings in the rate of increase or decrease.

7. In 1968 Congressman Henry Reuss complained that M1 had grown at a 9 percent annual rate from January to August 1967 and urged "as a basis for discussion" expanding M1 by 3 to 5 percent yearly.

8. In 1968 the House Banking Committee published a *Compendium on Monetary Policy Guidelines and the Federal Reserve Structure,* which provided broad academic support for the idea of setting guidelines for monetary growth.

9. In 1974 Dr. Weintraub presented a staff report, based on interviews with the presidents of the twelve Federal Reserve banks and five of the Federal Reserve governors, which recommended that Congress treat monetary policy in the same way that the 1974 Budget Control Act mandated that it treat fiscal policy. "Specifically," said Weintraub, "I recommended that the Federal Reserve annually present to Congress a plan for M1 growth expressed as target ranges for each of the next twelve months and delineated in terms of percentage changes from the same month a year previously."

10. In March 1975 Congress passed the famous House Concurrent Resolution 133, which obliged the Federal Reserve to issue targets for money growth and to report to Congress on the achievement of those targets.

11. The trend toward imposing greater accountability on the Fed-

eral Reserve culminated in PL 95-188 on November 16, 1977. This law provided that the governors of the Federal Reserve would publish annual targets for the growth of monetary aggregates and consult with Congress at the semiannual hearings before the House and Senate Banking committees.

The Dawn of Hope in a New Era for Monetary Policy

It took more than a decade after Meltzer and Brunner's 1964 report to the House Banking Committee before the passage of any formal congressional resolution that would give effect to the widespread fear that the Fed did not have a plan for the control of money. Not until thirteen years after the Meltzer-Brunner report did Congress pass an act making it obligatory for the Fed to publish targets of monetary growth over the next twelve months and to report to Congress on its stewardship in relation to those targets.

The lapse of time needed to bring the issue of the plans, policies, procedures, and accountability of the Fed to the point of actually passing a law about it indicates the powerful resistance to any such moves. As it subsequently emerged, the Federal Reserve had no intention whatever of allowing its "discretionary power" to be truncated in any way at all by the Congress—or by anyone else.

That did not stop informed people from expressing great hopes and enthusiasm about the passage of HCR 133 in March 1975. In his February 1982 article in the *Journal of Money, Credit and Banking,* Milton Friedman reported how he felt:

> At the time, I believed that this resolution was a major breakthrough, describing it as "perhaps the most important change (in the structure of monetary policy) since the banking acts of the mid-1930's." In justifying this judgment, I wrote: "Though superficially innocuous (because it has no teeth), the resolution represents the first time since the Fed began operation in 1914, that the Congress has (1) specified monetary and credit aggregates as the Fed's immediate target; (2) enjoined it to produce steady monetary growth in line with output growth; (3) required it to state its objectives publicly in advance; and (4) required it to justify publicly any departure from them. All four elements are major changes. The Fed has shifted among alter-

native targets—monetary aggregates, interest rates, exchange rates; it has produced widely varying rate of monetary growth; it has never specified long-range numerical objectives and has decided its short-term objectives in camera, making them public long after the event; it has reported to Congress in vague terms that have resisted strict accountability.

Milton Friedman was not the only one who was hopeful that the Fed would change. In its December 1976 report, the House Banking Committee's Subcommittee on Domestic Monetary Policy reported that Arthur Burns, then chairman of the Fed, had told it in May 1975 that "the Federal Reserve System is presently seeking a moderate expansion in the monetary aggregates . . . of 5 to 7½ percent in M1 over the twelve months March 1975 to March 1976." The subcommittee, after reporting on the trend of money growth to October 1976, said: "The steadiness of recent Fed policy is commendable."

Dr. Weintraub himself was delighted. In the 1978 *Journal of Monetary Economics* he wrote: "Under the new oversight procedures established by HCR 133 and Public Law 95-188, money supply growth can no longer be ignored."

Four Years of Disillusion: 1976–80

It was soon obvious that the arrangements introduced in early 1975 would not yield results like those anticipated by the starry-eyed optimists at the time. The Federal Reserve officials were more than a match for the reformers, who had tried to introduce objective standards of performance for monetary policy, standards that would allow outsiders a clear basis on which to judge the Fed's success or failure.

Milton Friedman, in the February 1982 article referred to, wrote:

In the event, my judgment [that the new HCR 133 procedures represented a new hope for a better monetary policy] proved wide of the mark. The Federal Reserve had strongly opposed the resolution and had tried to prevent its passage. When it was passed, it pledged cooperation but then proceeded to undermine it so subtly and effectively that the resolution has proved to be a noteworthy minor step rather than the major breakthrough that I have mistakenly interpreted it as being.

94

After four years of the new arrangements it was obvious that they had not yielded any improvement in monetary management. On the contrary, despite formal monetary management supposedly being conducted in the period 1976–80 under the rules of HCR 133—targeting and congressional accountability of the Federal Reserve—it was clear that the whole plan had been a grotesque failure. The House Banking Committee's Subcommittee on Domestic Monetary Policy in its 1980 report told the sorry story:

> In concluding the 1976 Report we commended "the steadiness of recent Fed money policy" and concluded optimistically that "we can bring inflation under control and keep it in check by achieving moderate M1 growth, commensurate with our potential to increase production."
>
> We recommended 4–6 percent M1 growth for 1977 and a gradual deceleration thereafter to 2–4 percent per year. We said that in time this would "reduce inflation to the attainable 1–3 percent rate."
>
> Our optimism was based on the hope that the Federal Reserve was embarked on a course for money growth much like the one we were recommending.
>
> *It was not* [my italics].
>
> Although we had noted a spurt of money growth in the month of October 1976, we did not think that this portended a new inflationary surge of money growth; a surge that would persist well into 1979, propel inflation upwards once again and set the stage for the recession that now [summer 1980] afflicts our economy.
>
> *Unhappily, it did* [my italics].
>
> M1 growth accelerated sharply, beginning even as that [1976] Report was being written in the fourth quarter of 1976. Quarter to quarter M1 growth, which had been kept between 2.9 and 5.8 percent a year, and averaged 4.4 percent a year in the four quarters ending the third quarter of 1976, was suddenly increased to 7 percent per year in the fourth quarter of 1976. In 1977 it ranged between 6 and 8.8 percent per year and averaged 7.5 percent per year. M1-B growth remained high in 1978 and through summer or third quarter of 1979. Quarter to quarter M1-B growth ranged between 4.8 and 10.7 percent per year and averaged 8.2 percent per year during this period.
>
> In the wake of the acceleration of money growth, inflation, which had been checked and reduced, increased again. The

gross national product deflator [the measure of the average increase of prices for the volume of goods produced nationally each year] increased 6.2 percent in the four quarters ending with the fourth quarter of 1977; 8.2 percent in the four quarters ending the fourth quarter of 1978; 8.9 percent in the four quarters ending the fourth quarter of 1979 and 9.6 percent in the four quarters ending the fourth quarter of 1980.

What Went Wrong?

The subcommittee of the House Banking Committee, in its explanation of this scandalous episode in monetary policy administration, let the Federal Reserve off very lightly. In the December 1980 report, the subcommittee said:

The acceleration in the growth of M1-B that began in October 1976 and led inexorably to the acceleration of inflation and in turn to the recession that now [summer of 1980] afflicts the economy, does not appear to have resulted from a deliberate decision to accelerate money growth. The Federal Reserve's targets for money growth were not raised when the acceleration began. They were not raised later. What happened was not planned or even projected.

However, given the Federal Reserve's policy, it was a predictable event.

The acceleration of M1-B growth that began in October 1976 was the predictable corollary of the Federal Reserve's deemphasizing money supply control and placing more emphasis on interest rates changes beginning around April 1976.

Federal Reserve monetary policy is reviewed and determined roughly once a month by the System's Open Market Committee. The Committee is comprised of the seven members of the Board of Governors of the Federal Reserve System and five of the twelve Reserve Bank presidents who, apart from the President of the New York Reserve Bank (who serves as a permanent member of the Open Market Committee), serve in rotation.

At its roughly monthly or near-monthly meetings, the Committee sets inter-meeting or immediate targets for both money growth and the Federal Funds rate.

These targets are used to guide and constrain the manager of the System's Open Market accounts in the New York Reserve Bank until the next Open Market Committee meeting. From

March 1975 through March 1976, the manager usually (12 out of 13 times) was directed to keep the per year money growth band within 2½–4 percentage points wide and the Federal Funds rate within a band 1¼ percentage points wide.

However, beginning in April 1976, the Open Market Committee narrowed the band in which the manager was instructed to keep the Federal Funds rate and widened the inter-meeting target range for money growth.

Thereby, the Committee *deemphasized control of the money supply* [my italics] as an operating goal and increased the importance of resisting interest rate movements. Money growth subsequently emerged primarily as the *incidental corollary* of the Committee's Federal Funds interest rate goals.

The Collapse of the Federal Funds Rate Control in 1979

It could be argued—and I certainly will argue later—that there was much more to the Fed's decision to narrow the range of its federal funds targets and to widen the range of its money growth targets in 1976. That was, after all, an election year. Chairman Burns was at the helm of the Fed.

The subcommittee's comments point to the following conclusions:

1. The Federal Reserve not only failed to pursue its targets for monetary growth with anything that could be described as honest diligence but went farther, taking steps (notably the decision to narrow the permitted range of fluctuation of the federal funds rate in April 1976), which had the effect of actively undermining control of the monetary aggregates.

2. Although the subcommittee was far too polite to say so, there is no getting away from the fact that the April 1976 policy change was a deliberate and arrogant flouting by the Federal Reserve under Chairman Arthur Burns of the intention of the whole discussion and external pressure on the Fed, for the previous twelve years, directed at attaining control over the growth of monetary aggregates. The April 1976 decision was taken in time for the federal election later in that year, when President Ford was defeated by Jimmy Carter.

In any event, the willful refusal of the Federal Reserve officials to attempt to carry out the intentions implicit in the HCR 133 and subsequent legislation PL 95-188 led to the inflationary boom of 1976–79 and to the abandonment of the whole external trappings of the "federal funds targeting" policy which applied up to October 1979. Once the Fed began in 1976 the process of inflationary expansion of the money supply, through the device of narrowing the federal funds band and widening the money growth band, then in its increasingly frantic efforts to control the uptrend in the federal funds rate which it had initiated, it rapidly lost control over the whole monetary situation.

The House Banking Committee's subcommittee 1980 report described the panic that developed at the Fed during 1979:

The results of the mode of operating [that was initiated in April 1976] proved unwelcome. Strong credit demands put upward pressure on the Federal Funds rate almost continuously from April 1976 to early 1980. These pressures should have been allowed to dissipate by keeping money growth and hence spending on GNP goods and services from rising. Instead they were fueled.

Given its policy of resisting short term changes in interest rates, the Federal Reserve was obliged to supply banks with increasing input of reserves. This input provided the base for accelerated money growth and ultimately resulted in faster inflation and weakness of the dollar on foreign exchange markets. With faster inflation, credit demands and interest rates rose higher and higher. The Federal Funds rate climbed from a daily average of 4.82 percent in April 1976 to a daily average of 10.29 percent in June 1979. In the summer of 1979, the rise of interest rates became intolerably difficult to contain.

Even between Open Market Committee meetings, control could not be obtained over the Federal Funds rate.

At its July 1979 meeting, the Open Market Committee set the inter-meeting Federal Funds rate target at 9¾–10 percent.

However, it proved necessary to raise the upper limit to 10¾ percent before the August meeting.

At its August meeting, market conditions compelled the Committee to set the inter-meeting Federal Funds rate at 10¾–11¼ percent.

But before the September meeting, it became necessary to raise the upper limit to 11½ percent.

At the September Open Market Committee meeting, conditions compelled still another boost in the targeted range to 11¼–11¾ percent.

By the end of September, it was clear, even inside the Federal Reserve, that interest rates had not been kept from rising by focusing open market operations on keeping them from rising and subordinating control of money growth to that end.

A new approach was needed.

Fortunately for the Federal Reserve, a new chairman, Paul Volcker, had been appointed in August 1979, and he was able to present the inevitable capitulation of the Fed as some sort of reform. It was clear that the whole policy of interest rate targeting had failed. An excuse for changing that policy had to be found because it had become an embarrassment to, and a potential source of criticism against, the Fed, *affecting the central bank's independence.*

On October 6, 1979, the whole edifice of Federal Reserve policy for the previous three and a half years collapsed in a shambles. The so-called new policy described in the previous chapter was announced. Henceforth interest rate targeting was to be given a lower priority, and money aggregate control a higher priority. This was exactly what the Fed had been told to do by Congress back in March 1975 and exactly what had been the essential criticism of the Fed's policies for the previous several years.

But change came only when the costs associated with the traditional policy became a threat to the Fed's own standing. I am convinced that the Federal Reserve Board or the Federal Open Market Committee would never have changed its policy without the possibility that a catastrophe would raise the dreaded prospect of a massive increase in external controls over the Fed.

Milton Friedman said of this episode, in his February 1982 article:

On October 6, 1979, the Federal Reserve made a dramatic announcement of a change in procedure. Like all previous major moves by the Fed, this one too was a delayed reaction to external events or pressure, on this occasion, a collapse of the dollar abroad because of a lack of confidence in monetary policy and rising U.S. inflation. Chairman Volcker flew back from the meeting of the International Monetary Fund in Belgrade, where the foreign pressure came to a head, in order to issue the announcement. Despite that announcement of a change in operating procedures, the Fed reverted briefly to a straight Federal Funds target in the spring of 1980.

As it was, the Fed did in fact widen the range of the federal funds rate. It had little or no option but to do so, in view of the appalling failure of its previous policy of four years. But there was worse to come. After the inflationary spiral set off in 1976 had gained momentum, a mere switch in the Fed's policy procedures would not solve the nation's economic problems.

The Crisis of March 1980

Although the Federal Reserve was *obliged* in October 1979 to abandon interest rate targeting as previously practiced and to announce changes in policy procedures that would give it an excuse for abandoning its previous long-term policy of very narrow control over the federal funds rate, it certainly has not *entirely* given up control over the funds rate, with all that implies. Although the range of variation of the federal funds rate has been widened substantially, a floor still exists under the funds rate, and this floor caused havoc in the second quarter of 1980.

The House Banking subcommittee 1980 report tells us:

> Beginning in late March 1980, the public suddenly and substantially increased its demand for coin and currency, vis-à-vis demand (checking) accounts. This was not an accident. Switching from checking accounts to currency was impelled by the higher costs of using credit cards that were imposed by new regulations issued by the Federal Reserve pursuant to President Carter's invoking of the Credit Control Act of 1969, on March 14, 1980.

The public needed a lot more cash because it could not pay with checks the bills it previously paid with credit cards. The money supply M1-B fell sharply, by $6.6 billion from the four weeks ending March 12, 1980, to the four weeks ending May 14, 1980, or at an annual rate of nearly 10 percent.

The 1980 subcommittee report stated:

> No harm would have resulted, indeed the money supply would have continued to grow, if the Federal Reserve had made open market purchases in sufficient volume to replace reserves that banks lost at this time, because of the currency drain that resulted from the higher cost of using credit cards.

But until late May, the Federal Reserve failed to replace the reserves that were drained as a result of the imposition of credit controls. It did not supply replacement reserves because it was afraid that doing so would cause the Federal Funds rate to fall precipitously.

[This was virtually a complete replay of the disastrous Federal Reserve policy in the early 1930's, when the Fed withdrew reserves from the banks at the very time the demand for credit was collapsing. This action was taken because the Fed at that time was frightened of the "inflationary consequences" of the fall in interest rates. The following passage from the speech by Emmett J. Rice could have been given in 1932 by a Fed governor during that earlier debacle. Note Rice's preoccupation with preventing the fall in the federal funds rate in 1980—a throwback to fifty years earlier.]

As put by Federal Reserve Governor Emmett J. Rice in a New York City speech on May 7, 1980:

"When the aggregates registering growth fell substantially below their target ranges, we could, of course, increase reserves by an amount sufficient to bring them within the announced target ranges. However, the increment in reserves necessary to achieve this could imply a Federal Funds rate that is far lower than seems prudent under present conditions. Such a provision of reserves would run the risk of creating too much liquidity too soon. Moreover, it might be interpreted by market analysts as indicating an abrupt shift by the Federal Reserve towards monetary ease, possibly thereby encouraging inflationary pressures."

It may seem laughable that a governor of the Federal Reserve could express concern about the inflationary consequences of providing reserves to the banking system in the middle of a liquidity crisis, as in the second quarter of 1980. The Fed then turned around and made exactly the opposite error in the second half of 1980, when in an attempt to hold the federal funds rate *below* its *ceiling,* it put out so much cash that in the six months ending November 1980, M1-B grew at an annual rate of 15 percent, the highest in any six-month period since the end of the Second World War.

Fighting Free from HCR 133—The Fed Confuses the Issues

To summarize what we know about the attempt to *oblige* the Fed to institute procedures which would bring about a slow, steady growth of money, no more than needed to finance noninflationary feasible economic growth, the main points are:

1. After about ten years of development of thinking outside the Fed, Congress was persuaded in 1975 to impose a control system on the Fed, requiring it to announce and meet targets.

2. The plan failed. The Fed instituted an inflationary boom beginning about a year after the new House Concurrent Resolution had been passed by Congress.

3. This inflationary boom was initiated by means of the Fed's narrowing the permissible band in which the federal funds rate could move and widening the band in which money growth rates could move.

4. As money growth developed, it was persistently reinforced as the Fed poured out more and more cash in its attempt to hold down the federal funds rate. A massive inflationary boom developed, culminating in a collapse of the whole Fed policy.

5. This collapse of policy was not presented to the American people as such. Rather, in October 1979 a "new" policy of permitting more variation in the federal funds rate band was introduced. This was merely a face-saver for the Fed, an attempt to get out of what had become a disastrous commitment to holding down the federal funds rate without the public disgrace of admitting the disaster for what it was.

6. Even after that terrible admission of failure the Fed continued in 1980 to try to hold the federal funds rate *up* during the second-quarter liquidity crisis and recession of that year (thus making the recession worse), and by attempting to hold the federal funds rate *down* during the second half of 1980, thus making the inflationary boom of that period worse.

In all this, an underlying concern by the Fed, influencing all its actions, was the attempt by its officials to undermine the intent of the House Concurrent Resolution of March 1975 and the congressional supervision and loss of "discretion" which that involved.

In its counterattack against the threat to its discretionary independence implied by HCR 133, the Fed took two broad lines of attack:

1. It presented the Congress with a *number* of targets, referring to differing definitions of *money*. All told, five different categories—

M1-A, M1-B, M2, M3, and L—were presented to Congress, as part of the annual targeting procedures. There was a target (there still is) for each of M1-A, M1-B, M2, and M3.

2. It constantly changed the *base period* from which the target growth ranges were to be measured.

The use of multiple definitions of *money* allowed the Fed to be able to say at any particular point that one of the "M's" was on or near target. The confusion caused by this practice remains deeply embedded in all public discussion of money. Fortunately, studies have indicated that the use of M1-B (which since January 1982 has been described as M1 again) gives the best forecasting results and hence discussion about monetary control should center on this aggregate. This is discussed in detail in a later chapter.

As for the changes in target bases, here is a list of the occasions during the first year of the target system on which a target base changed:

- March 1975—system initiated
- Late spring 1975—base changed
- Early fall 1975—another change in base
- Winter 1975—another base change
- End winter 1976—base changed again
- Summer 1976—another base change

Commenting on this in September 1976, Karl Brunner said:

> The authorities have accustomed the public and Congress to a deliberately "flexible" approach. Every quarter, the base for the target cone is redefined in terms of the most recent actual values observed. Moreover, the Fed also changes with some frequency, the width or boundaries of the target range for one or another of the aggregate measures.
>
> This procedure forms in a sense a rational response by the policy institutions to the inquiries and potential constraints emanating from Congress. It protects its operational freedom and requires relatively small adjustments for internal procedures.

The Fed thus succeeded in confusing Congress and indeed in confusing most of the American people about two crucial issues:

1. What was the money the growth of which was being controlled?
2. What was the evidence that the Fed was on target for controlling whatever money one happened to be talking about?
As a result, the Fed succeeded in protecting itself against informed criticism and certainly left Congress standing.

"The Myth of Congressional Supervision of Monetary Policy"

I can think of no better way to summarize the experience of the last seventeen years of attempts to achieve congressional supervision of monetary policy than to quote James Pierce, the former high official of the Fed who is professor of economics at the University of California at Berkeley. Writing in the *Journal of Monetary Economics* in 1978, Pierce said:

> For years, Congressional committees have attempted in varying degrees to oversee monetary policy. Chairmen of the Federal Reserve Board have been interrogated intensively by some members of Congress, attempting to learn what the Fed was doing and why it was doing it. These efforts were frustrated by the Fed's unwillingness to divulge its plans and objectives for monetary policy. The Fed was able to keep its intentions to itself. It apparently believed that to expose its policy decisions to public scrutiny would be detrimental to the Federal Reserve and its policies. In effect, it told Congress not to ask too many questions; just "trust us."
>
> The Federal Reserve was able to imbue its activities with a mystical quality, arguing in effect that secrecy was required for effective central banking.
>
> This ploy was successful, because many potential critics of monetary policy were fearful that greater disclosure might result in some calamity for domestic or even international money markets.
>
> The lack of public interest and the mystical quality of American central banking could be combined with the Fed's considerable political power to withstand attacks by those who demanded greater disclosure of policy objectives and plans.
>
> It is difficult to understand how monetarists, or anyone else, could conclude that any substantive changes have occurred in the execution of policy or in the supervision of that policy [since the passage of HCR 133]. The evidence points clearly to the conclusion that the Federal Reserve has *not* placed greater

emphasis on monetary aggregates in its actual—as opposed to its stated—policy-making. In fact, the evidence suggests that the Fed has placed an even greater reliance on stabilizing the money market, frequently at the cost of losing control over the monetary aggregates, since HCR 133 was passed.

Whatever can be said for Congressional supervision of monetary policy, it has not produced closer control over the monetary aggregates and it has not lessened the Fed's penchant for stabilizing short-term interest rates. It appears safe to conclude that Congressional oversight has not altered the conduct of monetary policy.

Milton Friedman's Correspondence with Martin and Burns

In discussing the gradual change from a formal commitment by the Fed to "controlling money market conditions" to "trying to control monetary aggregates," Milton Friedman, in his February 1982 article, reported on correspondence with William McChesney Martin (chairman of the Fed from 1951 to 1970) and with Arthur Burns (chairman from 1970 to 1978):

> In 1969 I wrote a letter to William McChesney Martin, noting that two issues were under discussion: first, whether a monetary aggregate ought to be the policy target; second, whether, if it were the target, the system could control it. I suggested that the issues be separated, and that there be carried out at the New York Fed "a dry run to test the possibility of achieving money supply targets and to develop and calibrate the necessary techniques." Such procedures would then be available when and if the first issue was decided in favor of monetary aggregates.
>
> I refer to this letter, not to advertise the suggestion I made, but rather because of the reply that I received from Chairman Martin. I quote from his reply: "I seriously doubt that we could ever attain complete control [of monetary aggregates] but I think it's quite true that we could come significantly closer to such control than we do now—if we wished to make that variable our exclusive target. But the wisdom of such an exclusive orientation for monetary policy is, of course, the basic question."
>
> That's a very instructive statement. First of all, it says that the Fed had repeatedly denied and was to deny throughout the rest of the period that I'm talking about [up to 1981] that it *could* control the monetary aggregates. But second, the Fed

didn't really mean it. The reply was simply designed to immobilize me—as I later learned from an economist in the Fed's
Research Division, who boasted to me about his cleverness in
constructing that reply. And of course it did immobilize me.
Why conduct a study to figure out how to do something the Fed
already knew how to do?

Almost simultaneously, Alan Holmes, who ran the Desk in
New York and Sherman Maisel, who was at that time a member of the Federal Reserve Board, were proclaiming, at a June
1969 monetary conference in Nantucket, that the Fed could not
in fact control the money supply.

On November 26, 1970, I repeated to Arthur Burns [then
chairman of the Fed] the recommendation I had made to Chairman Martin. I also recommended that the Fed establish two
committees of outside and inside people, one to study procedures for controlling the money supply and the other to study
the measurement of the money supply. The first committee was
never established; the second was appointed three years later
and turned in its report in early 1976.

In 1970, the directive [to the Open Market Desk] was
changed after Arthur Burns became chairman. Monetary
growth was put first and money market conditions second.
However, that change turned out to be pure lip service, and was
later deemphasized.

Congressional Initiatives Actually Made Things Worse

The conduct of monetary policy since 1975 has actually been far
more disastrous for the American economy—and for the world economy—than was the case before then. In the United States inflation
has been much worse, interest rates have been much higher, and
monetary movements have been much wilder and much more destructive.

One important factor behind this grave deterioration in the degree
of monetary control was the struggle being waged by the Federal
Reserve during the latter half of the 1970's to remain free of congressional control. Rather than make any attempt to cooperate with the
intentions of Congress, the Fed actually went even farther and more
vigorously toward the traditional policy of interest rate control.

As we have seen, the Fed made two important changes in its
operating procedures after the passage of HCR 133 in March 1975:

1. It narrowed the range of permitted movement of the federal funds rate. This would necessarily have the effect of intensifying movements in the monetary aggregates, whether up or down.

2. It widened the range of permitted movement of the monetary aggregates, thus giving its Desk officials in New York the necessary freedom to allow the monetary aggregates' fluctuations needed to ensure even stricter control over the federal funds rate.

Over the period from January 1974 through March 1975 the mean federal funds rate range was 1.29 percentage points and the mean absolute change in the federal funds rate was 80 basis points. In the period between March 1975 and the end of 1977 the mean federal funds rate range was 0.84 percentage points and the mean absolute change in the actual rate was 20 basis points.

Before the passage of HCR 133, the mean width of the range of growth for M1 was 3.0 percentage points. Between March 1975 and the end of 1977, it was 3.9 percentage points. In the period from January 1974 to April 1975, M1 was in its two-month growth range 47 percent of the time, but between March 1975 and the end of 1977 it was in its *expanded* range only 37 percent of the time.

The Fed willfully opposed Congress through the use of confusion and actually put itself even more vigorously up against its critics by intensifying the use of the very policies which were the source of the disagreement. When the Fed's policies finally culminated in the disaster of October 1979, it became apparent, by its own admission, that it had been acting against the law for the previous four and a half years.

Yet no action was taken against any Fed official. No move was made to restrict the Fed's freedom. The Fed could perpetuate the still further disasters of the June quarter 1980 and the second half of 1980. It was a remarkable story of impunity in the face of illegal and utterly destructive policy actions.

Needless to say, the Fed has a great continuing need for political protection and influence. It has been able to develop a wide range of influence throughout the federal bureaucracy and in the various administrations. Let us examine some of these policies and practices of the Fed as it seeks to obtain and use political and bureaucratic influence.

5 The Fed and the Presidents—Who Is Manipulating Whom?

The more one understands about the *possible* success that would attend a well-run monetary policy in the United States, the more difficult it is to accept the *actual* performance of the Federal Reserve in running the monetary policy of the country. We know that well-established relationships are at work. We know there is a constant and highly predictable relationship between the monetary base (currency and banks' reserves with the Fed) and the money supply (currency plus demand deposits at commercial banks and checkable deposits at all depository institutions). This means that there is a highly stable relationship between one item which the Fed *can* control with great ease—the monetary base—and another item which most of us would *like* the Fed to control—the money supply M1. (In Chapter 7 I have included a technical note which sets out very clearly these simple relationships, the very heart and soul of a practical, thoroughly tested system of monetary control.)

Over the last twenty years, as we have seen, there has been a continuing development of thinking, outside the Fed, by famous economists and government officials. The group includes Milton Friedman and Anna Schwartz, the historians of money in America; Allan Meltzer and Karl Brunner, the theoreticians of monetary reform, going back at least to 1964 in their presentations to Congress; the Shadow Open Market Committee; the House Banking Committee and its Subcommittee on Domestic Monetary Policy, in which Dr. Robert Weintraub played such a valuable and continuing role in analyzing the Fed's performance and making suggestions for reform; congressional leaders such as Wright Patman, Henry Reuss, Stephen Neal, and Parren Mitchell; Homer Jones and his many disciples at the St. Louis Fed Research Department, including James Meigs and Denis Karnosky; David Meiselman, professor of economics at Virginia Polytechnic Institute; and James Pierce, professor of economics at the University of California at Berkeley, and William Poole, professor of economics at Brown University, both former senior officials of the Fed.

Very little of this mass of work has had any effect on the procedures adopted by the Federal Reserve. That institution remains indifferent to outside pressure and to the huge volume of criticism which has accumulated over the last twenty years.

Instead the Fed is loathed and feared in the money markets of America and the world. This fear and loathing are the result of the experiences suffered by money market participants. Owners of fixed-interest securities such as bonds—public and corporate—have suffered huge losses as interest rates have progressively increased, along with inflation. But owners of stock have not escaped, as I have shown. By early 1982 the real (inflation adjusted) value of the Dow Jones industrial index was back to the levels prevailing in the early 1950's, a quarter of a century earlier. In the last two years the variability of interest rates and of money supply have increased. There has been more and more instability.

Why, we must ask ourselves, has the Federal Reserve permitted such chaos and destruction to develop? Some would argue that the Fed has been caught up in the failures of the economic policies of presidents. Others would argue that the Fed's hands have been tied by a need to finance the extraordinary expansion of government spending which has taken place in the last twenty years. Since 1965 federal spending as a proportion of gross national product has risen from 17 to 23 percent.

Fed officials have given many excuses for their failures, including some of the above. They have also said money is not controllable and that even if it were, there would be no point in doing so (as William McChesney Martin told Milton Friedman).

I do not believe any of these excuses gets to the heart of the issue of why the Fed has failed. I believe that the answer to this question: How could such a massive organization, endowed with limitless funds and an extraordinary staff of highly talented people, make such a mess of things? is: *The Fed has always had other fish to fry.* It has never been interested in the control over the money supply as its principal priority. The principal—and unstated—top priority of the Fed is its survival as an expanding and largely unfettered bureaucracy, providing power and promotion for its members.

Undoubtedly the Fed has accommodated its actions to the dominant political themes of the day, particularly when the president of the day expressed urgent interest in a certain course for monetary policy. But this means only that the Fed has been able to bend with the political winds. This willingness to bend explains some of the fantastic somersaults performed by Fed officials, notably that performed by Arthur Burns, who was transformed, upon accession to the position of chairman of the Fed in 1970, from an economist who had a lifetime commitment to free market policies, with an abhorrence of wage-price controls, and a leading exponent of the dangers of inflation, to the most inflationist central banker the country has known. Burns spent his years at the Fed twisting and turning with the political currents of the day. He emerged with a tarnished reputation, a name for accommodating dirigiste ideas (wage-price control) and for using the great financial powers of the Fed to support President Nixon's political ambitions. He was prepared to support Carter with even more inflation than he had given Nixon, but Carter got rid of him.

"The Burden" of Budget Deficits

Fed officials and members of the Federal Reserve Board—as in a recent example of Governor Wallich—have long complained that they have a "burden" of financing the debts of the federal government. This, it is argued, makes it difficult, if not impossible for the Federal Reserve to carry out "responsible" monetary policy.

Yet the Federal Reserve has been granted extraordinary independence from the pressures of the government of the day. Any favors the Fed may have done for governments would have been done for reasons which suited the Fed. There is very little in an immediate sense that the president can do to the Fed if it defies him. Certainly, when the time comes around (every four years), it is possible for the president to dismiss a chairman of the Fed, as Carter in effect dismissed Burns in 1978. But this takes time. Even upon dismissal from the position of chairman, a former chairman does not have to leave the Federal Reserve Board unless his term as a member of the Federal Reserve Board has expired. The seven members of the board are appointed for terms of fourteen years. So there is no urgent need for the Federal Reserve to do the government of the day any favors. Nor, in fact, is there any evidence to suggest that in the matter of buying government debt, the Fed has been notably accommodating to governments.

Richard Harris, of the Chicago Harris Bank, has pointed out that in the last eleven years the Fed has "monetized" only a small proportion of the federal deficits. This means that it has purchased, net, only a small proportion of the increase in the stock of government securities—bonds and bills—that have been issued from time to time to finance the federal government's deficits. The proportions are set out below.

**The Fed Has "Monetized" Little
of the Federal Deficit
(Proportion of Federal Deficit
Purchased by the Federal Reserve)**

1971	37%
1972	39
1973	30
1974	114
1975	19
1976	6
1977	18
1978	37
1979	6
1980	15
1981	9

The Fed's track record of the actual proportion of the federal deficit which has been "monetized" indicates that it has actually been quite restrained in any net purchases of government debt. We must therefore put the argument that the Fed has a terrible "burden" of financing government debt into the category of convenient excuses

III

to justify its general failure to provide effective control over the growth of money.

The Fed Has Been Very Helpful in Federal Elections

In every presidential election since that of 1968, the Federal Reserve has ensured that there has been a very strong increase in the money supply during the election year. In some cases this extraordinary coincidence has been more blatantly obvious than in others. But there is no getting away from the fact that in every presidential election since 1968, the Fed has "accommodated" the incumbent president with a huge rise in money growth. These episodes have often been followed by a very sharp reduction in money growth once the election was out of the way.

In all presidential elections the Fed certainly could not have been accused of being neutral. It was invariably on the side of the incumbent. Inasmuch as the incumbent lost in 1968, 1976, and 1980, one could argue that the Fed had bad political judgment. But one would be hard put to argue that it was not very deeply involved in the election process.

One would be equally hard put to argue that the Fed officials of the day were immune to the grand sweep of the so-called New Economics, which placed such a supreme priority on full employment and economic growth while drastically downgrading the importance in policy of sound money and free markets (even though these were truly prerequisites for the very growth sought by the practitioners of the New Economics under Presidents Kennedy, Johnson, and, after a short change of emphasis in 1969, Nixon).

A short outline of some of the dominant trends in economic policy since President Johnson will put the Fed's role as willing handmaiden of inflation into perspective. In 1968, the Nixon versus Humphrey election, the Fed presided over a major rise in money growth. The rise in M1-B in the year ended April 1967 had been only 1.4 percent. (This embraced a period in which the Fed actually imposed a severe "credit crunch," for which it was to pay dearly in the impetus this error gave to moves to impose congressional limits on Fed discretion.) But in the twelve months to March 1968, money growth (M1-B) rose to 6.2 percent and to 7.2 percent between December 1967 and December 1968. In its 1968 economic report, issued early in the year, the Council of Economic Advisers had stated:

> After a hard look at the alternatives, it has been and remains the conviction of both the Administration and the Federal Reserve System that the Nation should depend on fiscal policy, not monetary policy, to carry the main burden of additional restraint on the growth of demand that now appears necessary for 1968. In present circumstances, the accompanying further rapid expansion of credit demand would impose severe strains on financial markets—even under an expansionary Federal Reserve policy—to the extent that policy was aimed at moderating inflationary pressures, the more interest rates would rise and the more homebuilding would be depressed.

The administration thus indicated it wanted interest rates kept down, and presumably the way to do that was to refrain from restricting the growth of money. (The Council of Economic Advisers was of course wrong in this belief, as much bitter experience since those times has taught us. We now know that an expansionary monetary policy induces higher interest rates, by its effect on inflationary expectations.)

Despite the rapid growth in money that took place in 1968, the policy not surprisingly failed to achieve its result. By the end of 1968 interest rates were higher than at the end of 1967, and for the year 1968 as a whole the average yield on a ninety-day Treasury bill was up to 5.33 percent from 4.3 percent average in 1967.

It was obvious in 1968, even from the published statements of the Council of Economic Advisers, that the administration and the Federal Reserve System were acting totally in concert toward a common goal, that of achieving ever faster real economic growth and low interest rates. The Federal Reserve System was, in fact, being caught up increasingly in the so-called New Economics of the times. This New Economics included as its main elements a commitment to "maximum employment and rapid economic growth" to be stimulated by an expansionary fiscal policy (the Kennedy tax cuts) and a benign or overtly stimulatory monetary policy. Any problems of an inflationary kind were seen to be the result of "excessive wage growth" or "exploitative pricing policies" and hence to be contained by price and wage controls, either overt or exhortative (jawboning).

The Fed was swept along by the fervor of this New Economics. Between 1956 and 1963, the years of Eisenhower and Kennedy, the average growth of money supply (M1-B) was 1.5 percent (these days we consider ourselves fortunate when money supply growth is *only four times* that rate). From 1964 to 1967 annual growth of M1-B accelerated to 4.2 percent. As a result, the GNP price deflator (the price index of the gross national product and a good general indicator of the rate of increase of the average price level for the national income), which had risen only 1.7 percent a year from 1958 to 1965, increased 3.3 percent in 1966, 2.9 percent in 1967, and 4.5 percent in 1968. This acceleration of prices carried interest rates up with it.

Thus, in participating as a willing handmaiden of the Age of Inflation, the Federal Reserve under President Johnson set in train the process that would lead to the stagflation of today. Excessive monetary growth led to price inflation and higher interest rates. This in turn led to a progressive shortening of the debt structure throughout the nation and a reluctance to make long-term investments. In its turn this led to a stagnation of production and of employment. Eventually, by this route, we reached the Great Recession beginning in 1978. That their starry-eyed policies would culminate in high money growth, high interest rates, virtually zero average economic growth, and persistently mounting unemployment would have seemed unthinkable, perhaps, to the zealots who thought they had found a magic means to ever-growing employment and output through the New Economics.

President Nixon initially set out to follow the same general economic policy lines as were set down and largely implemented under President Reagan in *his* first year. In his 1970 economic report Nixon said:

> 1969 was a year of progress in the fight against inflation. For the first time since the price spiral began, there was a sustained period of combined fiscal and monetary restraint. During 1969, the rise of Federal expenditures was slowed to an increase of $9 billion, compared with an annual average of $20 billion in the three preceding years. Instead of the rising budget deficits, of early years, there was a surplus in 1969. Instead of the money

supply expanding by 7 percent as in 1968, it grew at a 4.4 percent annual rate in the first half of 1969 and at a 0.7 percent annual rate in the second half.

President Nixon's Council of Economic Advisers also roundly criticized the Johnson policy of imposing "price and wage guideposts" as an instrument to contain inflation. In its 1970 annual report, which accompanied Nixon's economic report in February of that year, the CEA said:

> The Administration's plan of policy for 1969 did not include an attempt to revive wage-price guideposts, such as those existing in 1962–66. By the Fall of 1966, the policy was widely recognized to be unworkable and it was allowed to fade away. In subsequent years, there were only episodic actions with specific companies regarding prices.
>
> The guidepost policy clearly did not work once the economy ran into strong and serious pressures of inflationary demand.

The Federal Reserve cooperated fully with the Johnson inflationary monetary policy, culminating in the huge buildup of monetary growth in the election year 1968. The Fed (under the same chairman, William McChesney Martin) also cooperated in the switch to a tough policy of monetary restraint in 1969.

It then switched again in 1970 to turn on the money spigots when Burns went to the Fed in February of that year. By that month the Nixon administration's nerve broke and, with Arthur Burns at the helm as chairman of the Fed (having been appointed on February 1, 1970), the Federal Reserve instituted a major expansionary money policy. The Nixon team could not withstand the political pressure that followed the rise in unemployment in 1970 in the recession of that year. Thus ended the first serious attempt to curb inflation by means of a restrictive monetary policy.

The collapse of the Nixon attempt to beat inflation in 1969 was followed by the rapid growth of money initiated in 1970, which culminated in another boom in money growth in 1972 and in the crisis of 1973 and thereafter in the serious 1974–75 recession. The Federal Reserve Open Market Committee at its February 10, 1970, meeting, stated: "In light of the latest economic developments and current business outlook, it was appropriate to move gradually toward somewhat less restraint with a view to encouraging moderate growth in money and bank credit over the months ahead."

Robert Weintraub, writing in his capacity as staff director of the House Banking Committee's Subcommittee on Domestic Monetary Policy, said of this decision:

It is noteworthy that three of the Committee's members [Hayes, Brimmer, and Coldwell] dissented from the associated February 10, 1970, policy directive "because they felt that any overt move toward less firm money markets was premature. . . . They were impressed by the strength of inflationary expectations . . . concerned about the prospects for adequate fiscal strength . . . they agreed . . . that some growth in the monetary and credit aggregates was called for but in their view this objective could have been adequately met by a directive similar to the one the Committee had adopted at its January meeting." That directive called for "maintaining firm conditions in the money market" while taking account of the Committee's desire to see a modest growth in money and credit.

Further moving to abandon its earlier disinflationary economic policies, the Nixon administration in August 1971 installed its version of the New Economics under the title of the New Economic Policy. This was nothing more or less than a return to the inflationary policies of President Johnson. As stated by Robert Weintraub, in "Political Economy of Inflation" (a 1981 symposium of the Graduate School of Administration, University of Rochester, New York),

The Nixon remake contained the usual fiscal and monetary elements and an incomes policy:
    Specifically, Nixon's "New Economic Policy" (August 1971) included:
    (1) Tax reductions and expenditures increases to increase aggregate demand.
    (2) Commitment to expansionary monetary policy which necessitated, as a corollary, the suspension of conversion of dollars into gold and other reserve assets. In his 1972 Economic Report, President Nixon proclaimed that monetary expansion was underway. He reported, "The Federal Reserve has taken steps to create the monetary conditions for rapid economic

expansion." The growth of money supply (M1-B) had accelerated from 2.4 percent in the year ended February 1970 to 8.2 percent in the twelve months ending July 1971.

(3) "A 90-day freeze on wages, prices and rents" which was followed by a "comprehensive, mandatory system of controls with more flexible and equitable standards than were possible during the first 90 days."

Following the abandonment of budgetary and monetary restraint in the summer of 1971, further major expansion of money was instituted during 1972. Money supply growth accelerated to 9.4 percent in the first eleven months of 1972, ensuring that the economy would be buoyant during the presidential election year. That money boom of 1972 was part of the program initiated in the summer of 1971 to provide the economic conditions to ensure Nixon's reelection. Once the election was over, the whole policy had to be put into reverse because its results were proving so disastrous.

Inflation began to bolt ahead. The consumer price index, which had risen only 3.3 percent in 1972, down from 5.4 percent in 1969 and 5.9 percent in 1970, jumped up 6.2 percent in 1973 and 11.0 percent in 1974. The decline in the growth of prices in 1972 reflected the delayed results of the monetary restraint which had been imposed in 1969 and early 1970. The subsequent boom in inflation in 1973 and 1974 represented the effects of the abandonment of monetary restraint by Burns and Nixon in 1970 through 1973.

By July 1973 it was obvious a major change in policy would have to be initiated, and Burns at the Federal Reserve instituted a money squeeze. The annual growth rate of M1-B, which had averaged 8.2 percent in the 1972–73 period, fell to 5.3 percent in the twelve months ended January, February, and March 1974 and stabilized in the 4.6 to 5.0 percent range between then and late 1974.

More Money Explosions in the 1976 and 1980 Elections

The blatant expansion of the money supply in 1972 exposed the strong political connections between the Federal Reserve and the White House. The 1976 federal election would see a similar extraordinary money boom.

Under President Ford, a semblance of a restrained monetary policy had been instituted briefly. During the time Ford was president, and Burns was still chairman of the Federal Reserve, the rate of growth of money dropped heavily, down to 3.5 percent in the year ended the first quarter of 1975. The result was the 1974–75 recession, at that time the worst since the 1930's and very much the product of the gyrations of monetary policy in the years since Nixon and Burns had abandoned restraint in 1970, in the face of the mild recession of that time. The sharp drop in M1-B growth after July 1973 began to reverse inflation in 1975. The deceleration of inflation continued from the first quarter of 1975 to the end of 1976. In the year ended the first quarter of 1975, the GNP deflator price index peaked at 11.6 percent; in the year ended the fourth quarter of 1976, it had fallen to 4.8 percent. This was the payoff for the tight money policy that had been instituted between July 1973 and 1975.

But in April 1976 the Federal Reserve Board, under Burns, instituted another booming period of monetary expansion. As was pointed out in Chapter III, in April 1976 the Federal Open Market Committee, the supreme monetary policymaking body in the Federal Reserve System, instructed the Desk operations manager in New York that he must sharply narrow the range in which the federal funds rate was to be permitted to trade. This was a back-door way of ensuring a rapid growth of money. From March 1975 through March 1976 the open market Desk manager in New York was instructed to keep the per year *money* growth band within 2½ to 4 percentage points wide and the *federal funds* rate within a band 1¼ percentage points wide. However, beginning in April 1976 the Open Market Committee narrowed the band in which the manager was instructed to keep the federal funds rate and widened the intermeeting target range for money growth. Thereby the committee *deemphasized control of the money supply* as an operating goal and increased the importance of resisting interest rate movements. The effect was to provide a powerful stimulus to money growth at a time when economic activity was expanding.

"Snatching Defeat from the Jaws of Victory"

All told, from 1968 to 1980 the Federal Reserve produced roller coaster money growth superimposed on high average money growth.

That, in turn, helped produce stagflation—recessions in 1969–70, 1974–75, and 1979–80, and rising inflation. The ultimate irony is that fast money growth did not keep interest rates down or financial markets calm. The volatility of financial markets increased and interest rates skyrocketed.

Commenting on the experiences of the last fifteen years, Robert Weintraub wrote in the report of the Joint Economic Committee of Congress in March 1982:

> The fight against inflation requires patience, perseverance and courage, especially in the conduct of monetary policy. Money growth is the sustenance of inflation. Inflation will endure as long as money growth exceeds the nation's long-run real growth potential. Courage is required to fight inflation because the initial effect of slowing down money growth is likely to be a slowdown in economic activity and real hardship for many people. Patience is required, because it takes time for reduced money growth to reduce inflation. Perseverance is required because reaccelerating money growth will reignite inflation. Unfortunately, twice since 1968, defeat was snatched from the jaws of victory by abandoning the fight. Money growth was slowed in 1969. That triggered a recession starting in the fourth quarter of 1969. Then the Federal Reserve reversed course early in 1970, just as the 1969 deceleration in money growth started to reduce inflation. Money growth was again slowed in mid-1973. The deceleration was sharp enough, and kept in place long enough, to dramatically reduce inflation. Between 1974 and 1976, the year-on-year rate of inflation dropped from nearly 10 percent to just over 5 percent. But the effort was not sustained. Year-on-year money growth was increased from under 5 percent in 1974 and 1975 to 5.6 percent in 1976, 7.5 percent in 1977, 8.2 percent in 1978, 7.8 percent in 1979 and 6.4 percent in 1980. As a result, inflation was reignited and surged to new post World War II highs.

Despite the "help" from the Fed and Arthur Burns, Ford lost the 1976 election, and in December 1977, President Carter replaced Burns with G. William Miller as chairman of the Fed.

There was another massive drive for money growth in 1980. On this occasion the panic at the Fed to ensure favorable economic conditions by election time was even more evident than in 1968,

1972, or 1976. As explained earlier, the attempt by the Federal Reserve to maintain a tight control over the federal funds rate led to increasing monetary disorder, and by the middle of 1979 the Fed was having to make huge injections of cash in its attempt to hold down the federal funds rate. The inflationary process thus generated was bound to lead to some sort of collapse, and interest rates were bound to leap beyond the confines of Federal Reserve control bands. It was, as stated in Chapter 3, in an attempt to evade the responsibility for the sharp upward movement that had become inevitable, that the Federal Reserve announced on October 6, 1979, that it was downgrading the importance of interest rate control and upgrading the importance of monetary growth rate control. The explosion of interest rates that followed the lifting of the lid in October 1979 was followed by the recession of the second quarter 1980, which was in turn exacerbated by the failure of the Federal Reserve to take any steps to feed cash into the system at a time of extreme cash shortage (the product of ill-conceived and panicky credit controls imposed in March 1980).

A wildly expansionary money policy was finally set in train in the middle of 1980 to try to make good, by the end of the year, the damage that had been caused in the year ended the middle of 1980. During the first quarter of 1980, money supply (M1-B) had risen at an annual rate of 6 percent; in the second quarter it fell at an annual rate of about 2 percent, and in the last half of 1980 it rose at an annual rate of some 12 to 13 percent.

During all these years the Federal Reserve was fooling around with procedures such as interest rate targeting, federal funds narrow banding, and a general refusal to concede that Congress should be able to impose targets on its prospective permitted money growth ranges. The Fed did not have its collective mind on the job of defeating inflation by a strong monetary policy. Rather, it was preoccupied with the issue of its own survival, which led the Fed and its officials (including the chairmen, Martin, Burns, and Miller) to spend a disproportionate amount of effort in inventing schemes to *get around* the well-intentioned and, as experience has shown, *very relevant* attempts by a tiny group of members of Congress and their aides to get the Fed to concentrate on monetary control.

The Federal Reserve, when it was not preoccupied with ensuring its own survival during this period from 1965 to 1980, was intellectually committed to the very policies—the New Economics and the Nixon New Economic Policy—which were bound to undermine any prospect of monetary stability. As part of its survival program the Fed did not merely attempt to curry favor with presidents and to confuse Congress. It was also active in constructing its own apparatus of influence within the administration. In this, Fed efforts were notably concentrated on ensuring total hegemony over the one power center within the administration which could provide a significant challenge. That was the United States Treasury.

The Federal Reserve and the Treasury

No president operates monetary policy in a vacuum. He does not think it up himself. Hence, the views and policies of the central bank are bound to have their influence in the mix of policies eventually adopted by any administration. Accordingly, the Federal Reserve has of necessity developed its own lines of influence within the federal economic policy civil service. The key position in this regard is that of under secretary for monetary affairs in the U.S. Treasury. This position is the focal point of possible intervention in monetary policy and one area that could provide a base for a challenge to the authority of the Federal Reserve.

Federal Reserve sympathizers filled the position for most of the period from 1945 to 1980, thus obviating any concerted criticism from within this key area of administration policymaking. As a result, there was no development, over that time, of an alternative to the Federal Reserve's broad policy lines. Alternatives came from the Council of Economic Advisers under Johnson, where the policy of monetary permissiveness, which was to prove so destructive of financial and price stability, was developed.

Under Nixon, there was no threat to the Federal Reserve's broad policy lines, as Burns and Nixon shared the same aims, summarized in an impatience with criticism of Nixon and a dominating need to ensure Nixon's political survival. But it was under Nixon that the Congress developed into a source of criticism of monetary policy as administered by the Federal Reserve, and the movement of thinking associated with the House and Senate Banking committees (outlined in Chapter 3) came to be seen by the Federal Reserve (led by Burns) as a threat to the independent use of the central bank's power.

Under Carter the Federal Reserve had a very docile chairman, G. William Miller, who presided over the disastrous buildup to the crisis of October 1979.

It was not until the appointment of Beryl Sprinkel to the position of under secretary for monetary affairs in the Treasury early in 1981 that a powerful alternative voice to that of the Federal Reserve was developed within the administration. He led the move to develop policy lines that would form the basis for a breakdown in the monopoly control by the Federal Reserve over U.S. monetary policy.

Sprinkel's challenge to the Federal Reserve was serious because for the first time a very senior federal official, in a key position, was committed to a line of policy thinking totally at variance with the traditions of the Federal Reserve. Sprinkel had worked for most of his career in the Harris Bank and Trust Company in Chicago. During the 1970's he was an influential member of the Shadow Open Market Committee, an unofficial body of economists formed by Karl Brunner, professor of economics in the Graduate School of Management at the University of Rochester, and Allan Meltzer, professor of economics at the Carnegie-Mellon Institute of the University of Pittsburgh. Sprinkel had become a member of the Shadow Open Market Committee in 1973 and remained so until his appointment to the Treasury by President Reagan in 1981.

In the Treasury, Sprinkel moved quickly to bring about changes in monetary policy. He argued forcefully for tough monetary policies and "hands off" free markets. He recruited to his side as director of the Office of Domestic Monetary Policy Denis Karnosky, an outstanding monetary economist and a former staff economist with the St. Louis Federal Reserve. Karnosky had worked for the St. Louis Fed since 1967, in the Research Department. The St. Louis Fed under its famous chief economist Homer Jones had been for long the source of much of the research on the relationship between money and prices, output and interest rates. Immediately before going to the Treasury position in 1981, Karnosky had been from 1975 through 1979 vice-president of the bank, with responsibility for administration of the operation of the Research Department and for the editorial management of the St. Louis Fed's influential monthly *Review*.

These changes in the Treasury were volcanic in their possibilities for the Federal Reserve because they indicated the establishment of a powerful countervoice to that of the Fed in administration policy-making. Before that time, however, the Federal Reserve had maintained a tight grip on the Treasury Monetary Affairs division.

From 1945 through 1957 the under secretary for monetary affairs was W. Randolph Burgess, who had been a vice-president with the New York Federal Reserve Bank from 1920 to 1938. From 1961 through 1964 Robert V. Roosa held the post. He had worked for the Federal Reserve Bank of New York from 1953 to 1960, principally in the Research Department. Roosa was followed in the Treasury slot by Frederick Deming, who was president of the Minneapolis Federal Reserve Bank from April 1957 through May 1974 and who took a leave of absence to assume the position of under secretary for monetary affairs in the Treasury from 1965 through 1969.

Deming was followed in the Treasury position by Paul Volcker from 1969 through 1974. Volcker had also worked for the Federal Reserve Bank of New York, as an economist from 1952 to 1957, and subsequently was president of the New York Federal Reserve Bank from 1975 through 1979, when he was appointed chairman of the Fed by President Carter. From 1977 to 1980 the under secretary for monetary affairs in the Treasury was Anthony M. Solomon, who left the job to take over as president of the New York Fed from Volcker in 1980. It was a comfortable little group. Movement to and from the Federal Reserve System—particularly to the New York Federal Reserve Bank—was arranged, and the Fed was able to have its "own man" in the key Treasury position.

This happy little game of musical chairs lasted thirty-five years.

How the Fed Controls the Composition of the Federal Reserve Board

The control of the Federal Reserve policy apparatus is vested in what is in fact a self-perpetuating oligarchy. The Fed has thus managed to resist any significant external threat to its deep-seated policy traditions.

Consider the composition of the Federal Reserve Board at the beginning of 1981. The chairman, *Paul Volcker,* born in 1927, had spent his entire career as an official, with a few brief interludes outside the world of government service. Volcker's first association with the Federal Reserve was as a summer employee at the Federal Reserve Bank of New York in 1949 and 1950. He returned to the New York bank in 1952, at the age of twenty-five, as a full-time economist and remained with the Federal Reserve until 1957, when he became a financial economist at the Chase Manhattan Bank. In 1962 he joined the United States Treasury as director of financial analysis and in 1963 he became deputy under secretary for monetary affairs. From 1965 to 1969 he was a vice-president of the Chase Manhattan Bank. In 1969 he was appointed under secretary for monetary affairs at the Treasury where he remained until 1974. During this time he was the principal U.S. negotiator in the development and installation of a new international monetary system, following the collapse of the Bretton Woods system under Nixon.

After a short stint during the academic year 1974–75 at his alma mater, Princeton, as a senior fellow, he was appointed president and chief executive officer of the Federal Reserve Bank of New York on August 1, 1975. He continued in that office until he was sworn in to a four-year term as chairman of the Federal Reserve Board on August 6, 1979, appointed by President Carter.

Volcker is thus the complete government official. By 1981 he had been a government employee for about twenty-five years. Furthermore, he is a government employee steeped in the traditions and practices of the Fed. It would have been unfair to expect Paul Volcker to institute radical changes in Federal Reserve policy or practices. His whole training and his personal attitudes must push him in the direction of maintaining the existing policies of the Fed, with only minor adjustments.

Appointed by President Nixon, *Henry Wallich* was sworn in on March 8, 1974, at the age of fifty-nine as a member of the Federal Reserve Board, with a term ending in 1988, by which time he will be seventy-three. Wallich is a German who became a U.S. citizen at the age of thirty. Educated at Oxford University in England from 1932 to 1935 and at Harvard, where he took a Ph.D. in 1944, Wallich was in private business in Argentina, Chile, and the United States from 1933 to 1940. He was on the staff of the Federal Reserve Bank of New York from 1941 to 1951 and was chief of the bank's Foreign Research Division from 1946. He was a professor of economics at Yale from 1951 to 1974. Wallich also worked as a member of the Council of Economic Advisers from 1959 to 1961.

Charles J. Partee was appointed in January 1976 by President Ford to fill an unexpired term which ends on January 31, 1986, when he will be fifty-nine. He joined the Federal Reserve Bank of Chicago in 1949 at the age of twenty-two as an economist specializing in consumer finance, mortgage markets, and savings. After seven years he went to the Northern Trust Company of Chicago, where he spent five years as an associate economist and then as second vice-president. He returned to the staff of the Board of Governors in 1962, at age thirty-five, and served as chief of the Capital Markets Section, Division of Research (1962–63); adviser in charge of financial sections, Division of Research (1964–65); and then director of the Division of Research and Statistics and adviser to the board (1969–74).

In November 1973 Partee was appointed managing director for research and economic policy of the board, which office he held until he became a member of the board. He was the second member of the staff to be appointed to the board. Before joining the board, he also served as senior economist of the system's Federal Open Market Committee and as its representative on the board of directors of the Securities Investor Protection Corporation. Partee clearly has been steeped in Federal Reserve traditions for virtually his entire career. He has been working for the Federal Reserve System, with the exception of his five years with the Northern Trust, since he was twenty-two. What is more, he has been responsible for the secretariat side of the board's research and economic policy work for the last eight years.

Nancy Hays Teeters was appointed a member of the Federal Reserve Board by President Carter in September 1978, when she was forty-eight years old. She was a staff economist in the Government Finance Section of the board's Division of Research and Statistics from 1957 to 1966. She worked as an economist, on leave from the Federal Reserve, for the President's Council of Economic Advisers in 1962 and 1963. Teeters worked in the Office of Management and Budget from 1966 to 1970, after which she spent three years at the Brookings Institution in Washington. From late 1974 to the time she joined the Federal Reserve Board as its first woman member, Teeters was assistant staff director and chief economist for the House Budget Committee. Here is another member steeped in the traditions of the Fed.

Emmett J. Rice was appointed to the Federal Reserve Board at age sixty by President Carter in June 1979 for a term expiring in 1990, by which time he will be seventy-one. At the time of his appointment Rice was senior vice-president at the National Bank of Washington, where he had worked since 1971. He first became associated with the Federal Reserve System as an economist at the Federal Reserve Bank of New York (1960–62). Thereafter he spent most of his career working in the area of developing nations' problems. From 1964 to 1966 he was in the U.S. Treasury, in the Office of Developing Nations. From 1966 to 1970 he was alternative executive for the United States at the World Bank.

Lyle E. Gramley was appointed by President Carter on May 28, 1980, at the age of fifty-three. He had joined the Federal Reserve Bank of Kansas City in 1955, when he was twenty-five, as a financial economist. He stayed at the Kansas City Fed for seven years, at which point he took a job for two years as an associate professor of economics. In 1964 he rejoined the Federal Reserve as a senior economist for the board and was subsequently an adviser, associate director, deputy director, and director of the board's Division of Research and Statistics. He served as a member of the Council of Economic Advisers from 1977 to his appointment to the board in 1980. Here is another dyed-in-the-wool Federal Reserve career official.

Frederick H. Schultz, appointed by President Carter in 1979, was a businessman who had an active career in banking and investments in Florida. He left the Federal Reserve in early 1982 and was succeeded by another career businessman, *Preston Martin.* Schultz had the title of vice chairman of the board, as does Martin. Neither gentleman may be seen as a threat to the traditional policies and practices of the Fed. They have not had any experience in playing the game. They have not had any professional knowledge of what goes on. They are on the board principally to give it "balance."

The composition of the board thus breaks down into the following groups:

- One woman—Nancy Teeters, who has also worked for the Federal Reserve System for ten years and is steeped in the traditions of Washington officialdom.
- One black—Emmett Rice, who has virtually no experience in the world of central banking or indeed in serious economic policy areas of government.
- One businessman—Schultz/Martin, who is no threat.
- Four fully blooded Fed officials—Volcker, Wallich, Partee, and Gramley. These know the Federal Reserve System and its history and practices backward. They have the full control of the Federal Reserve Board in their hands. They know where the bodies are buried, how the Fed apparatus works, and where to look.

When it comes down to it, the full-time experienced officials on the Federal Reserve Board could hardly be expected to experience much difficulty in getting their way with part-timers who have not been steeped in the bureaucratic experience enjoyed by the likes of Volcker, Partee, Gramley, and Wallich. At the same time there is a clear majority of "Fed types" on the board. We are looking at a very inbred board, on which the "insiders" must be expected to be able to get their way virtually all the time.

What is more, Wallich, Teeters, and Gramley all have worked for the Council of Economic Advisers, indicating the continuing links between the Federal Reserve Board staff and the Council of Economic Advisers.

We also know that the Federal Reserve appointments in the outlying provinces, the "other" Reserve banks (outside the Federal Reserve Board in Washington and the New York Federal), are subject to effective veto by the Washington officials of the system. We merely have to consider the circumstances under which Jerry Jordan was proposed for the job of president of the Federal Reserve

Bank of Atlanta in 1980, only to have his candidature quashed by the disapproval of "Washington." Jerry Jordan is a prominent young monetarist economist with a very close connection to the powerful vein of criticism of the Federal Reserve emanating from the Shadow Open Market Committee, of which he was still a member when appointed to the Council of Economic Advisers by President Reagan in 1981.

It is, of course, open to the president of the United States to make changes in the Federal Reserve Board. The seven members of the Federal Reserve Board are nominated by the president and confirmed by the Senate. A full term is fourteen years. One term begins every two years on February 1 of even-numbered years. The chairman and vice chairman of the board are named by the president from among the members of the board and are confirmed by the Senate. They serve a term of four years.

Thus, the president of the United States does have considerable *potential* leverage. But the process of change can be very slow. Of the Carter appointees on the board, Volcker does not *have* to leave until 1992, Rice does not have to leave until 1990, Teeters does not have to leave until 1984, and Gramley does not have to leave until 1994.

As it is, the Federal Reserve Board is dominated by Democratic appointees in terms of political affiliation and by Fed officials in terms of effective power over policy and practice. It is hardly an encouraging picture for those who state that the whole Federal Reserve System and its officials need a powerful shock of change. It is not surprising that there is a pervasive fear in the money markets that this group of officials will at some point suddenly reverse any policy of moderation in money growth and revert to the wild policies of monetary expansion which distinguished the Carter years.

How Powerful Is the Influence of the President on Fed Policy?

Undoubtedly the president can have his way with the Federal Reserve, in the sense that he can lay down general guidelines for monetary policy which it will not openly ignore. But that is not the end of the matter. If we believed that were indeed the end of it, then we should not need to concern ourselves about the policies and practices of the Federal Reserve, except as a matter of recording the manner in which it carries out the president's wishes.

The truth is that the Federal Reserve has developed a body of policies and practices, of traditions and ingrained ways of thinking about money, that profoundly affect the manner in which monetary policy is carried out. These policies and practices exist *no matter who the president is.* They affect the Fed's actions in the marketplace very profoundly. A case in point is the practice of interest rate targeting, which goes right back to the traditions of thought of the Fed in the 1920's and those about central banking practice initiated during the nineteenth century in England.

If the Fed were merely the president's handmaiden, why concern ourselves with it?

The truth is that the Federal Reserve is a tremendously influential and powerful institution, the thoughts and recommendations of which pervade the whole area of economic policy thinking. It is not a mere operational tool of presidential policy. It is part of the policy process—part of the problem of inflation. Some would say that it *is* the problem.

No one suggests the president is without influence over the Fed. Robert Weintraub, staff economist with the Joint Economic Committee of Congress, said, in discussing this issue in 1978:

> The Federal Reserve shifted course in the fundamental sense, easing or tightening significantly, in 1953, 1961, 1969, 1971, 1974 and 1977. Except for 1971, these were years when the presidency also changed hands; and except for the changeover from President Kennedy to President Johnson, these were the only years when the presidency changed hands. Considering further that the thrust of monetary policy, which began to ease in 1961, eased significantly during Johnson's presidency from its first year (1964), it may be reasonably urged that the dominant guiding force behind monetary policy is the President. Congress plays only a "watchdog" role.

Yet the Federal Reserve's policies and practices profoundly affect the manner in which general presidential monetary policy aims are translated into action.

The Fed

An Example: The Fed Itself Was the Problem in 1982

President Reagan knew when he came to power that he wanted a *less expansionary* monetary policy than that of President Carter or President Nixon or President Johnson. His views were clearly stated by Beryl Sprinkel in testimony to the Monetary and Fiscal Subcommittee of the Joint Economic Committee of Congress on April 8, 1981, when Sprinkel called for "a steady and predictable decline" in the rate of monetary growth. He said this would have a prompt effect on inflationary expectations and a minimum disruptive effect on economic activity. Short-term variation in money growth has a strong effect on growth and spending in the economy, he said. This effect has been translated into temporary shocks to production. He also stated that this volatility in money growth has induced sharp gyrations in interest rates. But the short doses of monetary restraint we have experienced have had no effect on either the expected or the actual rate of inflation. "We hope," he said, "that current monetary control procedures will prevent such oscillations in the future."

Clearly the president was looking to the Fed to provide a steady and certain decline in the rate of money growth. There was to be a decline in the growth rate of money, but it was to be a steady decline. What is more, the rate of growth of the adjusted monetary base was to be reduced "smoothly and persistently by about one half between 1980 and 1984, with little further downward movement by 1986."

Those were the president's orders. How did things work out?

1. *There Was No Stability in Monetary Growth.*

Between June 1980 and December 1980, money supply (M1-B) had risen at an annual rate on the order of 14 percent. Following this buildup to the 1980 federal election, the Fed sharply reduced the rate of growth of money so that between the end of November and the end of January 1981 there was a *decline* in the stock of money. Beginning in early February 1981 and extending to the end of April, the money supply (M1-B) rose at an annual rate of 15 percent. Between the end of April and the end of October, money supply (M1-B) did not grow at all. Finally, from the end of October to the middle of January 1982 the money supply (M1, being the same as M1-B with its name changed) rose at an annual rate of over 20

130

percent. It is not overstating the matter to say that this is an appalling record of instability in money growth. It was completely counter to the expressed demands of the president, as outlined by Sprinkel in April 1981.

There were *five* distinct phases of money growth between the middle of 1980 and the middle of January 1982. To summarize they were:

Period	Annual Growth Rate of Money (M1-B)
June 1980–December 1980	+14%
December 1980–February 1981	Decline
February 1981–April 1981	+15%
April 1981–October 1981	Zero
October 1981–Mid-January 1982	+21%

2. *The Federal Reserve Was Chasing the Federal Funds Rate.*

Corresponding to these phases of monetary growth were phases of increase and decline in the federal funds rate. Remember, the Fed had stated in October 1979 it intended to allow bigger movements in the federal funds rate in order to allow itself to concentrate more on controlling the monetary aggregates (the money supply).

From June 1980 to December 1980 the federal funds rate rose from 9 to 20 percent. From December to March 1981 the rate dropped from 20 to 15 percent. From March to May 1981 it rose from 15 to 19 percent.

From March 1981 to November 1981 the funds rate fell from 19 to 13 percent. From November 1981 to mid-January 1982 it remained stable around 12½ percent.

We are familiar with this general story. I outlined part of the recent history in the first chapter, where I showed how interest rates and money supply growth tend to go in the *same direction*.

This is how I think things worked themselves out in 1980 and 1981, during the period from June 1980 to mid-January 1982. Beginning in June 1980, the Fed was very concerned about the precipitous drop in real gross national product in the second quarter, so measures were taken to stimulate money growth. Money started to grow rapidly in July, and in response to the inflationary expectations this growth immediately generated in the minds of the movers and shakers in the money markets, interest rates, including the federal funds rate, started to rise. The Fed, looking at the rise in the funds rate, said to itself: money is tight; therefore, we must give more reserves. This process went on for six months, with the Fed chasing its tail. The more reserves it put out, the more money grew, the greater was the increase in the funds rate. The process was halted by the merciful intervention of the federal election, which removed the pressure from the Fed to "keep interest rates down."

After a brief cessation in money growth—during the month of December 1980—the Fed returned to the task of trying to get interest rates down by promoting massive money growth. Remember that between June and December 1980, the rate on 90-day Treasury bills had boomed from just under 7 percent to nearly 16 percent. So in January 1981 rapid money growth resumed as the Fed tried to get interest rates down. The annual rate of growth of M1-B was 10.9 percent in January 1981, 5.9 percent in February, 13.9 percent in March, and a fantastic 24.7 percent in April.

This madness had to stop. It was brought to an end by the intervention of the Treasury and of President Reagan, who called Volcker into his office in April 1981 to ask him whether he intended to control the growth of money.

From April to October the Fed ensured that there was no growth in money at all. The result was a sharp decline in the funds rate. In October it became apparent that the economy had been gravely harmed by the extreme money squeeze of the previous six months. It was also subsequently learned that at its October 1981 meeting the Federal Open Market Committee had assumed—wrongly—that the fourth-quarter decline in real gross national product would be very modest. This was certainly the "consensus" forecast at the time, but it was not the forecast of those, including the U.S. Treasury Office of Monetary Affairs, which believed that the money freeze that began in April had been seriously overdone. Beginning in October, therefore, the Fed started to take steps to hold down the federal funds rate.

The process was extremely successful. Indeed, between the end of November 1981 and the third week of January 1982, this rate was locked in a vise.

Over that period of nine weeks, the funds rate hardly moved from the average of 12½ percent. It was as if in one bound the Fed had reverted right back to its practice of before October 1979 of putting an extremely tight straitjacket on the federal funds rate.

"Stepping Back into the Past"
Federal Funds Rate in
a Straitjacket (1981–82)

Week Ending	Federal Funds Rate Average
November 25	12.42%
December 2	12.48
9	12.04
16	12.26
23	12.43
30	12.54
January 6	12.98
13	12.42
20	12.97

In the four weeks ended December 23, the average weekly figure for the funds rate was 12.3 percent; in the next four weeks it was 12.73 percent; and in the whole nine weeks it was 12.5 percent.

The tight control over the funds rate necessitated the Federal Reserve's putting out more and more cash in order to hold the rate down. This stimulated a rapid growth in money supply, which culminated in a mammoth rise of over $10 billion in M1 in the week ended January 6. At his press conference on Wednesday, January 20, 1982, the president openly rebuked the Fed, stating that the rapid growth of money was giving the "wrong signals" to the money markets. He also refrained from giving his public support to the chairman of the Fed, Paul Volcker. On the following Monday, January 25, the fed funds rate suddenly shot up to a range of 14½ to 15 percent, and yet another episode in the continuing saga of the Federal Reserve's attempts to use the federal funds rate both as an indicator of money conditions and as a target for policy came to a close.

3. *Presidential Intervention, Yes—But the Fed Cannot Deliver the Results.*

In the brief period covered by the above story, a little more than eighteen months, from June 1980 to mid-January 1982, the following major changes occurred:

a. The president intervened three times. President Carter intervened to get the Fed to give him lower interest rates and more prosperous conditions in time for the 1980 election. Prosperity improved a little, but interest rates rocketed and the prevailing pattern of stagflation was not seriously interrupted. On the second occasion, President Reagan intervened in April 1981 to demand lower and more stable monetary growth. He got a money freeze and a severe recession, beginning in the middle of 1981. On the third occasion, the president intervened in public, to demand a cessation of a gargantuan rise in money supply.

b. The Federal Reserve was clearly still giving a very high priority to stability of the federal funds rate over the whole period and in the last nine weeks of the period reverted completely to type by putting a vise on the funds rate.

c. Monetary growth was extremely unstable over the whole period. Interest rates fluctuated violently.

Conclusion? You may ask the Federal Reserve for certain policy outcomes, but it is very unlikely you will get them. *The president proposes, the Fed disposes.*

6 *The Nixon-Ford-Burns Disaster*

Much of the fundamental work in debasing the money of America was accomplished during the time of Presidents Nixon and Ford. Until Nixon-Ford, there had been relative price stability and relatively effective control over money growth. Of course, President Johnson's New Economics, with its emphasis on maximizing the growth of output, stimulated by expansionary fiscal policies and accommodative monetary policies, contained the seeds of the disaster that was to come. But the disaster did not make its appearance under President Johnson, and it is unfair to state that the disaster was *inevitable* as a result of his expansionary policies. The disaster certainly was *not* inevitable. It was initiated by deliberate acts of policy carried out by two presidents and a number of key officials, including the chairman of the Federal Reserve Board, Arthur Burns.

The Explosion of Prices and Money

Let me first briefly fill in the statistical framework, so that you can readily see and understand the extent of the cataclysm that occurred under Nixon-Ford-Burns. Between 1948 and 1968, a period of twenty years, the consumer price index in America rose from 72 to 104—an increase of 44 percent, or less than 2 percent a year. Between 1968 and 1977, the Nixon-Ford-Burns years, the consumer price index rose from 104 to 182, an increase of 75 percent in nine years, or about 7½ percent a year. And between 1977 and 1981— the Carter years in which the process reached its climax—the consumer price index rose from 182 to 270, an increase of 48 percent in four years, or about 11 percent a year.

While the Carter years from 1977 to 1981 showed a worse price inflation than occurred under Nixon-Ford-Burns, *the break with the past* under Carter was nothing like that which occurred under Nixon-Ford-Burns. I have no sympathy for President Carter and his economic team, as is clear, but I have to say that in many respects, Carter had already been set up for failure by the extraordinarily violent events that took place under Nixon-Ford-Burns. The essence of what occurred under Nixon-Ford-Burns was a cynical sacrifice of monetary stability in the United States—and hence in the world— under the pressure of achieving certain political goals. The principal and overriding political goal was, of course, the reelection of President Nixon in 1972.

During the Nixon-Ford-Burns years there was a massive expansion in the supply of money. In the twenty years preceding 1968 the stock of money (M1 or M1-B) rose from $112 billion to $191 billion, an increase of 71 percent or less than 3 percent a year. Between 1968 and 1977, the stock of money rose to $325 billion, an increase of 70 percent or more than 7 percent a year. Between 1977 and 1981, the stock of money rose to $429 billion, an increase of 32 percent or about 7½ percent a year.

The violent shock administered in the Nixon-Ford-Burns years stands out very clearly. Under Carter, the growth of money was not, on average, significantly different from the average growth of money

Growth of Money and Prices Under Nixon-Ford-Burns
Percent Per Year

	Money (M1-B)	*Consumer Price Index*
1968	+7.1%	+4.2%
1969	+5.9	+5.4
1970	+3.8	+5.9
1971	+7.4	+4.3
1972	+7.2	+3.3
1973	+7.3	+6.2
1974	+5.0	+11.0
1975	+4.7	+9.1
1976	+5.7	+5.8
1977	+7.7	+6.4

under Nixon-Ford-Burns. Carter did nothing to repair the damage done under Nixon-Ford—he stood there impotently watching inflation rage on. There are several distinct phases in this trend:

Johnson's Election: Money supply growth was boosted up sharply in 1968, coinciding with the effort to elect Hubert Humphrey president. That left a legacy of monetary expansion which Nixon inherited.

Nixon-McChesney Martin Money Squeeze 1969: The Nixon administration had come into office with promises to combat inflation and balance the federal budget. Under William McChesney Martin, the Federal Reserve kept money under very tight control in 1969, in an attempt to clean up the mess caused by the big money expansion of 1968. In the closing months of 1969, money growth was held to zero. The year 1970 emerged as one of recession.

Slow growth in money in 1970—down to 3.8 percent from 5.9 percent in 1969 and 7.1 percent in 1968—intensified the recession. Burns was appointed chairman of the Federal Reserve on February 1, 1970, and he initiated the expansion of money policy at the meeting of the Federal Open Market Committee on February 10. Even before that, Nixon had been in a panic about the recession and the slow growth of money. Burns had already stated in his Senate confirmation hearings in December 1969 that he was in favor of relaxing money "under normal conditions." At a May 1970 convention of the American Bankers Association Burns had stated that the administration's exclusive reliance on monetary and fiscal policy to combat inflation could cause a "very serious business recession." He had, of course, already begun to expand the money supply in February 1970, and that expansion was to carry on for three years.

While the growth of the money supply dropped sharply between 1968 and 1970, prices did not respond so quickly because of the normal two-year lag between money and prices. Indeed, the annual rate of increase of prices continued to grow during 1969 and 1970, from 4.2 percent through 5.4 percent to 5.9 percent. Thus, the Nixon team in early 1970 could see recession spreading (reflecting the McChesney Martin tight money policy of 1969) but inflation *growing.* The acceleration of inflation in 1970 was the result of the Johnson money boom of 1968 to elect Hubert Humphrey.

The March 1982 report of the Joint Economic Committee describes what happened:

> During 1968, monetary policy remained expansive, putting the entire burden of anti-inflationary restraint on fiscal policy. As stated by President Johnson: "The cost of monetary restraint is high and unfair, imposed on a single industry—homebuilding." To carry out its assignment, the Federal Reserve accelerated money growth. It acted under the traditional Keynesian assumption that the creation of new money will decrease interest rates. Measured year over year, M1 money growth was increased from 3.9 percent in 1967 to 7.0 percent in 1968. In the second half of 1968, M1 growth averaged over 8 percent per year. The result of the combination of the tight fiscal policies and loose monetary policy of that time was very different from what had been planned. Interest rates were higher by the end of 1968 than they were in June 1968. In 1969 the incoming Nixon Administration temporarily departed from the game plan in order to fight inflation. Monetary restraint—true monetary restraint, the slowing of monetary growth—was applied. The tax surcharges imposed by President Johnson in June 1968, and which were scheduled to expire in June 1969, were extended. The growth in Federal spending was slowed. Incomes policy (wage and price guidelines) was forsworn. In time, inflation fell. Measured from four quarters earlier, inflation topped out in the first quarter of 1970. However, before it did, the deceleration of money growth, together with the depressing effects of the surtaxes and the still accelerating inflation, which was raising producer costs and narrowing profit margins, had brought about a recession. That recession began late in 1969.

For Nixon this was the worst of both worlds. He was getting a recession and worse inflation at the same time. It was not hard for Nixon's critics then to allege that his policy of monetary and fiscal restraint in 1969, his first year in office, was a failure.

Nixon was, of course, particularly sensitive to the effect of economic trends on political events. Back in 1960 when he was vice-president, Burns, who had been chairman of the Council of Economic Advisers from 1953 to 1956 under President Eisenhower, had told Nixon that unless there was an alleviation of tight money, Nixon would lose the 1960 election to John F. Kennedy. Nixon blamed his narrow defeat in that election largely on the excessively restrictive monetary policy of the time.

As Nixon recounted his experience in his book *Six Crises* (1962):

Two other developments occurred before the [1960] conventions, however, which were to have far more effect on the election outcome than all the carefully considered strategy decisions put together. Early in March, Dr. Arthur F. Burns, the former Chairman of the President's Council of Economic Advisers, and probably the nation's top authority on the economic cycle, called me in my office in the Capitol. In January [1960] virtually all the economists in the country had been bullish about the prospects for the economy throughout 1960. But when Burns came to see me in March, he expressed great concern about the way the economy was then acting. Steel, in particular, was in trouble—new orders were lagging after the strike. Production was barely over half of rated capacity. Burns' conclusion was that unless some decisive governmental action were taken, and taken soon, we were heading for another economic dip which would hit its low point in October, just before the elections. He urged strongly that everything possible be done to avert this development. He urgently recommended that two steps be taken immediately: by loosening up on credit, and where justifiable, by increasing spending for national security. The next time I saw the President, I discussed Burns' proposals with him and he in turn put the subject on the agenda for the next Cabinet meeting.

The matter was thoroughly discussed by the Cabinet, but for two reasons, Burns' recommendations that immediate action be taken along the lines he had suggested did not prevail. First, several of the Administration's economic experts who attended the meeting did not share his bearish prognosis of the economic prospects. Second, even assuming his predictions might be right, there was strong sentiment against using the spending and credit powers of the Federal Government to affect the economy, unless and until conditions indicated a major recession in prospect.

In supporting Burns' point of view, I must admit that I was more sensitive politically than some of the others around the Cabinet table. I knew from bitter experience how, in both 1954 and 1958, slumps which hit rock bottom early in October contributed to substantial Republican losses in the House and the

Senate. The power of the "pocketbook" issue was shown more clearly perhaps in 1958 than in any off-year election in history.

Unfortunately, Arthur Burns turned out to be a good prophet. The bottom of the 1960 dip came in October and the economy started to move up again in November—after it was too late to affect the election returns.

In October, usually a month of rising employment, the jobless rolls increased by 452,000. All the speeches, television broadcasts and precinct work in the world could not counteract that one hard fact.

In 1970 it was very clear that Nixon did not intend to allow an excessively tight money policy to lose him the 1972 election.

Nixon-Burns Money Boost, 1970–73

Beginning early in 1970, therefore, Nixon abandoned tight money and Burns did the deed. Money supply growth doubled its rate between 1970 and 1971, from 3.8 to 7.4 percent. In the 1970 midterm elections continuing inflation and unemployment near 6 percent helped the Democrats do extremely well. The growth of money was accelerated by Burns at the Fed during 1971 and on into 1972 and 1973.

In 1970 real gross national product had declined by 0.3 percent, following a string of solid increases in real GNP under Johnson—6.0 percent (1966), 4.4 percent (1968)—and a rise of 2.6 percent in Nixon's first year, 1969. By the end of 1970 gross national product was clearly on the increase, and in 1971 real GNP rose 3.0 percent. Yet there was no intention whatever by the Nixon-Burns alliance to moderate money growth. As the table on page 136 shows, money growth remained very high through 1971, 1972, and 1973. It was a policy of vigorous inflation, to meet a tight political deadline, the elections of 1972.

Nixon, 1971—The New Economic Policy

Before the results of the 1970 monetary boost program could be fully evaluated, Nixon and Burns conceived and implemented a complete about-face on economic policy, the so-called New Economic Policy of August 1971. Burns had played a major role—most

likely *the* major role—in bringing about the abandonment of monetary control and its replacement with a program of price and wage
controls. In December 1970, when the U.S. economy was still in
recession and inflation was high, Burns had proposed an eleven-point
anti-inflation plan that included as a key element a wage-price review
board. In August 1971 Nixon called a meeting at Camp David, at
which Burns and he hammered out the New Economic Policy of tax
reductions and expenditure increases, a wage-price freeze and wage-
price controls, and a commitment to an expansionary monetary
policy (which was of course already in place; M1-B growth had
accelerated from 2.4 percent in the twelve months ending February
1970 to 8.2 percent in the twelve months ending July 1971).

The Panicky Reversal of Mid-1973

Following the continuing expansion of the money supply in 1972
and into 1973, real gross national product increased—by 3.0 percent
in 1971, 5.7 percent in 1972, and 5.5 percent in 1973. The old
Johnson magic seemed to be working.

There was one new problem. The progress on the inflation front
was not as good as the progress on the stimulation-of-output-at-any-
cost front. In 1971 and 1972 inflation had receded markedly as a
result of the money restraint in 1969 and the early months of 1970.
The rate of growth of consumer prices was cut in half between 1970
and 1972, falling from 5.9 to 3.3 percent.

So, initially Nixon's new policies appeared to be successful. The
recession ended late in 1971 and inflation continued to slow. However, the seeds of later destabilization had been planted by the expansionary monetary policy that Burns had initiated in 1970.

In 1973 the delayed effects of Burns's huge money boosts in 1970
and 1971 started to show up in price increases. The "dream time"
phase of monetary expansion—when output increases but prices fall,
reflecting an earlier phase of monetary restraint—was over, and
Burns and Nixon were back into the nightmare phase, when inflation
was accelerating and monetary restraint imposed to control inflation
gave as its initial result a sharp fall in the growth of output.

By mid-1973, inflation was once again seen as the main economic
problem and once again money growth was slowed. Then, late in

1973 and early in 1974, OPEC raised the price of oil fourfold. Inflation and interest rates, already heading sharply upward as a result of Burns's expansionary money policies, soared still higher. However, money growth began to decline, and by the fall of 1974, buffeted by inflation and the initial effects of slowing money growth (which temporarily reduces output), the economy was in the throes of the worst recession since the 1930's.

By late 1974 the policy of monetary restraint imposed in 1973 (following the 1972 elections), combined with the effect of the recession, had brought about a plunge in interest rates. The slower money growth also caused inflation to decelerate sharply, beginning in the spring of 1975.

Economic recovery began in the second quarter of 1975. In spite of OPEC's supply shock and even though unemployment rose to a post World War II high in the spring of 1975, monetary growth was kept relatively low in 1974 and 1975. Measured year over year, it was 4.9 percent in 1974 and 4.6 percent in 1975. That policy of monetary restraint laid the groundwork for sustained economic recovery.

By 1976 the benefits of all the foregoing pain, in the form of unemployment and recession, were being felt. President Ford had managed to battle his way through the difficult period following the resignation of President Nixon in August 1974. He maintained monetary restraint until early 1976. Thanks to the moderation of monetary growth between 1973 and early 1976, inflation, as measured by the GNP deflator (the price index of the gross national product), was only 4.7 percent at the end of 1976, compared with a year previously. Interest rates drifted down and by the end of 1975 the Treasury bill rate, which had risen to nearly 9 percent at the end of 1974, was down to little more than 5 percent.

For a brief period Ford held the line on monetary growth and on inflation. Between mid-1973 and early 1976 the Federal Reserve managed to reduce the rate of growth of money very substantially. But by early 1976, as already stated, the Fed had taken measures which had the effect of abandoning monetary restraint. This was the policy of drastically narrowing the permitted range of variation of the federal funds rate, as a back-door method of booming the money supply up again. That was begun in April 1976.

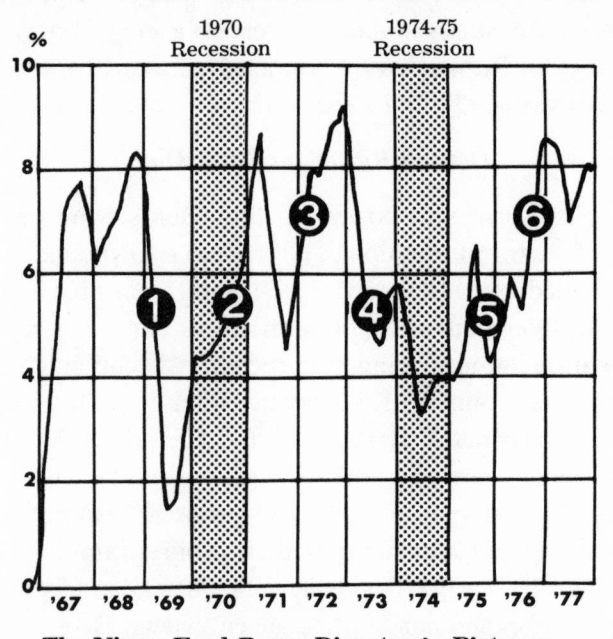

The Nixon-Ford-Burns Disaster in Pictures

The graph shows the two-month average growth rate of M1 or M1-B. The shaded areas represent the 1970 and 1974-75 recessions. The horizontal lines are the annual rate of growth of money.

(1) The McChesney Martin — Nixon money restraint, following the big Johnson money buildup in 1967 and 1968 to elect Hubert Humphrey.
(2) Nixon-Burns abandon restraint in 1970.
(3) All stops out to reelect the president, 1971-72.
(4) Inflation and dollar crises force restraint on Nixon-Burns in 1973, leading to the 1974-75 recession.
(5) President Ford tries to restrain money growth to fight inflation.
(6) Another money boom — to reelect President Ford in 1976.

By the time Nixon-Ford-Burns finished, the United States had experienced the following:

1. There was a major change in inflationary expectations. In the 1960's a 1 to 3 percent average rise in consumer prices was the rule. By the late 1970's 7 to 10 percent was the norm.

2. A major change occurred in the level of interest rates. In the 1960's a rate of 4 to 5 percent on twenty-year bonds was the rule. By the late 1970's a rate of 8–10 percent was the average.

143

3. During the period 1960–1968 the growth of output per man-hour in private business in America rose an average 3½ percent. In the Nixon-Ford-Burns years it averaged an annual growth of 1.7 percent. Between 1977 and 1980 inclusive, it averaged 0.3 percent.

Getting Rid of the Good Guys

When Nixon came to power in 1969, Burns, who became the architect of the transformation of Nixon into a Keynesian, was origi-nally appointed counsellor to the president, responsible for advising the president on domestic policy matters. Three committed free market, anti-inflationary, and even monetarist economists were ap-pointed to the Council of Economic Advisers. They were Paul McCracken (chairman), Herb Stein, and Hendrik S. Houthakker.

McCracken advocated a policy of "gradualism" in economic pol-icy, eschewing extremes of monetary and fiscal restraint or expan-sion. He favored a gradual implementation of restraint in money and in the budget. The early Nixon policy of monetary and fiscal restraint was the general expression of McCracken's views. He was fifty-three when he took over at the Council of Economic Advisers and ad-vocated budget cuts in spending (implemented by Nixon in July 1969, when he ordered a $3.5 billion cut in federal expenditures), monetary restraint (also implemented in the year to the March quar-ter 1970), the achievement of a budget surplus (also achieved in 1969), and the abandonment of wage-price controls. During 1970 and 1971, however, it became more and more apparent that McCracken's formula would not do for Nixon.

Burns had begun to balloon the money supply in early 1970; in January 1971 Nixon introduced an "expansionary" budget, and in August 1971 the New Economic Policy completed the defeat of McCracken's ideas.

Long before that, however, Nixon had moved to downgrade McCracken's influence on economic policy. In December 1970 Nixon appointed John Connally to succeed David Kennedy as secre-tary of the Treasury. Nixon was trying to position himself to get out of the trouble the bad results in the December 1970 midterm elec-tions presaged. Connally took over from McCracken the role of economic spokesman for the administration. Under increasing pressure from Nixon, McCracken started a modest program of "jawbon-ing," the practice of trying to talk down price increases. This was in contrast with all of McCracken's public statements about the futility of wage-price guideposts or controls. But by the end of 1971 it was all over. McCracken resigned on November 24, 1971, conceding that his policy of gradualism had failed to bring inflation under control. There is no doubt that McCracken is highly respected as one man who was not prepared to sit still for the disastrous turn of events set in train by Nixon-Ford-Burns.

That August 1971 program included, in addition to a ninety-day wage-price freeze, tax cuts and the formal acceptance of an expan-sionary monetary policy, the first in a series of devaluations of the dollar under Nixon-Ford-Burns. In August 1971 the end of the convertibility of the dollar into gold was announced, along with a surtax on imports. That devaluation of the dollar by 8 percent and the imposition of a 10 percent surcharge on imports were other steps along the path toward the elimination of market forces in the Ameri-can economy. It was another sign of the underlying failure of an anti-inflationary policy. The New Economic Policy was decided on at Camp David, Maryland, on August 13–15, 1971. Present were Connally, Burns, Nixon, Office of Management and Budget Director George Shultz, McCracken, and Paul Volcker, who was then under secretary of the Treasury for monetary affairs. Connally argued forcefully for the closing of the "gold window" (the ending of gold convertibility of the dollar) and won.

Also present at the August 1971 Camp David meeting was Herb Stein, a member of the Council of Economic Advisers who had also advocated the tough policies against inflation sponsored by McCracken. He was strongly opposed to wage-price controls. When McCracken quit in November 1971, Stein took over as chairman of the Council of Economic Advisers. Stein stayed on until July 1974, quitting just before the accession of President Ford. But long before that, his influence and that of monetarist and free market economists generally had long been eclipsed in the Nixon administration by the inflationists typified by Arthur Burns.

The abandonment of monetary control in the United States initi-ated by Nixon-Burns in February 1970 led to a dollar crisis culminating in the devaluation of August 1971. The persistent increase in inflation soon led to another dollar crisis, that of February 1973, when another speculative surge against the dollar culminated in a further 10 percent devaluation. In early March 1973 Shultz, as secretary of the Treasury, met in Paris with other monetary officials, and, after foreign exchange trading had been suspended for two chaotic weeks, agreed to the abolition of fixed exchange rates. Thus did the Federal Reserve Board of the United States, under Arthur Burns, preside over the collapse of the external value of the dollar as well as over the collapse of its domestic value. Shultz quit the Treasury in March 1974, as the Watergate scandal moved toward its denouement.

Volcker Was in the Key Treasury Job During This Debacle

Another very significant player was involved in the disastrous turn of events from 1969 to 1974—Paul Volcker, who had been appointed under secretary of the Treasury for monetary affairs in 1969.

A Treasury official in Washington in 1981 told me: "Until he became chairman of the Fed, Volcker had been associated with every major financial and economic policy disaster in the last decade." He was certainly up to his ears in the very core of monetary policy—domestic and international—during the crucial period up to the departure of Nixon.

Volcker was part of the tiny group of men who decided on the abandonment of free market policies in the historic New Economic Policy switch in August 1971. He was at Camp David for those talks. He was also deeply involved in the whole process of devaluation of the dollar, abandonment of any link between the dollar and gold, and the abandonment of fixed exchange rates, which had been the foundation of the Bretton Woods system of international exchanges since the Second World War. His official Federal Reserve biographical notes state: "Mr. Volcker was from 1969 through 1974 the principal United States negotiator in the development and installation of a new international monetary system, departing from the fixed exchange rate system installed following World War II."

The official biography does not note, however, that this "new international monetary system" was the result of the collapse of worldwide confidence in the U.S. dollar, following the growth of inflation in America under Nixon-Burns. After Nixon had been forced out Volcker went into semiretirement for a while, spending the academic year 1974–75 at Princeton University as a senior fellow at the Woodrow Wilson School of Public and International Affairs. After the dust had settled, he came back into the public eye and took the job of president of the New York Federal Reserve Bank until he was appointed chairman of the Federal Reserve Board in August 1979.

Burns—The Transformation of Principle by the Experience of Power

At the August 13–15, 1971, meeting at Camp David, where the Nixon-Burns New Economic Policy was planned and decided on, the following were present: Nixon (left the White House in August 1974, three years later); John Connally (left the administration May 1972); George Shultz (left the administration March 1974); Volcker (left the Treasury mid-1974); McCracken (quit November 1971); and Stein (quit July 1974). Burns stayed on in Washington at the head of the Federal Reserve Board until February 1978, three and a half years after the disappearance of all the main players in the U-turn policy switch of August 1971.

Even at the last there was really no need for Carter to get rid of Burns. The chairman was still willing and able, as the actions of the Fed in 1977 showed, to accommodate the president with an excessive growth of money. That this would be the tragic end to the career of Arthur Burns as a central banker was not apparent in his writings —always voluminous—or in his actions *before* he went to the Fed. Even in Nixon's first year, when monetary and fiscal restraint were the order of the day and when Burns was the exalted counsellor to the president, there was little sign of the decline into the wild expansion of money and the debasement of the dollar which were to be the mark of Burns from 1970 through 1978.

Arthur Burns dominated the landscape of central banking in America for almost the whole decade of the 1970's. He was the supreme figure in monetary policy. There can be no understanding of the extent of the failure in monetary policy in America without an understanding of how this remarkable man came to acquiesce in the monetary debacle that occurred during the years when he had the power over monetary policy. Burns's failure has produced a sense of bitterness throughout the ranks of those concerned with money in America. Most particularly, he is criticized for his skill in *seeming* to be responsible, in *seeming* to be a tough, unrelenting central banker, while in actuality he was, more than any other official, responsible for the massive inflation which has occurred.

Burns the Anti-Keynesian in Earlier Times

Burns emerged as a strong and informed critic of Keynesian thought after the Second World War. In 1930 at age twenty-six he became a research associate at the National Bureau of Economic Research, a private institute for the study of business cycles. In 1941 he returned to his old school, Columbia (where he had taken his doctorate in 1934), as a visiting professor, and he became a full professor in 1944. The following year he became director of the NBER.

At a time when Keynesian ideas were almost completely dominant in the economics profession, Burns made severe criticisms of them. In the thirty-second annual report of the NBER in May 1952, Burns said of Keynes's *General Theory* that it was a "highly original work that met the needs of the despondent Thirties for a theory that was at once simple and reassuring, clothed with the symbols of science and yet equipped with a handle for economic reform." He went on to criticize the notion that there is a stable relationship between consumption spending and income, or between savings and income. "If it was approximately true," he said, "that consumer spending is linked passively to income, economics was at last on the threshold of becoming an engineering science. In the years immediately follow-ing the publication of Keynes's 'General Theory,' it came to be widely believed that once the desirable level of income was specified, the economist would be able to estimate, with tolerable reliability, what amount of investment—or of some practical equivalent—would bring that income into being."

He went on to show that this so-called stable relationship did not exist. In the aftermath of World War II a massive miscalculation by economists foresaw a postwar recession instead of the postwar boom in consumer spending. He referred to a more recent example, the 1950 economic report of the president, which stated: "Consumer spending is the most uncertain factor determining the general inflationary outlook for 1952."

Another major strand of post-Keynesian thinking was the so-called secular stagnation theory, which implied that modern capitalist economies were chronically incapable of reaching full employment of resources. Said Burns:

> The doctrine of secular stagnation, which stirred economic circles only a short time ago, owed some of its popularity to inadequate appreciation of the historical fact that the spending of the average family at a given level of family income has shown a progressive tendency to increase across the decades. One of the main explicit pillars of stagnationist theory was of course the absolute decline in the year-by-year increments of our population. But this decline ceased just about the time when the theory was first articulated.

Burns was way out of line with the dominant Keynesian thought of the times.

A Favorite of Eisenhower

In 1953 Burns was recruited, at the age of forty-nine, to the position of chairman of the Council of Economic Advisers under Eisenhower. Sherman Adams, Eisenhower's chief of staff, said of Burns:

> As devoutly as he believed in a free economy, Eisenhower as President watched and studied the trends in the nation's business constantly, always ready to modify his "hands off" policy whenever he felt that the public good demanded it. He met regularly with his White House staff economist, Gabriel Hauge, and Arthur Burns, Chairman of the Council of Economic Advisers, and listened to them about the stock and commodity markets, the significance of business and trade statistics, credit figures, the trend in farm prices and merchants inventories.
>
> To me, Arthur turned out to be a pleasant surprise. He and Eisenhower got along fine. They shared the same outlook and philosophy. Far from being the abstract and impractical profes-

149

sor, Burns has his feet planted solidly on the ground and had no difficulty in more than holding his own in arguments at the Cabinet table. The President was particularly impressed by the importance that Burns placed on the time factor in his analyses of business conditions. Going back, as he often did, to his Army experiences, Eisenhower remarked that a commanding officer could recover lost men and weapons or a strategic position on high ground, but he could never recover time.

One morning, after Burns finished a detailed outline of the contributions the various government departments could make to strengthening the economy, Eisenhower said to him admiringly: "Arthur, my boy, you would have made a fine chief of staff overseas during the war."

Here was Burns entirely at home with a president whose policies were those of caution, restraint, fear of inflation, and concern for the preservation of the free and open market economy.

In 1954, while chairman of the Council of Economic Advisers, he laid down some of the rules which in his view should determine government action in economic policy.

> The government must conduct its affairs so as to inspire favorable expectations concerning the future, on the part of the people generally. This means the government must avoid extravagance and make-work schemes; it must use monetary policy in a flexible manner and assign it a very high priority in the arsenal of counter-cyclical weapons; it must give priority to tax reductions over expanded expenditures when an unbalanced budget becomes difficult to avoid.

A Naive Belief in the Purity of Politicians' Motives

After leaving the Council of Economic Advisers in 1956, at the age of fifty-three, Burns wrote the following comment in the *Columbia University Forum* about "life at the top" of government in America:

> When I was invited by President Eisenhower to serve as the Chairman of his Council of Economic Advisers, I was in the midst of some research to which I was devoted. But that was not my only reason for thinking twice before accepting the opportunity. Another was a feeling of uncertainty whether a professional economist could function well in a political envi-

ronment. In performing his duties under the Employment Act, a member of the Council will, to be sure, work with technical staff and numerous experts both within and outside the government. But the great bulk of his time is of necessity taken up by conferences or preparing for conferences, with the President, with members of Cabinet or their principal deputies, with heads of independent agencies, with the White House staff and with members of Congress.

Now these men are generally known as politicians. The term is a good one, to the extent that it indicates they are all concerned with issues of public policy. The term politician, however, sometimes suggests an absorbing pursuit of partisan interests, or of personal power and gain, by cynical men with uncultivated minds.

Such men exist. But I have found that they are fewer than I had supposed before I became a government official. As a group, politicians in high office are men of outstanding ability. They usually bring good minds, wide knowledge of affairs and considerable experience in handling practical problems to their special tasks. Their minds are receptive to fact and reason. They work hard at their jobs and seek to promote the general welfare, rather than the advantage of this or that group. They are not lacking in vanity or personal ambition but as a rule they seek to advance their fortunes by performing honorably and well at their appointed tasks. True, they are prone—perhaps excessively prone—to identify the interests of the nation with the interests of their party, yet they do so in the sincere belief that their political party is the best instrument for promoting the general welfare.

I have spent the last quarter of a century writing about politics and I would be very hard pressed to identify any successful politician who would qualify for Burns's lofty and idealistic description. Rather, I would characterize that statement by Burns as indicative of a lusting and longing for the company of men of power. To me, the statement is very revealing, pointing as it does to a sort of ingratiating view of politicians. Burns's years in power were years in which he turned on the whole tradition of thinking which he had developed up to 1969, by which time he was sixty-five years old. The experience of such enormous power at such a late stage in his life could have explained the manner in which, unlike all the other officials who were influential in economic policy in the 1970's, he hung on to the bitter end and only went, at the last, because he was told to go.

By 1958 Burns was becoming more and more concerned about the prospect of growing inflation. He was very much ahead of his time in this preoccupation. He was also formulating a range of justifications for the Federal Reserve's being able to contain inflation on its own. In an important address on "Monetary Policy and the Threat of Inflation," given to the American Assembly in October 1958, he said: "Although efforts to check inflation have increased in recent years, there has been a tendency on the part of the government to leave the job of fighting inflation during times of economic exuberance very much to the Federal Reserve System. This, however, is a greater burden than the System is equipped to carry, or should be expected to carry."

Burns—The Leading Critic of the New Economics of Kennedy-Johnson

After the election of President Kennedy, Burns became a critic of the New Economics, which was based on the theory that the American economy was suffering from chronic and growing slack, or, as the economists of the day put it, a growing gap between actual and potential output. Burns disagreed, believing that the theory was based on a misinterpretation of the recovery in the 1958–60 business cycle, which was exceptionally short and was interrupted by special factors, including a violent shift in federal finances after the first quarter of 1959, a sharp tightening of credit conditions, and the protracted steel strike.

Instead of going along with the New Economics theory, which seemed to justify almost any measures to expand spending, Burns warned of the danger of secular inflation and made some suggestions for reform. These included the reduction of government obstacles to growth (rather than incessantly devising new government stimuli to growth), the need to amend the tax rules to take much more account of the effects of technical change and inflation on depreciation deductions, and the need to reduce the rates of taxation on personal incomes. If it proved too difficult to make such sweeping reductions in personal income tax, a broadly based excise tax should be introduced to make up some of the lost revenues. He also demanded an amendment to the Employment Act so that the government would be specifically required to promote reasonable stability of the consumer price level. These were far-sighted ideas.

When the Kennedy-Johnson tax cut of 1964 was passed, Burns applauded it. In October 1964 he said:

> I would like to express the hope that the recent tax law may prove to be the first step in a long-range continuing process of tax reduction. I can think of no policy that is better designed to stimulate the growth of our economy than a continuing policy of year-by-year reductions of tax rates. The policy that I speak of implies, of course, that the growth of federal expenditures will be curbed effectively.

Burns also emerged as a strong critic of the so-called wage-price guideposts. He wrote in the *Harvard Business Review* in March–April 1965:

> The guideposts have been a major part of the Administration's economic policy since 1962, when they were first set forth by the Council of Economic Advisers. What are these guideposts or guidelines?
>
> Once the government looks to trade unions and business firms to stave off inflation, there is a danger that it will not discharge adequately its own traditional responsibility of controlling the money supply and of maintaining an environment of competition. In the past, our own and other governments have often found it convenient to blame profiteers, corporations or trade unions for a rising price level. Only rarely have they pointed the finger of blame at their own policies—such as flooding the economy with newly created currency or bank deposits.
>
> To the extent that the Government relies on private compliance with its guidelines for prices and wages, it may be more easily tempted to push an expansive monetary and fiscal policy beyond prudent limits. We must remain mindful of the lessons of past experience—particularly the need for prudent control of the money supply and the need for maintaining and enhancing the forces of competition.

Milton Friedman Endorses Arthur Burns

By the time Burns was appointed to the job of chairman of the Federal Reserve Board he had acquired a reputation as a free market thinker, an opponent of wage-price controls, a powerful critic of the New Economics, which had dominated economic thinking since the Second World War, and a prestigious holdout against the stifling command over economic thought which had been attained by Keynesian ideas.

He was thus seen as, and had represented himself as, a counter-Keynesian, a member of a vanguard of thinkers who would challenge the Keynesian orthodoxy and turn back the tide toward a corporate state.

In the February 2, 1970, issue of *Newsweek,* a few days before Burns attended his first meeting of the Federal Open Market Committee as chairman of the Fed, Milton Friedman wrote the following ringing endorsement:

This week, Arthur F. Burns takes over as Chairman of the Board of Governors of the Federal Reserve System, replacing William McChesney Martin, who is retiring after nineteen years as chairman—the longest period anyone has held that post. The Chairman of the Board has only one vote out of seven on the board itself and only one vote out of twelve on the all-important Federal Open Market Committee. Yet this greatly understates the influence that the chairman can exert—especially when he is a man with the extraordinary intellectual qualities and personal force of the incoming chairman.

My close friend and former teacher, Arthur Burns, is not just another Chairman. *He is the right man in the right place at the right time* [my italics].

Arthur Burns is the first person ever named Chairman of the Board who has the right qualifications for that post. Prior chairmen have been able, public-spirited men with high standards of integrity and service. But none has had any training or special competence in the problems of the economy as a whole. All have come with a background of experience in individual business or financial institutions.

This distinction is crucial.

It so happens that in the monetary area—as in many other parts of economics—the whole is very different from the sum of the parts. An individual bank does not "create" money—as it sees matters. It simply borrows from some and lends to others. It is a financial intermediary operating in the market for credit.

In contrast, the banking system as a whole plays a minor role in the market for credit but is the primary creator of money.

The difference between the individual bank and the banking system is a basic source of the erroneous philosophy that has guided the Fed these many years.

Generalizing from the individual financial institution, the men who run the Fed have regarded monetary policy as concerned primarily with credit.

This preoccupation, which has been strongly reinforced by the Fed's special concern with the Federal debt, is reflected in the use of interest rates as a guide and criterion of policy. It is reflected also in the importance the Fed attaches to limiting interest rates on deposits and margins on stock purchases and to regulating the lending and investing activities of the banks.

For the economy as a whole, this is all a sideshow. The key function of the Fed, the function that it and it alone can perform, is to control the quantity of money.

Yet the Fed's concentration on credit conditions has led it to pay little attention to the effect of its actions on the quantity of money. The result has been highly erratic movements in the quantity of money that have produced economic instability and price inflation.

Arthur Burns will not make this mistake [my italics].

His training, experience and special competence are precisely in the relation between the individual enterprise and the economy as a whole—as a college professor; as one of the world's leading scholars in the analysis of the business cycle; as Chairman of the Council of Economic Advisers and most recently as Counsellor to the President.

He understands the *monetary system* and its relation to the economy at a depth and subtlety that has not been equalled by any past Chairman of the Board.

Arthur Burns is at the right place, because of the extraordinarily important influence monetary actions exert on the economy as a whole—and also because the Fed is the preeminent financial institution in the world. In the heat of debate, critics have attributed to those of us who have stressed the importance of money the view that "money is all that matters." This is an absurd position—and it is one that we have never held. But even the critics now concede that money matters and matters very much.

In particular, inflation is always and everywhere a monetary phenomenon. And inflation today is our major economic problem.

The time is ripe for a change in the Fed's basic philosophy. Even as recently as three or four years ago, the erroneous credit view was so firmly entrenched that the alternative monetary view was ridiculed. But the past few years have forced an "agonizing reappraisal." It has become painfully obvious that the use of interest rates as a guide to policy produces wide swings in monetary growth and that these swings can be a major source of monetary instability.

The shift in view is far from complete. More important, *the shift has as yet had a negligible effect on the operating procedures at the open market desk of the New York Federal Reserve Bank* [my italics].

These procedures are well adapted to smoothing short-term movements in interest rates. They are poorly adapted to controlling smoothly the quantity of money.

This is also a critical time in a more immediate, if less fundamental, sense. Burns takes office as the economy is not only slowing down, but seems on the verge of sliding into a full-fledged and fairly severe recession—thanks to an unduly restrictive monetary policy.

The Fed can no longer prevent this outcome. The damage, if damage it be, is already done. Because of the delay between monetary actions and their effects, what happens to the economy during most of 1970—insofar as it is affected by monetary policy—is already determined.

What the Fed can do is shift promptly to a less restrictive policy and thereby build now a base for a healthy recovery from the recession.

The real test will come during the next six months or so, if and when the recession becomes a clear and present reality and shows every sign of deepening further. The temptation will then be strong for the Fed to overreact as it has so often done in the past, to go from too slow a rate of monetary growth to too high a rate.

If it acts that way, it will simply set off another round of inflation.

Let us hope that this time, the Fed will have the foresight, the patience and the courage to hold to a steady and moderate course, to keep the quantity of money expanding at a rate high enough to encourage recovery from the recession but low enough to avoid renewed inflation.

If, under Burns' leadership, the Fed can meet this immediate challenge and also modernize its philosophy and operating procedures, the nation will, for the first time in its history, have a monetary framework for stable economic growth.

Such an achievement would be a worthy capstone to Arthur Burns' distinguished career.

It is some measure of the catastrophic results Burns actually achieved at the Fed that its operating procedures are still largely as they were in 1970—and 1960 and 1950 and 1940 and 1930. The nation has been through the most disastrous inflation in its peacetime history. Earnest government officials and even the president are still openly and insistently demanding that the Fed provide "steady and moderate" money growth. In the closing nine weeks of 1981 the Fed reverted totally to the practice of "narrow band interest rate targeting" (meaning effectively *no* control over money growth at all), which was the one Fed operating procedure most trenchantly criticized by Friedman in his endorsement of Burns.

The contrast between "what Burns did" and "what Milton Friedman said he would do" could not have been more complete. We now go on to try to make sense of the reasons for Burns's failure. It may be that Burns's performance in office turned out to be one of the biggest disappointments in Milton Friedman's life.

7 Burns at the Fed—A Decade of Self-Deception

Burns came to the Federal Reserve as its chairman in January 1970, having been appointed to the position by Nixon in October 1969. Speaking at Burns's inauguration, Nixon said: "Dr. Burns, please give us more money!"

Burns did not take long to answer the plea, and the meeting of the Federal Open Market Committee on February 10, 1970, concluded that "in the light of the latest economic developments and current business outlook, it is appropriate to move toward somewhat less restraint with a view to encouraging moderate growth in money and bank credit over the months ahead. " Three of the FOMC members, Hayes, Brimmer, and Coldwell, dissented from the associated policy directive, "because they felt that any overt move toward less firm money markets was premature. They were impressed by the strength of inflationary expectations, concerned about the prospects for adequate fiscal strength. They agreed that some growth in the monetary and credit aggregates was called for, but in their view this objective could have been adequately met by a directive similar to the one the Committee had adopted at its January meeting." That directive called for "maintaining firm conditions in the money market while taking account of the Committee's desire to see a modest growth in money and credit."

As the years went by, Burns increasingly laid the blame for the excessive growth of money during the 1970's on the Kennedy-Johnson policies of rapid expansion of government spending, on budget deficits, and on the "philosophical currents of the times." It is important to remember this, as we follow his path during the decade, because it was Burns's actions, views, and domination of the monetary policy arena that led to the extraordinary explosion of money. This money explosion was the cause of the inflation.

Burns was also, as we have already seen, a leading figure in the adoption of policies of wage-price controls and devaluation of the dollar in international payments. Later he would attempt to argue that these revolutionary changes in his own actions, when compared with his lifetime publicly expressed convictions, were required by the overwhelming force of the political and philosophical currents of the times.

There are those who would blame not Burns but rather "the system" for the disasters that occurred. Thus, Milton Friedman, in his February 1982 article in the *Journal of Money, Credit and Banking,* wrote:

> I do not believe an answer for the extraordinary record of bureaucratic inertia and mistakes that have not been corrected [at the Fed] can be found in terms of the particular personalities who have been in charge, because the resistance to learning from experience has persisted [at the Fed] for more than six decades.
>
> Why the enormous resistance of the Fed to moving to monetary aggregates [as the means of monetary control]? Fundamentally, I believe, because monetary aggregates permit far more effective monitoring of performance and accountability for achieving targets than money market conditions. Who of us wants to be held responsible for our mistakes? It's not very nice to have a bottom line. If we don't have a bottom line, why should we introduce one?
>
> The annual or more frequent statements by chairmen of the Federal Reserve to congressional committees have a common script. If things have gone well in the economy, the Fed takes full credit and the chairman explains that it was all due to the wise policies followed by the Fed. If things have gone badly in the economy, the chairman explains that the reason was the limited powers of the Fed to offset external disturbances that were beyond the Fed's control.
>
> He then assures the committee that the Fed will now be able to correct any of its past deviations from desirable policy and that, next year, all will be well—subject of course to unpredictable events. The statements of general principles and desirable policies are always excellent—both wise and theoretically

sound. The explanation of defects in past performance is always ad hoc and exculpates the Fed.

Robert Weintraub, senior economist with the Joint Economic Committee of Congress and a long-standing participant in the struggle for improved monetary policy, told me in an interview in October 1981:

As soon as Burns came to power, the monetary base growth rate rose sharply and it stayed there for the whole of his term. That is absolutely right. They started pumping up the money supply as soon as Burns became chairman. They kept on pumping it up for three years until they finally had to change in 1973. Burns went with the winds of the day. There isn't any doubt whatever about that.

It seems difficult to reconcile so many of Burns's statements before he came to power with what happened when he gained power. I have often said Burns was long on talk and short on action. I mean, it's clear Burns gave Carter everything he wanted. But Carter could not reconcile keeping Burns on, with the political implications of doing so. It would have indicated to the liberal wing of the Democratic party that Carter was a Hooverite, back in 1978, and there was no need for him to do that.

I think Burns's big error was in thinking that if he gave Carter what he wanted and in the meantime had a tough-sounding rhetoric for the financial markets, he'd be allowed to stay.

In 1970, when the economy was suffering from recession and inflation was still moving ahead strongly, Burns put forward an eleven-point anti-inflation plan. Among his proposals were more vigorous use of antitrust regulations, expanded federal training programs to produce more skilled workers in high-wage sectors of the economy, a liberalized depreciation allowance for corporations, a suspension of the Davis-Bacon Act requiring union wages to be paid on federal construction projects, and compulsory arbitration of public interest labor disputes. He also voiced his support for wage-price controls. At this time the very idea of controls was rejected by the Nixon administration.

Burns Demands Wage-Price Controls

In May 1970 Burns announced his conversion to the need for wage-price controls and elaborated the foundations of his justification for the whole of his policy of neglect of monetary control while he was at the Fed. He told the American Bankers Association:

> One of the most serious economic blunders of recent years was the failure to alter the course of monetary and fiscal policies when early warnings of inflation began to flash. Late in 1964, signs of growing pressures on our nation's resources were already multiplying and these signs became stronger and more widespread in the first half of 1965. With the economy moving rapidly toward full employment, the time had come for backing away from the stimulative policies pursued in the early 1960's. But precisely the opposite course was taken—both fiscal and monetary policies became substantially more stimulative during 1965. The mistake of stabilization policy in 1965 reflected an unwillingness to face up promptly to the urgent need for restrictive actions on the fiscal and monetary front. It was soon found, however, that by eschewing an ounce of prevention, a pound of cure became necessary. Inflationary forces gathered such momentum that it took stern measures in subsequent years to eliminate excess demand.

It is hardly important to record that in comparison with the inflation he inherited, the inflation that Burns handed on to President Reagan and Paul Volcker was a good three times as great. Burns's ability to divert attention from his own actions was, however, one of his great strengths as a political survivor.

In May 1970 he was still laying the groundwork for his defense. As he told the ABA, "Another deficiency in the formulation of stabilization policies in the United States has been our tendency to rely too heavily on monetary restriction as a device to curb inflation." This was hardly a vote of confidence in William McChesney Martin, who had by one means or another managed to hold the rate of growth of money to little more than 3 percent a year for nearly twenty years up to 1969 and the rate of growth of consumer prices to 2½ percent. Burns was to give us 6 to 7 percent average inflation and 6 to 7 percent average increase in money. However, that record was not yet established. Burns in mid-1970 was still fresh in office at the Fed and was laying the groundwork for a major change in economic policy which would direct attention right away from the Federal Reserve System and drop the problem of fighting inflation in someone else's lap.

He said in his ABA speech:

There are several reasons why excessive reliance on monetary restraint is unsound. First, severely restrictive monetary policies distort the pattern of production. On the one hand, monetary restraint has relatively slight impact on consumer spending, or on the investments of large businesses. On the other hand, the homebuilding industry, state and local construction, real estate firms and other small businesses are likely to be seriously handicapped in their operations. When restrictive monetary policies are pursued vigorously over a prolonged period, these sectors may be so adversely affected that the consequences can become socially and economically intolerable and political pressures mount to ease up on the monetary brakes.

Second, the effects of monetary restraint on spending often occur with relatively long lags. Because the lags tend to be long, there are serious risks that a stabilization program emphasizing monetary restraint will have its major effect on spending at a point in time when excess demand has passed its peak.

The inflationary developments we are now experiencing do not reflect the present state of balance between aggregate demand and supply. Rather, they are the aftermath of overheating that existed earlier and which is still having a lagged effect on wage rates, on other costs and hence on prices. We are in a transitional phase of cost-push inflation. An effort to offset, through monetary and fiscal restraints, all of the upward push that rising costs are now exerting on prices would be most unwise. Such an effort would restrict aggregate demand so severely as to increase greatly the risks of a very serious business recession. If that happened, the outcries of an enraged citizenry would probably soon force the government to move rapidly and aggressively toward fiscal and monetary ease and our hopes for getting the inflation problem under control would then be shattered.

In the months ahead, we may be witnessing economic developments that will test patience—with costs and prices continuing to advance despite the slack that exists in markets for goods and productive services. It seems likely that we will hear an increasing number of suggestions that additional steps need to be taken to moderate the rise in wage rates and the advance in prices—steps that could involve the government more directly in the operations of the private economy. Other countries that have depended on specific wage-price policies—or incomes policies as they are frequently called—have achieved relatively little success and the same can also be said of our own experiment during the sixties. Nevertheless, *we should not close our minds to the possibility that an incomes policy, provided it stopped well short of direct price and wage controls, and was used merely as a supplement to overall fiscal and monetary measures, might speed us through this transitional period of cost-push inflation* [my italics].

Nixon's Commitment to Orthodox Anti-Inflation Policies (1969–71)

Burns's move to open advocacy of wage-price controls in 1970 may have laid the foundations for the survival of the Federal Reserve, in that it gave an excuse for the coming failure of monetary policy, but it was hardly in tune with the public policies demanded at the time by President Nixon and the White House.

Nixon had inherited plenty of problems from Lyndon Johnson. Johnson's expansionary fiscal policies had provided for expanded federal domestic programs as well as an increasingly expensive military campaign in Vietnam. The consumer price index rise had accelerated from an increase of 1.5 percent in 1965, 3.1 percent in 1966, and 2.8 percent in 1967 to 4.2 percent in 1968 and 5.4 percent in 1969, Nixon's first year in office. Nixon had made inflation a major issue in his presidential campaign. His own experience with price controls during World War II had made him detest them. He moved to adopt orthodox anti-inflationary policies, including a balanced budget in 1970. In his last year, 1969, McChesney Martin had moved to reverse the strongly expansionary monetary policy of 1968, initiated before the Nixon-Humphrey election.

As might have been expected, inflation continued to accelerate in 1969 and 1970, when the consumer price index rose a further 5.9 percent on top of the disturbing 5.4 percent rise of 1969. This was the result of the excessively expansionary monetary policy in 1968, the "Elect Hubert Humphrey" money boom, a 7.1 percent increase in that year, spilling over to another big 5.9 percent increase in 1969 as a whole (although in the last half of 1969 there was a virtual freeze on money growth, this did not stop the *average* of money growth in 1969 from being so high). Nixon was in the classic position of the "vicious cycle" of the inflationary process. He was getting all the bad things and none of the nice ones. He got a recession in 1970 (the immediate result of his policy of holding down money growth in 1969) and he also got more inflation (the result of the money boom in 1968). He got the worst of both worlds. But it was not until the middle of 1971 that Nixon finally resolved to make a fundamental switch in policy.

Before then, Burns's continuing public insistence that there was very little progress in defeating inflation and his advocacy of wage-price controls were getting him into trouble with the White House. White House officials such as Ronald Ziegler, then press secretary, appeared to be campaigning against Burns in early 1971. Ziegler implied that the White House was considering doubling the size of the Federal Reserve Board with Nixon's own appointees. Two days after Ziegler's remarks, Connally, who had been appointed secretary of the Treasury in February 1971, stated that "very substantial" progress has been made against inflation, thus contradicting Burns. Rumors appeared in the press that Burns was hypocritically seeking a $20,000 a year increase in his own salary.

This latter rumor was eventually traced to Charles Colson, then a White House aide, who was later one of the Watergate plumbers. In August, Nixon made a public statement to "set the record straight," calling Burns "the most responsible and statesmanlike" chairman of the Federal Reserve in history.

Burns did not let up on his advocacy for wage-price controls. On December 7, 1970, in a speech to the Pepperdine College Great Issues Series, at Los Angeles, he said:

> Many of our citizens, including some respected labor leaders, are troubled by the failure of collective bargaining settlements in the United States to respond to the anti-inflationary measures adopted to date. They have come to the conclusion, as I have,

that it would be desirable to supplement our monetary and fiscal policies with an incomes policy, in the hope of thus shortening the period between suppression of excess demand and the restoration of reasonable relations of wages, productivity and prices.

I would hope that every citizen will support the President's stern warning to business and labor to exercise restraint in pricing and wage demands.

(By that time, at the end of 1970, Burns had become so committed to the support of the Nixon administration that he apparently had forgotten his words back in March 1965 when in the *Harvard Economic Review* he had written: "Once the government looks to trade unions and business firms to stave off inflation, there is a danger that it will not discharge adequately its own traditional responsibility of controlling the money supply and maintaining an environment of competition.")

Burns was in open conflict with the Council of Economic Advisers under Paul McCracken. In its 1970 annual report the CEA had said:

The Administration's plan of policy for 1969 did not include any attempt to revive wage-price guideposts, such as those existing in 1962–66. By the fall of 1966 the policy was widely recognized to be unworkable, and it was allowed to fade away. In subsequent years, there were only episodic actions with specific companies regarding prices. The guidepost policy clearly did not work once the economy ran into strong and serious pressures of inflationary demand.

It had not worked in the 1960's, and it did not work in the 1970's. Yet Burns kept on promoting wage-price controls in 1970 and 1971. It would seem clear that at that juncture his overriding concern was the reelection of Nixon in 1972, and he knew that wage-price controls would give a *temporary* respite, a short-run bonus of price stability, which would disappear after a short time but would give a cosmetic result in time for the election. Burns was making sure that the Federal Reserve would not be blamed for the inflationary fire that had been lit in February 1970 and that would culminate in 11 percent inflation in 1974 and the maxirecession of 1974–75. The dilemma Burns had provided for himself, for the Fed, and for the president became apparent in his testimony to the Joint Economic Committee of Congress in July 1971.

Burns Presses Harder for Wage-Price Controls (July 1971)

In his testimony, Burns first explained how the Fed had contributed to excessive growth of money in 1970–71:

The shift toward monetary expansion in early 1970 [when Burns took over at the Fed and started to provide an offset to the restrictive monetary policy of late 1969] was rather promptly followed by a resurgence of bank deposits and in the flow of funds to other financial intermediaries. Late last year, there was a marked decline in the rate of expansion of the narrowly defined money supply—that is, currency plus demand deposits. In these circumstances, for a brief period a more rapid expansion in the money supply to compensate for the fourth quarter shortfall seemed appropriate. The System consequently provided bank reserves liberally over the winter months and interest rates—partly reflecting the increased supply of reserves —declined sharply further. Expansion of the narrowly defined money supply rose to a 9 percent annual rate in the first quarter of this year.

This March and April [1971] the Federal Reserve System faced a dilemma. Information available at that time suggested that high rates of monetary growth might persist under existing conditions in the money markets. Interest rates, however, were already displaying a tendency to rise, and vigorous action to restrain monetary growth might have raised them sharply further. In view of the delicate state of the economic recovery which was then just getting under way, it seemed desirable to prevent the possible adverse effects of sharply higher interest rates on expenditure plans and public psychology. The Federal Open Market Committee decided, therefore, to move very cautiously toward restraining the growth of the monetary aggregates.

With the benefit of hindsight, I now feel that stronger action was warranted this spring. For, as matters turned out, we experienced even faster monetary growth in the second quarter than had been anticipated, while interest rates also moved substantially higher. Present estimates indicate that the narrowly defined money supply rose at an 11 percent annual rate in the second quarter.

166

There is nothing surprising in what happened. The Fed was trying to hold down the rate of interest. It pushed out large amounts of reserves to the banks. This led to an increase in the money supply, which in turn encouraged inflationary expectations and a further rise in the rate of interest. What *is* of interest is that despite the statement Burns made to the Joint Economic Committee in July 1971, the Federal Reserve went on to increase the money supply by another 7.2 percent in 1972 and by yet another 7.3 percent in 1973. The money boom was arrested only following the panic of July 1973, preceded by yet another dollar crisis in February and March of that year.

At the conclusion of his July 1971 evidence, Burns made another plea for wage-price controls:

In my judgment *and in the judgment of the Federal Reserve Board as a whole* [my italics] the present inflation in the midst of substantial unemployment poses a problem that traditional monetary and fiscal remedies cannot solve as quickly as the national interest demands. This is what has led me, on various occasions, to urge additional governmental actions, involving wages and prices—actions that would serve, by moderating the inflationary trend, to free the American economy from the hesitations that are not restraining its great energy.

Burns Was an "Involved" Chairman and Laid the Ground for Attacks on the Fed

Burns was very dissimilar from his predecessor at the Fed, William McChesney Martin. Martin had adopted a relatively low public posture, generally eschewing public comments on economic policy. He was not an economist and he does not appear to have had a high regard for economic analysis, economic forecasting, or economists' advice on Fed policy. Martin worked for Truman, Eisenhower, Kennedy, and Johnson. Under his rule, the Federal Reserve maintained a low growth rate of money, on the average. The demands of the different presidents were met. Martin's position was not in doubt. The Fed was not the subject of incessant congressional criticism, as was the case in Burns's time, and has been indeed ever since.

Burns, by contrast, was an *activist* chairman. He was a voluminous

writer and speaker (to the point of being garrulous). He was fas-
cinated by an involvement in the government power apparatus.
Burns was naive, as was made apparent in his assessment of the
power hunger of most politicians (see page 150). He loved access to
the supreme presidential power. In his review of a book by Walter
Heller in the *National Banking Review* of June 1967, Burns spoke
of the position of chairman of the Council of Economic Advisers. He
gave a description of what things were like when he was chairman
from 1953 to 1956.

"The unique function of the Council of Economic Advisers,"
in Professor Heller's well-chosen words, is "to put at the President's disposal the best facts, appraisals and forecasts that economic science, statistics and surveys can produce." But, as he
explains, the activities of the Council extend beyond giving
advice to the President himself. Professor Heller discusses per-
ceptively the activities of the Council since 1961 but he again
fails to do justice to history. He conveys the impression that
prior to 1961, the Council pursued a "detached, Olympian,
take-it-or-leave-it approach to Presidential advice." This description may fit the brief period when Dr. Nourse was Chairman of the Council. Otherwise it is simply untrue. During
1953–56, for example, the Chairman of the Council had weekly
scheduled meetings with the President—a privilege that only
one other member of the government, the Secretary of Defense,
enjoyed. He had full access to the President at other times and
he used it when necessary. He represented the Council at
weekly Cabinet meetings, made frequent reports on current and
emerging policy requirements and participated actively in Cabinet debates on economic matters. He worked closely with the
Secretary of the Treasury and the Chairman of the Federal
Reserve Board. He served as Chairman of various Cabinet
committees and used the opportunity to advance the Council's
program. He and his Council colleagues spent a good part of
practically every day striving for consensus on policy issues
with representatives of various departments and agencies. The
Council thus fought tirelessly within the Executive establishment for the policies that it deemed needed and proper. The
Council did not, however, take to the stump and fight in the
public arena for the President's program. It refrained from this
essential political activity because it felt, by and large, that
professional economists should stick to their knitting.

Burns loved to be near the center of government power: he worked very hard at his job and was devoted to the president. He was extremely vulnerable to presidential flattery, particularly the flattery of being told the "inside story" or being "in the know." Burns was not unlike a million other vulnerable officials in that regard—whether in government or business. Burns was, however, chairman of the Federal Reserve for eight years. Hence, his attitudes were necessarily very important to the United States.

There is another aspect to this issue of the power wielded by Burns. We know that the U.S. economy is primarily controlled in its movements by the movement of the stock of money. This is true for production, employment, prices, and interest rates. Movements in the growth of the stock of money are the most important single factor at work. (See Chapter 1, page 36.)

Burns as chairman of the Federal Reserve was uniquely placed to control or largely influence those movements. It is clear that many of his policies were disastrous in their consequences; they promoted excessive growth of money, ever-escalating inflation, disorder in money markets, high interest rates, and a weak dollar. They contributed materially, if not uniquely, to the decline of America's economic power since 1968. Many times Burns argued strongly for the continued "independence" of the Federal Reserve. He presided over the successful moves within the Fed, from early 1975, to forestall the congressional attempt to make the Fed meet certain targets. Burns was the mastermind of the strategy that resulted in confusion and instability during that period.

Burns was the longest serving economic policy official in the 1970's. Other important officials came and went. Connally, Shultz, Volcker, McCracken, Simon, and Greenspan all lasted a couple of years, perhaps even three or four. Not one of them had the enduring term of office nor the supremely important power position held by Burns. Hence, Burns's errors, self-deception, and incessant maneuvering for self-justification were of quite crucial importance.

As the evidence of his failure at the Fed accumulated, he became more and more aggressive in demanding "independence" for the Federal Reserve against the attempts by Congress to impose rules—such as the many targets in HCR 133. Unfortunately his own record of close involvement with the president and the White House made it difficult to accept such self-righteous demands for independence at their face value.

After all, Burns had been active in President Nixon's presidential campaign in 1968; he had been a close adviser to Eisenhower; he had tried to get Eisenhower to "pump up" the money supply in 1960 to assist Nixon's chances (as Nixon states in his book *Six Crises*). While at the Fed he argued strongly and openly for a wide range of economic policies way beyond his narrow purview as its chairman. In doing so, he stood the risk of being accused of trying to take over a wide range of economic policy responsibilities. Nixon appointed him to head the Government Committee on Interest and Dividends the purpose of which was to keep bank and other interest rates and stock dividends at appropriate levels—a form of capital pricing control which carried with it overtones of major government interference in capital markets. He was up to his ears in the planning for the August 1971 New Economic Policy and had, of course, been the single most influential advocate of such a plan for over a year before it was adopted. He was responsible for pumping up the money supply before the 1972 campaign to reelect the president. He did the same in 1976 for Ford. He was an important central participant in the negotiations during 1971 to devalue the dollar and to negotiate the so-called Smithsonian Agreements in December 1971, which in effect led to the abandonment of the post-World War II Bretton Woods system of fixed exchange rates.

Burns was intimately involved in every aspect of presidential planning and politics affecting the economy. He was into everything he could reasonably get into. And he loved it. Indisputably, the Federal Reserve was dominated by him during his long term. "Independence" for the Fed really meant freedom for Arthur Burns from any significant interference with what he wanted to do.

Burns: Dominant—and Domineering

A former high official in the St. Louis Fed told me in confidence: "Burns exercised mental regimentation right down the line when he was chairman of the Fed. That is why Bill Poole [William Poole, formerly professor of economics at Brown University and now a member of the Council of Economic Advisers] and Jim Pierce [professor of economics at the University of California at Berkeley] left. Pierce in particular was right up there. They were both very senior officials. They both left in the Burns years. Burns was a source of turmoil and disorder in the Fed. They lost a president in St. Louis because of Burns. That was Daryl Francis. The day that Burns called him a son of a bitch was the day Daryl decided he just didn't need this any more. He left. Burns was a mean guy. He was mean. He's vindictive; he's revengeful."

In regard to this latter aspect of Burns's character, Sanford Rose, the well-known financial journalist now with the *American Banker* daily banking newspaper, got into a lot of trouble with Burns following the publication of an excellent article in the July 1974 issue of *Fortune* magazine. Rose wrote in that article:

> It is hard to credit the notion that the Fed simply blundered into the monetary overexpansion in each of the last several years. To my estimation, monetary policy did not seem to have strayed too far off the target in 1970 and 1971. Then along came 1972. The Fed's performance in that year baffles, indeed stupefies, monetary historians. The battle against both recession and inflation seemed to have been won. At the end of the first quarter, the economy had substantially recovered from its 1970–71 doldrums. The unemployment rate had begun to fall and real product was growing robustly. What's more, unit labor costs had stabilized. It is true that the unemployment rate did not fall much between July and October but there were strong indications that real gross national product would continue to rise at a rapid pace for some time to come. And, indeed, the unemployment rate came "unstuck" in late 1972 and continued to decline.
>
> Yet the money supply grew by 7.9 percent during calendar 1972, appreciably faster than the 6.6 percent of 1971. By supplying so much monetary stimulus for so long at such an inappropriate time, the Fed virtually guaranteed the resurgence of inflationary pressure in 1973.
>
> When they are asked what happened to policy in 1972, some Federal Reserve officials manage a nervous laugh and try to change the subject. Others say unhesitatingly (though not for attribution) that throughout the year the Fed was subjected to "unusual pressure" from the White House and Congress. It

seems that a majority of the Federal Open Market Committee recognized the need for a turn to a more restrictive policy in 1972. But Burns held out for continued stimulus, arguing that the Fed should do nothing that could snag the ongoing recovery or cause interest rates to rise any more rapidly than they were already rising. Burns appears to have had some real doubts about the durability of the recovery.

Burns' arguments were impressive, but not impressive enough to sway the FOMC. Throughout the year, the committee's economic staff steadily forecast very rapid rates of GNP growth. The committee also knew that the Administration's desire to prevent interest rates from rising rapidly was linked to the coming election.

In the circumstances, the dispute between Burns and the FOMC majority became fairly tense at times. At one point, frustrated by his inability to convince the committee of the need to hold down interest rates, Burns left a meeting in obvious anger. He returned in about an hour, announcing: "I have just talked to the White House."

The effect of this declaration on the committee must have been quite dramatic. Burns was invoking the aid of the White House in a manner rarely, if ever, employed by a Chairman of the nominally independent Federal Reserve System. It was undoubtedly a difficult moment for Burns, a man accustomed to swaying colleagues by the logic of his arguments. But the committee got the idea: the White House was determined to try to keep rates from rising.

Many of those who heard Burns' words could have interpreted them as an implied threat. That is, either the committee acquiesced or it risked the White House's maximum displeasure. And White House displeasure might easily have meant Republican backing for persistent southern Democratic efforts to limit the Federal Reserve's independence. In any case, Burns eventually succeeded in persuading the FOMC to continue providing that stimulus throughout 1972.

In a discussion with me about that article in July 1981, Sanford Rose said:

"That fact that the White House dictates to the Federal Reserve is well known. The article itself was not all that remarkable. The only remarkable thing was the effort that Arthur Burns put into getting me fired. That was quite remarkable. He made very strenuous efforts to get me fired. He had many influential figures call the Time Inc. editor in chief, Hedley Donovan. The Fed governors kept ringing up. They were mobilized by Burns, especially a man by the name of John Sheehan, who was then a governor and a very hot-tempered fellow. Then I was called upstairs, and I was told 'We've been threatened with being frozen out of Washington. No one's going to be talking to us, unless we recant.'

"I said, 'I'm not going to be doing any recanting.'

"But the pressure continued. And to the credit of Hedley they withstood the pressure very well. Then *The New York Times* picked up the article and wrote a piece about it and that got Burns really upset, because *Fortune* is nothing as compared to the *Times,* so we are told. So Burns mobilized even more support, and even Milton Friedman wrote a letter to *The New York Times,* saying this incident could not have taken place, because Arthur Burns is a man of great integrity.

"So I called Friedman and I said, 'Why did you do this? After all, you weren't there. You don't know what happened.'

"And Friedman had no response for me. He said: 'I liked your article, but there is no question that Burns would not have done this.' I said, 'How do you know? You know he loses his temper. You shouldn't have written this thing. You know, a letter from you, like this, is ridiculous because you are in effect saying that you have some private knowledge, which is what I allege—and I have witnesses.' And he said, 'Well, maybe I shouldn't have done it.'

"But Burns went to extreme lengths to put pressure on all the governors. The behavior of Andy [Andrew] Brimmer [Fed governor from March 1966 through August 1974] was particularly interesting. He was the only black governor at the time. He called me, very interestingly, before the article was printed, because I told the Federal Reserve what I was going to put into the article. I gave them the opportunity to refute it. And so I got a call from Brimmer, and he said, 'What you allege never took place.' So I said I had such and such evidence that I obviously could not identify. He went on talking and talking, and we have [*sic*] a very pleasant conversation. Then he called me the next day and told me the incident never took place. He then called me a third time and I said, 'You know, Andy, the more times you call me the more convinced I am that I am right.'

"Then he said one of the most peculiar things I have ever heard. He said, 'Are you sure this didn't take place during the coffee break?' And I said, 'I don't know when it took place. I know it took place during the meeting at some time. Maybe it did take place during the coffee break.'

"After the article was published, the Federal Reserve made a decision not to talk to me any more, which decision they have not adhered to.

"When I came to the *American Banker* to work, former Fed governor John Sheehan wrote a letter to the *American Banker,* saying that they should not employ such a disgusting person. This was six years after the [*Fortune*] article appeared. I joined the *American Banker* in 1979, but the letter was not written until 1980. It took him that long to catch up with me."

The former St. Louis Fed official whom I quoted earlier said of this incident:

"The reason Jim Pierce lost his job at the Fed was because [*sic*] he was blamed for leaking to Sanford Rose, when he was working for *Fortune,* the story that Burns left a meeting of the Board of Governors to ring up Nixon for orders. The door was slamming shut behind Jim, so he quit.

"Still, unless you have a very powerful personality at the head of the Fed, the chairman will simply be overwhelmed by the pressures of the job.

"After all, you have the Congress constantly pressuring you and from time to time calling for your impeachment. You have the President, and there is no way you are going to go against the President of the United States. You have a constituency of eastern bankers. This will overwhelm you unless you are an exceptional man.

"It did not overwhelm Arthur Burns. Arthur had a vision. His vision was that it was convenient to have Richard Nixon in the White House. Arthur saw it as a crusade—in favor of himself. This was his opportunity to play the grand master. I don't think he cared about the results. It was the game. After all, if you read his speeches and then look at the money supply figures, you would be entitled to think you were in a time warp.

"When Burns was appointed, we in the Fed didn't know much about him. We know about his reputation, but we didn't know much about the man. So we started calling people and we asked, 'Tell us about Arthur Burns.' And boy, were we misled. They told us Arthur has very, very strong opinions; he holds his opinions very, very strongly; but he is an empiricist and he is amenable to factual arguments. Don't try and snow him with philosophical arguments, we were told.

"In truth, of course, he wouldn't look at a piece of evidence to save his soul.

"Burns was a master at getting his own way. I remember a meeting of the FOMC which I attended. They had gone around the table and counted hands on some issue—money growth rate or something—and one of the FOMC members said to Burns: 'Mr. Chairman, what was the result of that vote?'

"To which Burns replied: 'We do not vote, we merely sample sentiment.'

"This allowed him to get around the legal requirement that the result of the *vote* had to be made public. A 'sampling of sentiment' does not have to be put into the public domain.

"Burns found out what the law required the Federal Reserve to do, and he then went out and redefined all the activity he didn't want anyone to find out about as not falling under the law.

"Another story sees Burns in the FOMC meeting and there has been a vote which comes up six to six. Arthur sits there and puffs on his pipe and declares, 'By the narrowest of margins, this six wins. I would like to have a recount, twelve to nothing.' He got away with it. They all exclaimed: 'Gee, oh, nobody explained it to me like that before.' "

The Failure of the Nixon New Economic Policy

It is not surprising that the Nixon New Economic Policy, introduced in August 1971, and the culmination of Burns's public and private lobbying for the previous year and a half, was a failure. It was nothing more or less than a stunt, aimed at holding down prices and wages temporarily, while Burns at the Fed and Connally at the Treasury could pump up the economy into a miniboom in time for the 1972 elections. It also involved recognition of the weakness of the dollar, brought on by the combination of the Johnson fiscal and monetary excesses and the new layer of monetary expansion brought in by Burns almost from the day he moved over to the Fed.

The New Economic Policy was a cynical exercise and its consequences were, of course, bound to haunt its perpetrators. Accordingly, Burns once again set about laying the groundwork for his self-justification. Having engineered the money explosion of 1972, to make it absolutely sure Nixon was reelected, he began arguing that the problem of inflation was due not only to the intractable upward movement of wages but also to the failure of the federal government to bring its budget under control. In a speech to the American Economic Association in Toronto on December 29, 1972, by which time Nixon was once again safely installed in the White House, Burns said: "The hard fact is that market forces can no longer be counted on to check the upward course of wages and prices, even when the aggregate demand for goods and services declines in the course of a business recession. Other countries have discovered, as we in the United States have, that wage rates and prices no longer respond to the play of market forces."

Like so much of Burns's argumentation when at the Fed, this was also a red herring. The facts of movements in wages, output per man-hour, and unit labor costs in the United States since 1960 are as follows:

1. Hourly compensation of workers in private business has grown at a steadily increasing rate over the twenty-year period. Between 1960 and 1965 hourly compensation grew about 4 percent a year, between 1965 and 1970 by about 7 percent, between 1970 and 1975 by about 8 percent, and between 1975 and 1980 by about 9 percent. The rate of increase in hourly compensation has not been sufficient to ensure that the growth of hourly compensation has kept pace with prices. Since 1970 real wages have remained virtually static.

2. Productivity has grown at a drastically slower rate since 1970. Between 1960 and 1970 output per man-hour in the United States rose 33 percent. Between 1970 and 1980 it rose 15 percent.

3. As a result, unit labor costs rose 29 percent between 1960 and 1970 while they rose 96 percent between 1970 and 1980.

What was happening during the 1970's in America was that workers were attempting to maintain their real wages by increasing their money wages. The increase in money wages took place steadily, as it always has in the United States, where multiyear labor contracts are the general rule. But two factors defeated the attempt by workers to maintain the growth of their real wages at anything like the rate that applied in the 1960's. These were the drastic reduction in the rate of growth of output per man-hour during the 1970's and the very rapid acceleration in the growth of consumer prices. Thus, between 1960 and 1970 the consumer price index rose 31 percent while hourly compensation rose 71 percent. Between 1970 and 1980 consumer prices rose 112 percent while hourly compensation rose 126 percent. In the former period hourly compensation rose more than twice as fast as consumer prices; in the second period it rose hardly faster at all.

The attempt by Burns to explain away the growth of inflation during the 1970's by reference to some increased intractability of the labor force is a sham. Real wages in America did not go up at all during the 1970's. In fact, when taxes are taken into account, there was a substantial decline in the real take-home pay of the American worker during the 1970's.

As Henry Wojtyla and Nicocles Michas, the economic strategists of the New York brokerage firm of Rosenkrantz, Ehrenkrantz, Lyon & Ross, pointed out in their January 1982 report, real take-home pay has fallen from approximately $90 per week in 1967 prices in 1970 to only $80 in 1981. This compared with a rise from about $75 to $90 per week between 1955 and 1970.

The barrier to the continuing growth of real wages has been a drastic decline in the growth of productivity. This has produced a freeze in the growth of real pretax wages. The growth of taxation as a proportion of income brought about the phenomenon of actually declining real take-home pay.

There may well be several causes for the cessation of growth of productivity in America, but one fact stands out. The escalation of money growth has produced an increase in prices which has steadily inhibited the growth of savings and investment. Excessive money growth has been behind the phenomenon of "bracket creep," which has produced such bounteous revenues for the federal government and in turn has meant the average worker has suffered an increasing proportion of his income going into taxes. With or without excessive money growth, the struggle by the workers to maintain their real wages would have continued. But there would not have been any rise in money wages such as occurred during the 1970's. The excessive money growth permitted money wages to rise so fast.

So there are two issues here. First, there was a very sharp drop in the rate of growth of real wages during the decade of the 1970's. This was fundamentally the result of the failure of productivity in America to grow. That in turn was a result of the inflation which frustrated investment in machinery and techniques to improve output per man-hour. Inflation also had the effect of stultifying the flow of savings, inasmuch as in an inflationary environment there is a special stimulus to spend what you have because tomorrow it will be worth less. Secondly, money wages rose rapidly, generally in line with inflation, because of the excessive money growth which took place during the period.

In blaming the unions for the inflation, Burns was, like the economists who controlled the levers of power under Kennedy and Johnson, blaming the symptoms, not the cause.

Blaming Full Employment for Inflation

The New Economic Policy was doomed from the start. It could not cure inflation because it was itself a principal cause of inflation, through its powerful stimulus to monetary growth, its expansionary fiscal policy, and its devaluation of the dollar.

This was not how Burns saw the situation in 1972, when he spoke to the American Economic Association.

The shock therapy applied by the President in the summer of last year [1971] had lasting benefits. The pace of business activity strengthened almost immediately after the announcement of the New Economic Policy and has gathered momentum over the past year.

It must be recognized, however, that the controls were aided

178

by continued slack in resource and product markets and by a pronounced rise in output per man-hour. Next year, further progress in moderating inflation will be more difficult to achieve.

Burns must have known that the "pumping up" process set in train in August 1971 could give only temporary relief. The abandonment of a steady, stable monetary and fiscal policy was bound to lead to an inflationary boom and a big reaction. So he argued,

> [A] major cause of inflationary bias in modern industrialized nations is their relative success in maintaining prosperity. Protection from the hardships of economic displacement has been extended by government to business firms as well. Workers who become unemployed can normally look forward to being rehired soon in the same line of activity, if not by the same firm. Institutional features of our labor and product markets reinforce these wage and price tendencies. Excessive wage increases tend to spread faster and more widely than they used to.

One would be able to put some credence in this theory if there were evidence of a *reduction* in the rate of unemployment in the 1970's. But this was not so. The rate of unemployment rose steadily during the decade. In 1967 and 1968 the rate of unemployment was under 4 percent. In 1972, when Burns was blaming the unions and full employment for the inflationary boom that was under way, unemployment was already up to 5.6 percent, and in Burns's last full year at the Fed, 1977, it was 7 percent. As inflation has persisted, there has been a steady increase in the rate of unemployment, and the argument that "full employment" is the problem in the battle against inflation has worn threadbare.

As in so many of his public statements, Burns in 1972 was looking for an excuse for the failure of his own monetary policy. He blamed escalating wages costs in 1970 and got the New Economic Policy. This blew up in his face in 1972 and 1973, so he blamed full employment.

Right along, we observe Burns trying to wriggle his way around the basic problem: who to blame for the inflation once he had decided that the monetary policies of the Federal Reserve could not be to blame.

179

He brought out the Kennedy-Johnson arguments that wages were the problem. This made the New Economic Policy wage-price controls look sensible. But this argument was bound to wear thin as the evidence piled up showing that real wages were not increasing at anything like the rates applying during the 1960's. He turned to the argument, which he used for years, that the problem was one of the rising aspirations of the masses for full employment. Yet mounting unemployment during the 1970's negated this argument. Then he turned to blaming the federal government for the inflation because of its excessive budget deficits.

All through this, Burns was actually grappling with the emerging and previously little known problem of stagflation. That was one part of his intellectual problem. There was a new and very difficult problem of economic policy coming to light. The other side of his problem was that he had to turn the spotlight of criticism always away from the Federal Reserve and away from monetary policy.

Another Self-Justification—Budget Deficits Are to Blame

The argument that the federal government is to blame for inflation, through its budget deficits, is one that has been favored by the Federal Reserve System since Burns enunciated it about a decade ago. It is, of course, a very shallow argument. The following facts are relevant:

1. There is no requirement for the Federal Reserve to "monetize" budget deficits by buying the government's debt. Indeed, one of the most important single justifications for the so-called independence of the Federal Reserve was and is to remove it from control by the administration and thus to oblige the administration to finance its expenditures by taxation, rather than by demanding cash from the Federal Reserve. That is the most fundamental reason for the "independence" of the Federal Reserve, and it is why central banks in other countries have also been granted great independence. They were made so independent in order to protect citizens from the greed and ambition of their rulers by denying those rulers access to the cash in the central bank.

2. There is no evidence that the Federal Reserve, as a matter of fact, has purchased a constant proportion of the debt created by

annual federal budget deficits. The table on page 111 shows that between 1971 and 1981 the proportion of the federal deficit purchased by the Federal Reserve fluctuated widely and without any noticeable pattern to it. Hence, even though the Federal Reserve is under no obligation to purchase federal debt (indeed, its charter strongly implies that it will not and must not aid in the financing of the federal government), the fact is that it has not done so in any case. The so-called burden of financing the federal budget deficits about which Burns, and latterly Volcker, talk, does not exist.

3. There is no evidence of any consistent relationship between the size of the budget deficit and inflation, or interest rates.

There has been no tendency for the budget deficit, as a percentage of gross national product, to increase over the last decade, even though over that period there has been a substantial escalation in the rate of growth of prices.

Federal Budget Deficit as Percentage of Current Prices GNP

1971	2.1%
1972	2.0
1973	1.1
1974	0.3
1975	2.9
1976	3.9
1977	2.3
1978	2.3
1979	1.1
1980	2.3
1981	1.9

If the budget deficit were going to be a cause of the increasing inflation of recent times, there would have had to be a tendency for the deficit to increase as a proportion of GNP. This has not happened. The deficit has drained away some of the nation's savings and to that extent has led to a less efficient use of those savings, but that is it.

The charts on the following two pages relate the deficit to the change in the money supply (page 182) in the United States and for various countries (page 183), and movements in the consumer price index to deficits. In neither case is it possible to find any significant relationship.

The chart below was prepared by Professor David Meiselman of Virginia Polytechnic Institute. It shows no consistent relationship between the budget deficit and money growth in America. The charts on page 183 show that in six major Western economies there is no consistent relationship between budget deficits and inflation. These graphs were prepared by Leon Taub of Chase Econometrics.

A similar conclusion is drawn from the table on page 184 published by Alan Reynolds, vice-president at Polyconomics, the economic consultants of Morristown, New Jersey, in the *Wall Street Journal* on October 5, 1981.

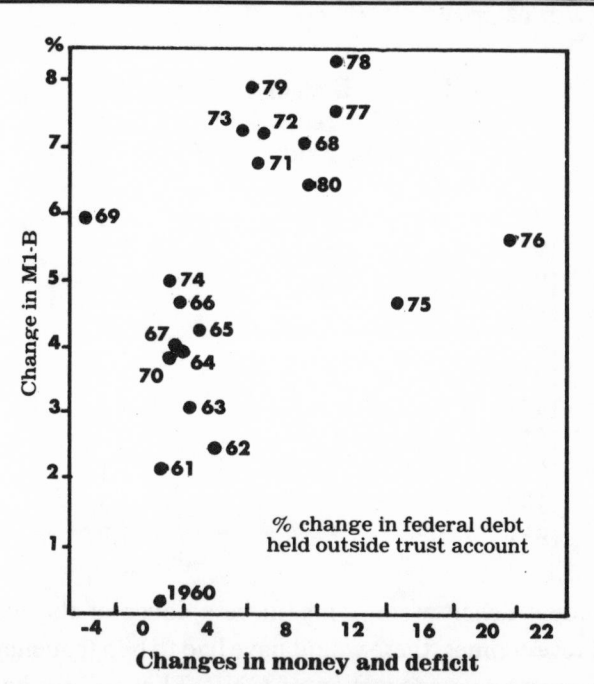

Source: David Meiselman, Virginia Polytechnic Institute

Each dot marks the relationship between increases in the money supply (M1-B) and changes in the federal debt, for the years 1960 to 1980. If budget deficits caused inflation—surging M1-B—the dots would adopt a straight-line pattern. They don't. Their pattern is random. So this chart's message is: don't blame inflation on the deficits.

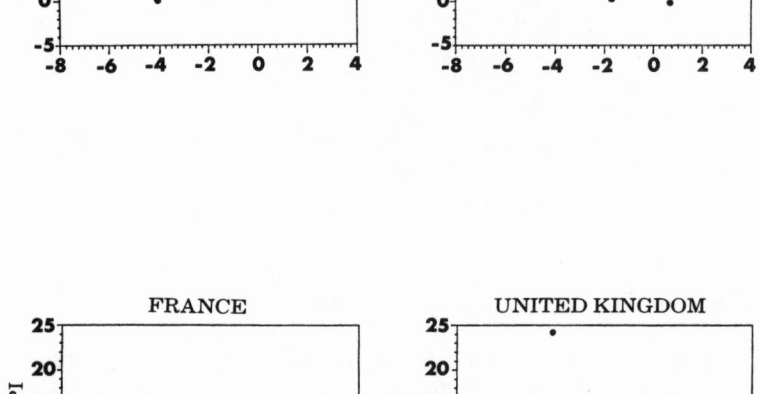

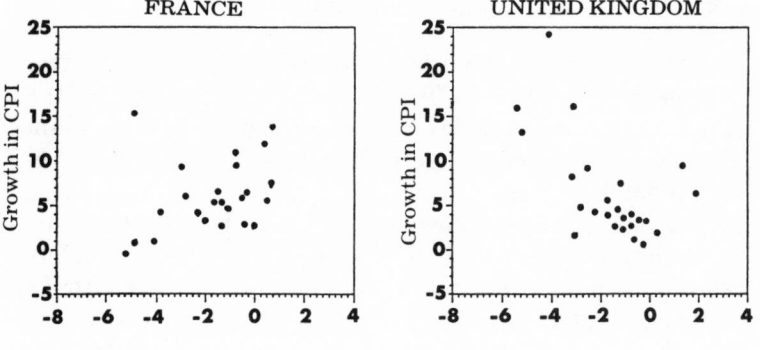

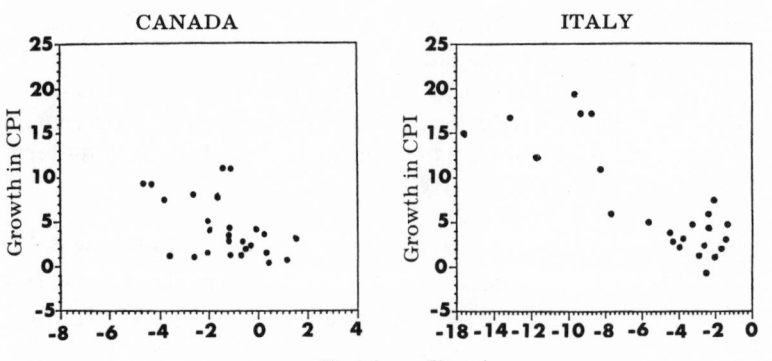

**Previous Year's
Government Surplus or Deficit / GNP
(Percent)**

The Fed

	Budget Deficit (-) or Surplus as % of Outlays	Annual Growth of Money Supply (M1)	Annual Consumer Price Inflation
	1977-79	1977-80	1977-80
Kuwait	84.7%	20.0%	7.5%
Colombia	5.5	28.5	25.5
Singapore	3.9	11.7	5.2
Switzerland	- 2.1	5.0	2.5
Brazil	- 3.2	50.9	54.5
France	- 3.3	9.8	10.6
Yugoslavia	- 4.1	23.4	19.9
Netherlands	- 6.9	6.7	5.3
Germany	- 7.0	4.0	4.0
Austria	-10.4	3.5	4.8
U.S.	-10.8	7.4	9.7
U.K.	-11.7	12.6	13.9
Belgium	-14.3	4.6	5.7
Japan	-32.0	7.1	5.9

Government Budgets, Money, and Inflation
Source: I.M.F.

Commenting on this table, Reynolds said:

The table indicates there is obviously no direct link between average deficits 1977–1979 and average inflation rates. Inflation was high in countries with small deficits (Brazil, France, Yugoslavia) and with large deficits (the U.S. and the U.K.). And inflation was low in some countries in each of these categories, like Singapore, Switzerland, and Austria. Growth of the money supply on the other hand explains relative inflation rates reasonably well but it does not appear even roughly related to budget deficits. Since deficits are not tied to inflation, they do not explain interest rates either. Countries with the slowest growth of money (relative to the growth of production) invariably have the lowest interest rates, regardless of their budgets.

The prime rate has lately been around 7 percent in Switzerland and Japan, over 14 percent in Singapore, and 120 percent in Brazil. Government bonds in late August were 5.8 percent in Switzerland, 9.4 percent in Japan, around 9 percent in the Netherlands, 11 percent in Austria, well over 14 percent in the U.S. and the U.K., 17 percent in France, and 148 percent in Argentina. Too much short-term money makes long-term credit scarce and expensive.

Burns used the argument that the Federal Reserve was "burdened" by the budget deficits again and again in the 1970's. It was never a sincere argument, but more an attempt to obscure the real

184

issue, which was the failure of the Federal Reserve under Burns to limit the growth money in the first place, thus arresting inflation at its source.

The Rising Cost of Money

As inflation escalated, interest rates increased. As in the case of wages, Burns tried to hold interest rates down with direct controls, but in view of the continuing escalation of money growth this also proved an impossible task.

Inflation and Interest Rates

	Annual Increase Consumer Price Index	Ninety-day Treasury Bill Rate
1967	2.8%	4.30%
1968	4.2	5.45
1969	5.4	6.66
1970	5.9	6.39
1971	4.3	4.33
1972	3.3	4.07
1973	6.2	7.03
1974	11.0	7.83
1975	9.1	5.78
1976	5.8	4.97
1977	6.4	5.27
1978	7.7	7.19
1979	11.3	10.07
1980	13.5	11.43
1981	9.3	13.3

There are two broad conclusions to be drawn from this table: First, the steady increase in the average rate of inflation in the last fifteen years has been accompanied by a steady increase in the average level of interest rates. Money has become more and more expensive until by 1982 we had moved into a period where the rate of interest routinely exceeds the rate of inflation by a substantial margin. Secondly, interest rates have moved in the same direction as the rate of growth of prices. When inflation increases, interest rates rise; when inflation decreases, interest rates decline.

During Burns's tenure at the Fed, interest rates declined in 1971 and 1972 (when inflation also declined, reflecting the tight money period in 1969 and early 1970, before Burns's influence at the Fed was in place). Interest rates also declined in 1975 and 1976, when inflation collapsed, following the tight money period put in place by Burns in the panic of mid-1973. Following the huge money growth buildup of 1972 to reelect Nixon, which was the culmination of two years of accelerating money growth, there developed in early 1973 a confrontation between the Government Committee on Interest and Dividends (of which Burns was chairman) and the banking system. In February 1973 Burns forced the banks to revoke an increase in the prime rate. In March, as inflationary pressure continued to build, Burns and the banks negotiated a "split rate" system of one rate for nationally known borrowers and another for small businesses. In April Burns, speaking in his capacity as chairman, sent a letter to all Federal Reserve member banks urging them to "avoid a credit crunch" and to be cautious in their lending. A week later, however, he was forced to concede that his "jawboning" efforts had resulted in artificially low interest rates, and by the end of 1973 the prime rate had risen from approximately 6.5 to 10 percent.

By that time Burns had realized that the Fed would at last have to take some action to arrest the inflationary boom. With the election of 1972 out of the way he instituted a serious reduction in the rate of growth of money, which had the effect of bringing the average rate of growth of money down from the 8.2 percent of the 1972–73 period to 3.5 percent in the year to the first quarter of 1975. This very rapid deceleration in money growth precipitated the 1974–75 maxirecession. It also caused a collapse of interest rates.

Commenting on the experience of 1972–73, the House Banking Committee Subcommittee on Domestic Monetary Policy stated in its 1976 report:

> Though it isn't all that matters, monetary policy matters very very much. In summary, the record shows that throughout the post World War II period, time and again excessively sharp, prolonged cuts in money growth helped to turn economic expansions into recessions. Between 1965 and 1973, a new twist was added. Sustainable expansions were turned into unsustain-

able inflations before monetary policy moved to cut them down. A full Committee staff report in August 1973 has proved to be sadly prophetic when it stated: "Beginning in early 1972, money supply growth was again accelerated to 8 percent a year and in the latest quarter, Spring 1973, has zoomed to nearly 11 percent a year. Inflation, which had tapered off, has resumed and prices are now advancing faster than before. Interest rates are skyrocketing. Financial intermediation is again underway. The future is even more bleak. Soon the Federal Reserve, in order to end the inflation it has fueled, will again cut back the growth of the money stock too sharply and too long. Interest rates will rise to unseen heights. Credit will become nearly unavailable to home buyers, consumers, small business and local governments. Economic activity will decline. Unemployment will rise."

We know now that this bleak monetarist scenario came true. Money growth was decelerated beginning in the second half of 1973 and sharply so after mid-1974. In the six months from September 1974 to March 1975, industrial production fell more than 15 percent. In May 1975, unemployment reached 8.9 percent.

The reason for these violent swings in money growth, inflation, and interest rates is to be found in the Federal Reserve's policy of trying to stabilize interest rates. As Professor James L. Pierce said in evidence to the House Banking Committee back in 1976:

Historically, the Federal Reserve, like other central banks, has exhibited a strong tendency to stabilize fluctuations in interest rates, particularly short-run fluctuations. The Fed's penchant for stabilizing interest rates has among other things helped to produce a procyclical behavior in the growth of the money stock; that is, money grows more rapidly during economic expansion and slowly during recessions. The reason for this is clear enough; when the economy is expanding rapidly, credit demands also expand, tending to put upward pressure on interest rates.

The Federal Reserve attempts to constrain these interest rate increases by providing more bank reserves through open market operations. The increase in bank reserves in turn leads to expansion in the money stock and underwrites an expansion in economic activity. During recessions, credit demands decline and interest rates begin to fall. The Fed attempts to constrain the decline in interest rates by retarding growth in the money stock. The retardation in money growth and constraint on interest rate declines tend to exacerbate the decline in economic activity. It seems clear that attempts to stabilize interest rates can and have produced greater cyclical fluctuations in income, production, employment and inflation than would have been the case had the Fed not been so concerned about interest rate fluctuations. If the Fed adhered more closely to a target growth for the money stock, interest rates would tend to move more quickly; that is, fall more rapidly in recession and rise more rapidly in expansion than has heretofore been the case. These sharper interest rate movements would serve to moderate the fluctuations in economic activity. If interest rates were allowed to react more quickly, aggregate demand would be affected more rapidly and hence would not probably fluctuate so widely. As a result, it is likely that interest rates would themselves actually fluctuate less widely.

None of these arguments convinced Burns. There is little or no evidence in the hundreds of pages of speeches and testimony he gave in public during his eight years at the Fed that he was even aware of them. His views were summarized in a statement to the House Banking Committee in April 1975: "The fact is that inflation started in the mid-1960's and was mainly caused by large deficits, continued year after year, in the Federal Budget. As a result of the excess demand created by a persistently loose fiscal policy, a spiral of wages got under way in the private sector and the rate of inflation began to quicken."

He never changed his tune. The record went around and around, and the same old song came out. In June 1976, when he was engaged in pumping up the money supply in time for the 1976 Ford-Carter election, he told the commencement class at the Florida Institute of Technology:

The current inflation in our country began in the middle years of the 1960's. The exuberant mood that then emerged in the business community soon gave rise to a series of inter-related and partly overlapping waves of speculation. The first involved corporate mergers and acquisitions. The second developed during the late 1960's in the market for common stocks. The third occurred in the real estate market. Between January 1970 and

January 1973, the volume of new housing starts doubled and a huge inventory of unsold homes was piled up.

It is inconceivable that Burns was unaware of the mounting toll of criticism of the Fed which culminated in the passage of the House Concurrent Resolution in 1975. He devoted a great deal of argument and effort in the second half of his term to the issue of the independence of the Federal Reserve.

Burns Fights for "Independence" for the Fed

It is not surprising that Burns faced increasing criticism of the "independence" of the Federal Reserve as the violent swings in money, the economy, and interest rates reflected the failures of monetary policy. Union leaders early criticized him for his advocacy of wage-price controls and with good reason. The advent of Nixon in the White House and Burns in the Fed was followed by a cessation of growth of real wages and a decline in real take-home pay. In 1971 George Meany, president of the AFL-CIO, charged that "Chairman Burns and others have been engaged in the shocking and blatant use of a double standard while providing subsidies and aid for the banks and big businesses."

In June 1970, following congressional opposition to a bailout, the Penn Central went bankrupt, upon which Burns organized a major rescue operation, with the Federal Reserve notifying all member banks it stood ready to issue standby credits to enable credit markets to operate smoothly.

Meany also called for the resignation of Burns at the beginning of the 1974–75 recession. Representatives Wright Patman and Henry Reuss repeatedly attempted to push legislation through Congress making the Fed more accountable. In May 1976, Reuss attempted to pass a bill that would have made the term of the chairman of the Fed roughly concurrent with that of the president. More fundamentally, Congress succeeded in trying to impose limits on the Federal Reserve's money powers by imposing targets for money growth in March 1975, but as we have already noted, these targets were evaded by the Fed through a combination of obfuscation and manipulation of base periods.

Burns expressed righteous indignation over these various unsuccessful attempts to make the Federal Reserve accountable to its supposed master, the Congress of the United States. In his commencement address to the students at Bryant College, Smithfield, Rhode Island, in May 1976, he said:

> There are two major reasons for the emphasis on monetary policy. In the first place, the manipulation of government expenditures has proved to be a rather clumsy device for dealing with rapidly changing economic developments. Secondly, the process of reaching a consensus on needed tax changes usually turns out to be complex and time-consuming. Experience has thus taught us that alterations of fiscal policy, once undertaken, frequently have a large part of their economic effect too late to be of much value in moderating fluctuations in business activity. Even when the economy is booming, legislatures are rarely willing to increase tax rates or to restrain the rising curve of governmental expenditures.
>
> Fortunately, monetary policy is relatively free of these short-comings. Flexibility is the great virtue of instruments of monetary and credit policy. Changes in the course of monetary policy can be made promptly and—if need be—frequently. Under our scheme of governmental organization, the Federal Reserve can make the hard decisions that might be avoided by decision makers subject to the day to day pressures of political life. And experience indicates that the effects of substantial changes in the supply of money and credit are rather speedily transmitted through the financial markets to the workshops of the economy.

On the defensive, Burns in 1976 had abandoned his earlier claims that too much emphasis should not be placed on monetary policy because its actions were subject to such substantial lags and because it hit discriminately on interest-sensitive industries such as autos and housing. Now, we are told, monetary policy works very fast and very effectively. That is part one of Burns's defense of the Fed—it is a very valuable instrument performing a crucial function in stabilizing short-term economic movements with unique success.

He then went on to lay down the case for the independence of the Federal Reserve:

> The founders of the Federal Reserve System were well aware of the dangers that would inhere in the creation of a monetary

authority subservient to the executive branch of government—
and thus subject to political manipulation. The principle of
independence of the monetary authority was embodied in the
original Federal Reserve Act in several ways. First, individuals
appointed to the Federal Reserve Board by the President were
to have ten-year terms and they could be removed from office
only for cause. A president could not, therefore, remove a
Board member from office simply because he disagreed with his
views and the term of office was long enough to minimize the
threat of covert political pressure on Board members. Moreover, the law provided for staggered terms in order to prevent
presidential "packing" of the monetary authority.

Second, the newly created Federal Reserve Board was required to report on, and to account for, its actions to the legislative branch of government, not to the administration.

Third, the operations of the Federal Reserve System were to
be financed from its own internal sources and thus protected
from the political pressures that may be exercised through the
congressional appropriations process.

Fourth, power was to be diffused within the Federal Reserve
System so that the interests of borrowers, lenders and the general public were to be recognized and blended in the new regional Federal Reserve Banks.

In the years that followed creation of the Federal Reserve
System, experiences—particularly during the Great Depression
—suggested that the degree of independence assigned to the
monetary authority was insufficient. The Banking Acts of 1933
and 1935 sought to rectify this and other defects in the financial
structure. Under the new legislation, the Secretary of the Treasury and the Comptroller of the Currency, who originally were
ex officio members of the Board, were relieved of this responsibility. The terms of the members of the Board were lengthened
from ten to twelve years and then to fourteen years, to insulate
the Board still more from political pressures. A new agency—
the Federal Open Market Committee, including representatives
of the regional Federal Reserve Banks as well as members of the
Board located in Washington—was established to conduct
open market operations which by the early 1930's had come to
play a major role in implementing monetary policy. Moreover,
the principle was reaffirmed that funds used by the Federal
Reserve to finance its operations were not to be construed as
government funds or as appropriated money. All of these legislative changes strengthened the ability of the Federal Reserve

System to resist the efforts of the Treasury, or the White House, or any other agency in the executive branch, to influence unduly the course of monetary and credit policy.

In the exercise of our adjudicatory responsibilities the members of the Board scrupulously avoid any contact with interested parties. In our deliberations on monetary and credit policies, not the slightest consideration is given to questions of political partisanship. Every member of the Board and every member of the Federal Open Market Committee weighs the issues of monetary and credit policy solely from the viewpoint of the public interest and the general welfare. My colleagues at the Federal Reserve are highly qualified individuals possessing a diversity of skills essential to the management of the nation's financial affairs.

They live and work under a Spartan code that avoids political entanglements, conflicts of interest or even the appearance of such conflicts. At the same time, members of the Board, particularly its Chairman, maintain close contact with members of the Executive and Congress, in order to assure that the activities of the Federal Reserve are appropriately coordinated with what other branches of Government are doing.

Nevertheless, there are now, as there have been over the years, some well-meaning individuals in our country who believe that the authority of the Federal Reserve to make decisions about the course of monetary policy should be circumscribed. The specific proposals that have been put forward over the years differ greatly, but they have usually had one feature in common—namely, the control by the executive branch of government over the monetary authority.

Milton Friedman Wants Executive Branch Control

Eleven years after he gave Burns the ringing endorsement in *Newsweek,* Milton Friedman, in a lecture to the Western Economic Association in San Francisco in July 1981, asked for total executive branch control over the Fed:

There is, I believe, only one realistic alternative [to the problem of the failure of the Fed to reform itself to produce a more efficient monetary policy]. That is somehow to establish a bottom line. One such policy, proposed by the Shadow Open Market Committee, that would do so is to require by law that the Federal Reserve Governors submit their resignations at the end

of any year in which the growth of a specified monetary aggregate has departed from the advance target by more than a
designated amount. Unfortunately, I do not really think that's
feasible. The only two alternatives that do seem to me feasible
over the longer run are either to make the Federal Reserve a
bureau in the Treasury under the Secretary of the Treasury, or
to put the Federal Reserve under direct congressional control.
Either involves terminating the so-called independence of the
system. But either would establish a strong incentive for the
Fed to produce a stabler monetary environment than we have
had.

Burns detested the very idea of such a reform. In his May 1976
speech he violently attacked the very idea.

A move in this direction would be unwise and even dangerous.
It is encouraging to find that, despite occasional outbursts of
anger, a majority of Congress share this belief. I doubt that the
American people would want to see the power to create money
lodged in the Presidency—which may mean that it would in
fact be exercised by political aides in the White House. Such a
step would create a potential for political mischief or abuse on
a larger scale than we have yet seen. Certainly, if the spending
propensities of federal officials were given freer rein, the inflationary tendency that weakened our economy over much of the
past decade would in all likelihood be aggravated.

Of course, in our democratic society, the independence of a
governmental agency can never be absolute. The Federal Reserve System is thus subject not only to the provisions of the
Federal Reserve Act but also to the Employment Act and
numerous other statutes. The original design of the Federal
Reserve System recognized this duty by requiring the Federal
Reserve to account for its stewardship to the Congress. The
oversight responsibilities of the Congress for the conduct of the
monetary authority do not, however, require congressional involvement in the details of implementing monetary policy.

The technical complexities of adjusting monetary or credit
instruments to the needs of a modern industrial economy are
far too great to be dealt with by a large deliberative body. At
the same time, there is a significant role for Congress in setting
forth the economic and financial objectives that the monetary
authority is expected to observe and honor. Over the past year,
the Congress has been exercising its vital oversight function

through a new and systematic procedure, spelled out in House Concurrent Resolution No. 133. That resolution requires the Federal Reserve to report to Congress at quarterly intervals on the course of monetary policy and to project ranges of growth in the major monetary and credit aggregates for the year ahead.

We at the Federal Reserve regard the dialogue between the monetary authority and the Congress stimulated by the Concurrent Resolution as constructive. It has given Congress a better opportunity to express its views on the appropriateness of our actions. It has also provided us at the Federal Reserve with an opportunity to explain fully the reasons for our actions and to communicate to the Congress and to the public at large our firm intention to adhere to a course of monetary policy that is consistent not only with continued economic expansion at a satisfactory rate but also with the gradual unwinding of inflationary tendencies.

Unfortunately the Federal Reserve has not acted with the restraint that might have been expected, given Burns's description of its "Spartan ideals" and its "adjudicatory responsibilities." Instead of holding back on money growth and providing a miserly output of new cash, it has provided vastly excessive amounts of money. It has consistently resisted all attempts to reform its operating procedures. It has confused and deceived Congress. The idealist picture painted by Burns does not exist in the real world. The acid test is the reaction of the financial markets to the actions of the Federal Reserve.

The slightest tendency for money to grow at any but a modest pace today throws the money markets into despair. They have so lost faith in the central bank that very high real rates of interest are the norm. There has been a complete disappearance of any belief that money will retain its value. The bond markets of America have been in ruins for years. They show any revival only when a really severe recession is fully in place.

In the Treasury there is, of course, outright opposition to the present independence of the Federal Reserve. As one senior Treasury official put it to me in late 1981: "One cannot watch the policies and practices of the Federal Reserve without experiencing a feeling of mounting anger and disgust."

The Anguish of Central Banking

Burns left the Fed in January 1978, when he was replaced by G. William Miller. In September 1979, Burns attempted to justify what he had done in his celebrated Per Jacobsson lecture at Belgrade. Gone, in this bitter speech, were the bombast, self-aggrandizement, and big talk about "Spartan codes" and the like. He began with a long exposition of the changing philosophical trends of the times, including the demand for full employment, the expansion of the welfare state, the growth of the power of unions, the wide acceptance of budget deficits, and the corrosive influence of Vietnam.

> The worldwide philosophic and political trends on which I have been dwelling inevitably affected the attitudes and actions of central banks. In most countries, central banks are an instrumentality of the executive branch of government—carrying out monetary policy according to the wishes of the head of government or the ministry of finance. Some industrial democracies, to be sure, have substantially independent central banks and that is certainly the case in the United States.
> *Viewed in the abstract, the Federal Reserve System had the power to abort the inflation at its incipient stage fifteen years ago, or at any later point, and it has the power to end it today. At any time within that period, it could have restricted the money supply and created sufficient strains in financial and industrial markets to terminate inflation with little delay. It did not do so because the Federal Reserve was itself caught up in the philosophic and political currents that were transforming American life and culture* [my italics].
> The Employment Act prescribes that "it is the continuing policy and responsibility of the Federal Government to use all its plans, functions and resources to promote maximum employment." The Federal Reserve is subject to this provision of the law and that has limited its practical scope for restrictive actions—*quite apart from the fact that some members of the Federal Reserve family had themselves been touched by the allurements of the New Economics* [my italics].
> Every time the government moved to enlarge the flow of benefits to the population at large, or to this or that group, the assumption was implicit that monetary policy would somehow accommodate the action. The fact that such actions could in combination be wholly incompatible with moderate ranges of

monetary expansion was seldom considered by those who initiated them, despite frequent warnings by the Federal Reserve that new fires of inflation were being ignited. If the Federal Reserve then sought to create a monetary environment that fell seriously short of accommodating the upward pressures on prices that were being released or reinforced by governmental action, several difficulties could be quickly produced in the economy. Not only that, the Federal Reserve would be frustrating the will of Congress—to which it was responsible—a Congress that was intent on providing additional services to the electorate and on assuring that jobs and incomes were maintained, particularly in the short run.

Facing these political realities, the Federal Reserve was willing to step hard on the monetary brakes at times—as in 1966, 1969 and 1974—but its restrictive stance was not maintained long enough to end inflation. By and large, monetary policy came to be governed by the principle of undernourishing the inflationary process while still accommodating a good deal of the pressures in the marketplace. The central banks of other countries, functioning as they did in a basically similar environment, appear to have behaved in much the same fashion.

In describing as I just have the anguish of central banking in a modern democracy, I do not mean to suggest that central bankers are free from responsibility for the inflation that is our common inheritance. After all, every central bank has some room for discretion and the range is considerable in the more independent central banks.

I have some comments to make:

1. There is no evidence that the Fed "undernourished" the economy with money. Far from it. Monetary growth was vastly excessive over the period from 1969 to the present day, as the figures cited demonstrate.

2. There is no evidence that the Congress persistently pushed the Fed into overproviding money. On the contrary, the House Banking Committee, to which the Fed was directly responsible, made many attempts to encourage it to *reduce* the rate of monetary growth. The evidence is indisputable.

3. During Burns's period at the Fed he had the opportunity of making slow and steady increases in money from a low base. He had that opportunity in 1970, when he inherited the squeeze on money

growth which was McChesney Martin's parting gift. He had a further opportunity to develop a slow and steady money growth after the 1974–75 maxirecession, and as has been shown in Chapter 3, the House Banking Committee thought this was what was going to happen.

4. It is not true that other central banks have felt obliged to provide money on the heroic scale of the Federal Reserve in America. The German and Swiss central banks, to take two examples of central banks working in a democratic environment, have not felt obligated to provide an excessive growth of money. Nor have they done so, to the great benefit of their economies' efficiency and growth.

5. Under Burns, the United States experienced steadily rising unemployment, not full employment. The cause of this escalation of unemployment was the barrier to economic growth erected by the excessively expansionary monetary policies for which he was responsible.

6. Burns never failed (as in May 1976—see pages 190–193) to assert how important was the "independence" accorded to the Federal Reserve and how essential this was to the implementation by the Fed of "hard decisions." In his "anguish" speech, he now tells us that he did not make any significant hard decisions at all but that he went along with what his bosses in Congress and the administration demanded.

Burns went on, at Belgrade in September 1979, to offer three more justifications for his failure:

1. "In a rapidly changing world, opportunities for mistakes are legion. Even facts about current conditions are subject to misinterpretation." He said that unemployment statistics are unreliable.

2. "While misinterpretations of unemployment statistics or other current information have consequences for all policymaking, there are other problems of interpretation to which the central banker's calling is peculiarly subject. Monetary theory is a controversial area. It does not provide central bankers with decision rules that are at once firm and dependable."

3. "There are other effects that raise doubts about the meaning of particular growth rates of the monetary aggregates. I have in mind changes in financial practices that evolved in the United States dur-

ing the 1960's—particularly during the bouts with tight money in 1966 and 1969—and that culminated in the financial innovations of the 1970's."

These further justifications are puny. All economic policy has to grapple with problems of economic forecasting. The Federal Reserve's economic forecasts have not been noticeably worse than those of any other major institution. The problem has not been one of economic forecasting. Rather the problem has been the unwillingness of those in supreme control at the Fed, the Federal Open Market Committee and the chief operating officials in New York, to adjust their policies and practices to take account of those changes. There has been a willful failure to take measures which will ensure that monetary policy does indeed act as a stabilizing influence in the economy. Because of inappropriate policies—notably that of persistently trying to moderate short-term movements in interest rates—the Federal Reserve has exaggerated fluctuations in the economy.

As for the "meaning of particular . . . monetary aggregates," this is a reference by Burns to the persistent confusion—encouraged and nurtured by the Fed—about the "correct" definition of money. As will be shown later, the best indicator of money growth as it affects economic fluctuations has been M1.

Burns himself admitted the Fed *could* control economic fluctuations in the statement emphasized on page 195. At Belgrade he made the following gloomy prediction:

> Central banks have indeed been participants in the inflationary process, in which the industrial countries have been enmeshed, *but their role has been subsidiary.* While the making of monetary policy requires continuing scrutiny and can stand considerable improvement, *we would look in vain to technical reforms as a way of eliminating the inflationary bias of industrial countries* [my italics].
>
> What is unique about inflation is its stubborn persistence, not the behavior of central bankers.

If those words were true, the outlook for the United States would indeed be grave, as it would mean the process of defeating inflation will require a complete metamorphosis of the American way of life and even of its political institutions. However, experience shows that inflation can be and has been defeated by appropriate monetary policies. That was the case in the immediate aftermath of the Second World War, when under President Truman there was a rapid decline in the money stock between 1946 and 1948. Burns's experience itself in 1973 and 1974 showed that a rapid deceleration of money growth could be achieved without precipitating revolution. The first eighteen months of President Reagan's rule saw a drastic decline in inflation, preceded by a sharp drop in money growth. The lesson has been learned in other nations.

In postwar America, under the traditions and practices of the Federal Reserve, however, there has been no continuing strong commitment by the *central bank itself* to a policy of low and stable money growth. In this nation of "laws" and "men," in the crucial area of the economy, the weaknesses of "men" have gravely hurt the country.

8 The Myopia of the Fed—Volcker Gets His Chance

We know that the process of postwar inflation in America was started by a political decision—the decision by President Johnson that it was possible to have both the Vietnam War and the Great Society at the same time. The expansionary budgetary policy that was necessary to achieve this political target was accompanied by an "accommodating" monetary policy.

In his 1965 economic report, President Johnson stated: "Monetary policy has supported fiscal measures. The supply of credit has been wisely tailored to the legitimate needs of a non-inflationary expansion, while care has been taken to avoid the leakage of short-term funds in response to higher interest rates abroad."

Johnson knew that he could not pursue his expansionary policies and maintain the gold coverage of the dollar. He took a vital step along the path which was to lead to the Nixon-Burns-Volcker devaluations of the dollar in 1971 and 1973. Johnson said in 1965:

> The Federal Reserve must be free to accommodate the expansion [of the Great Society and the Vietnam War] in 1965 and the years beyond 1965. Such an expansion needs to be supported by further orderly growth in money and credit. But this growth, as it is reflected in Federal Reserve note and deposit liabilities, could easily absorb—within two years or less, and without the outflow of a single ounce of gold—the present operating margin over the 25 percent "gold cover" required by existing law.
>
> I am therefore requesting the Congress to eliminate the arbitrary requirement that the Federal Reserve Banks maintain a gold certificate reserve against their deposit liabilities.

The Fed was *instructed* to participate in the inflationary process initiated by Johnson. The Fed cooperated pliantly with the Johnson demand for increased money supplies, including the provision of a sharply accelerated money growth in the 1968 election year.

We then had a brief period of monetary restraint in 1969. That experiment in monetary restraint was prematurely abandoned—after it had shown it was working. Nixon started to hold back on money growth as soon as the 1968 election was over, got a recession out of it, in 1970, and lost his nerve.

Burns came to power in February 1970, and immediately the monetary expansion started. From January 1970 to August 1971 monetary growth doubled. It was cranked up again in time for the 1972 elections. That was Burns trying to help Nixon. This went on well into 1973, when the continuing upsurge of inflation, combined with persistent dollar crises and a devaluation of the dollar, led Burns to impose a tough control on money growth.

Then, Burns started to accelerate money again, beginning in April 1976, in the buildup to the fall elections. Carter replaced Burns in early 1978 with G. William Miller, which was a case of sending a boy to do a man's job. During Miller's term at the Fed there was no monetary policy, beyond a policy of making sure there was an excessive growth of money.

The Miller episode had to come to an end as interest rates rose out of control during 1978 and on into 1979. Miller was given his leave in August 1979, and in came Volcker. Paul Volcker is a thoroughly experienced government official. The verdict is still out on him. In the period of his term under Carter, Paul Volcker gave the president just as big a money boost into the 1980 election as Martin had given to Johnson in 1968 or as Burns to Nixon in 1972 and 1976.

But through it all, Volcker did manage to reduce the *average* rate of growth of money. In 1980, his first year, the average growth of money fell to 6.3 percent (from the average of just short of 8 percent in the previous three years, which included one year of Burns and two years of Miller). In 1981, his second year, he held money growth at 6.5 percent. That is not a world-shaking achievement. But it was better than anything that had been achieved, with the exception of the 1974–76 recession years, since Martin's early Nixon squeeze in 1969. In the seven months ended July 1982, money growth (M1) fell to little more than 4 percent.

Are the Fed's Habits Too Ingrained to Change?

It is questionable, however, whether the Federal Reserve staff is capable of delivering stable monetary growth, at a low rate of growth, because it has become so attuned to operating procedures and traditions which go beyond the political events of the day. The Fed's thinking has developed to a point where it would seem possible, indeed likely, that only a complete cleanout of all its top officials will bring the chance of reform.

We have already seen in earlier chapters that the Fed has demonstrated it has its own priorities, which do not include control of the growth of money as a high priority on that list. Indeed, control of the growth of money has had a very low priority.

During all the violent changes in monetary policy in the last fifteen years, particularly in the period since 1969, Fed officials have maintained two policy priorities as their prime aims. The first of these has been to ensure the continuing independence and survival of the Federal Reserve in its existing form. Survival is the very top priority. This priority can be seen in action most clearly in the Fed's resistance to congressional invasion of its policy field.

The other top priority has been to "stabilize" interest rates. The Fed is a monopolist. It has the monopoly of money creation. The Fed's checks are uniquely regarded by the banks as cash. Hence, the Fed can buy a bond or a Treasury bill with its check and this check, when deposited in a bank, is regarded by that bank as good as cash. By expanding its purchases of bonds or bills, therefore, the Fed can expand the cash in the financial system. This cash, in turn, is used by the banks as a basis for financing their lending. As explained early in this book, the Fed officials have been in the habit of looking at the money markets and judging whether money is "tight" or "easy" by reference to the level and trend of interest rates.

This tendency is stimulated by the Fed's close relationship to the government securities dealers, reporting to the Federal Reserve Bank of New York. Fed officials are doing business with the government securities dealers—whom I will henceforth call bond dealers—almost every minute of every business day. Why? Because the bond dealers are the conduit through which the Fed manipulates interest rates.

Here is a list of the government securities dealers reporting to the Federal Reserve Bank of New York (as of August 28, 1980):

ACLI Government Securities, Inc.
Bache Halsey Stuart Shields, Inc.
Bank of America NT and SA
Bankers Trust Co.
A. G. Becker, Inc.
Briggs, Shaedle and Co., Inc.
Carroll McEntee and McGinley, Inc.
Chase Manhattan Bank NA
Chemical Bank
Citibank NA
Continental Illinois National Bank and Trust Company of Chicago
Crocker National Bank
Discount Corporation of New York
Donaldson Lufkin and Jenrette Securities Corp.
First Boston Corp.
First National Bank of Chicago
Goldman Sachs and Co.
Harris Trust and Savings Bank
E. F. Hutton and Co., Inc.
Kidder Peabody and Co., Inc.
Aubrey G. Lanston and Co., Inc.
Lehman Government Securities Inc.
Merrill Lynch Government Securities, Inc.
Morgan Guaranty Trust Company of New York
Morgan Stanley and Co., Inc.
Northern Trust Co.
Paine Webber, Jackson and Curtis Inc.
Wm. E. Pollock and Co., Inc.
Chas. E. Quincy and Co.
Salomon Brothers
Smith Barney, Harris Upham and Co., Inc.
Stuart Brothers N.Y. Hanseatic Division
United California Bank
Dean Witter Reynolds Inc.

Many of these names will be familiar to you. They are names you read every day in the newspapers. These bond dealers "make a market" in bonds. They are constantly buying and selling bonds and other Treasury securities. They also are underwriters of new bond issues. Obviously, the relationships between the Fed officials and the officials in the bond dealers' offices are intimate. They are doing business incessantly with each other.

In the New York Fed the so-called Desk officer controls the day-to-day dealings in bonds in which the Fed is engaged. The Federal Open Market Desk officer has extraordinary discretion.

In general terms, the Desk officer gets his marching orders from the Federal Open Market Committee, which is comprised of the seven members of the Federal Reserve Board plus five other Reserve bank presidents, including the president of the New York Fed, who is a permanent member. As explained by the Federal Reserve:

> The New York Reserve Bank conducts the actual daily open market operations for the system [that is, buying and selling of securities, bonds, bills, etc.] with primary dealers in U.S. government and federal agency securities and bankers' acceptances; conducts foreign exchange operations for the System and the U.S. Treasury; and conducts securities and foreign exchange purchases and sales for customers—foreign central banks and monetary authorities and official international institutions.
>
> These operations are almost always done in concert with the objectives of domestic open market operations. Sometimes they are carried out in the open market and sometimes internally, through the System portfolio.
>
> The manager for domestic open market operations and the manager for foreign operations are senior officers of the New York Fed. They are appointed to the "manager" posts annually by the Federal Open Market Committee.
>
> The account managers attend the FOMC meetings to report on operations and to receive the FOMC's directive. The records of policy actions of the meeting, including the directive, are made public two or three days after the following FOMC meeting.
>
> In addition, the manager of the domestic account, for example, speaks daily with the senior staff of the Board of Governors and a designated Reserve Bank president. The manager proposes a plan for the day and receives comment from the bank

president. Each day the Board staff issues a telegram to the voting and non-voting members of the FOMC, covering the discussion of the call.

The securities dealers and others voluntarily report their trading volume and portfolio positions to the New York Fed daily. In 1980, there were about three dozen reporting securities dealers, about one-third of which were commercial banks. When an institution believes it is performing the function of a government securities dealer and is a significant market participant, the institution may contact the New York Federal Reserve Bank and begin reporting activity and positions informally. After evaluating these reports, over a period, to determine a dealer's capabilities and volume of business, the Reserve Bank's securities department may add the dealer to the reporting list.

You can readily see from that description of the internal workings of the Federal Reserve open market accounts that there is a tremendous daily preoccupation by the most senior people in the Federal Reserve System with the movements in the bond markets. The dealings involved represent the meat and drink of the Federal Reserve's policy actions, on a day-to-day basis. Inevitably the Fed officials have become deeply preoccupied with movements in bond prices and in the prices of other similar securities. This means in turn that they are deeply involved with the day-to-day movements in interest rates (which are, of course, the inverse of bond or other securities prices: when bond prices go up, this means interest rates come down, and vice versa).

More than $800 Billion in Transactions a Year—for What?

Milton Friedman stated in his Western Economics Association speech in July 1981:

In the year 1980 the Federal Reserve made gross open market purchases of securities of something over $800 billion and gross transactions, including sales or maturities being rolled over, of more than double that amount. The net change in the portfolio was $4.5 billion. The open market desk therefore made $184 worth of purchases gross and roughly twice that amount of transactions (purchases plus sales) in order to add one dollar to its portfolio. Why all this churning? It accounts for something like one-quarter to one-half of all the transactions of U.S. government securities dealers other than the Fed itself. It generates millions of dollars of fees for the dealers involved. What function does it have for monetary policy and why has it occurred? It has occurred for only one reason: the mode of operations the Fed has adopted, including a reserve accounting period under which every bank in the United States settles on Wednesday.

Why [has there been such] opposition to staggering settlement dates or to other devices for reducing gross market transactions? Because churning gives the people who are involved in it a sense of great importance, makes them involved in big deals.

How can a person be in a position of buying and selling billions of dollars of securities every day, subject to pressure and influence from important people—and resisting that pressure—and yet believe that it is "full of sound and fury, signifying nothing"?

"Examining Sheep's Entrails"—The "Mystery" of the Fed

Karl Brunner, professor of economics at the universities of Rochester (New York) and Bern (Switzerland), who has been a leading student and critic of the Fed for the last twenty years, stressed the importance to the Fed of its massive open market operations.

"Take the example," said Brunner in an interview with me in December 1981, "of the Bank of England. The conception these people have of their monetary policy aims is very closely related to their prestige and power in the City [the "Wall Street" of London]. If, for example, they did what we tell them to do, namely, to become the lender of *last* resort instead of the lender of *first* resort, their relationship to the City would change radically. At the moment, they have a sort of sweetheart relationship with the City, and the City understands that very well. The Bank of England offers the City easy access to the Bank of England. When there is a little problem, you can always get your loan. So the City is able to run on virtually no reserves. It is really a subsidy to the City. The City understands that; the Bank of England understands that. Changing that would mean the City would have to change its behavior quite radically. It would mean that they would be less dependent on the Bank of England. So

206

the Bank of England bureaucracy would lose power, influence, and prestige as a result. To put the point differently, within such a monopoly organization as the Bank of England, issues about conceptions of policy are also invariably issues about *the power of the bureaucracy itself* [my italics].

"It is of the utmost importance, within these monopolistic bureaucracies, of which the Fed is one, that any young man of talent coming in is very promptly sat on, to stop him having unorthodox ideas. My good friend Jim Pierce left the Fed because of such pressures. He and I share very similar views and he came over to England with me last year [1980] with Allan Meltzer to talk with Mrs. Thatcher about her policies.

"In the case of the Fed, it is also clear how their policies and practices are inextricably bound up with their own power and influence. Consider the situation that would apply were there in operation a constant monetary growth rule, which we have told them to do. [Under such a rule, the Federal Reserve would be obliged simply to create a previously determined quantity of bank reserves, or to increase the monetary base by a previously determined fixed amount. That would be the be-all and end-all of its policy actions.] They cannot argue that this cannot be done.

"Instead, look at the way they fiddle around with the federal funds rate a bit and the way they hedge the discount window around with all sorts of restrictions and harassments. If you borrow too frequently from the discount window you are called on the carpet and some underling in the Federal Reserve can call a bank's president and demand more information and can call for more paper.

"The alternative to this procedure is to charge some interest rate which is specified in advance, say, one or two percentage points above the Treasury bill rate.

"Now consider the difference between the two situations. Under the first, a simple bureaucrat can call the presidents or the vice-presidents of major banks on the carpet or harass them by telephone. They can really push these people around—and they do. But under the other case, things would be very clear and simple. A girl could manage it, as the rules would be set in advance and the price of money from the Fed would also be set in advance.

"There would be none of the mystery and speculation which today constantly surround the actions and policies of the Fed. There would be none of the stories in the *Wall Street Journal* and *The New York Times.* There would simply be a report of a price or an interest rate at which the Fed would lend. And that would be that.

"Today, by contrast, there is always speculation and discussion. People are mystified as to what the Fed is up to. We metaphorically slaughter sheep and look into their entrails to discover what the Fed is thinking. The Fed seems very important. They get a lot of attention.

"Under the two systems, the position of the Fed bureaucrats is simply radically different. The Fed bureaucrats are only human. That is why they cling to the old system."

This preoccupation with the day-to-day movements of bond prices has led to the phenomenon known as the myopia of the Fed. Before going on to discuss that in more detail, I want to digress to discuss the decision by the Treasury under Donald Regan and Beryl Sprinkel to abandon intervention in the foreign exchange markets.

The Abandonment of the Management of Foreign Operations

As stated previously, the New York Federal Reserve Bank used to conduct foreign exchange operations for the U.S. Treasury. Under U.S. law, the United States Treasury has the responsibility for any intervention by U.S. officials in the foreign exchange markets. In the years before 1981 the New York Fed used to carry out vast operations in the buying and selling of foreign currencies, just as it still carries out vast buying and selling operations in the domestic U.S. Securities Market. These operations were generally aimed at "stabilizing" the market for the U.S. dollar and "stabilizing" its value in relation to other currencies. A multitude of schemes and stunts were invented, including huge "currency swaps," which were in effect arrangements between the Federal Reserve and the central banks and governments of other countries to advance each other quantities of their currencies as part of a worldwide attempt to "modify" movements in currencies. These operations were on a vast scale, and they were, in principle, little different from the daily open market operations which the Fed still carries out in *domestic* securities.

Upon the election of President Reagan, a decision was taken in the U.S. Treasury not to intervene any longer in foreign exchange markets. It was possible for the U.S. Treasury to make this decision because it had the legal authority to cease all foreign exchange intervention, whereas it does *not* have the legal power to cease all *domestic* market intervention in securities markets.

In Beryl Sprinkel's office at the Treasury in Washington, there is a telephone on a little table behind his desk. When he first came to his new job in Washington, as under secretary for monetary affairs in early 1981, the phone used to ring each morning. On the other end of the phone would be an officer of the New York Fed, asking for his daily instructions on what buying and selling he should engage in, to pursue the Treasury's aims in the foreign exchange markets. (For example, should he buy D-Marks, sell sterling, buy francs, etc.?) In answer to the question from the New York Fed: "What do you want us to do today in the foreign exchange markets?" Sprinkel would reply, "Nothing." "After a while," said Sprinkel, "they stopped phoning."

So ended a massive operation that had been going on for years, U.S. government intervention in the foreign exchange markets of the world. Sprinkel's reasoning was simple: free markets give the most efficient result in the allocation of resources. We in the Reagan administration believe in free markets. Therefore, there must be no intervention in the foreign exchange markets to try to twist and turn foreign exchange prices out of line.

The policy of nonintervention has produced a rise in the dollar such as has not been seen for over a decade. The importance of the policy decision is that it reflects what the Reagan team, through Donald Regan and Beryl Sprinkel, would likely do with the Federal Reserve's *domestic* operations if and when they are given the authority to do so. As clearly stated in the *Economic Report of the President, February 1982,* they would like to impose a constant monetary standard and abandon all open market operations by the Fed.

Needless to say, the nonintervention policy in foreign exchange has been roundly criticized, not least by foreign central banks which find that their *own* attempts to manipulate currency markets are being frustrated because under President Reagan, the United States "won't play."

By early 1982 the rise in the dollar and the policy of nonintervention by the U.S. Treasury had prompted a public denunciation of U.S. policy by the chancellor of the exchequer in Britain, the French prime minister, the West German chancellor, and the prime minister of Belgium.

Beryl Sprinkel gave an explanation of this contentious but reforming "noninterventionist" (or, perhaps better, "market-dominated") foreign exchange policy on February 1, 1982, in an address to the Reserve City Bankers of New York. In a rousing justification of the policy, Sprinkel went on to criticize the complaints from Europeans:

> In the international area, our views are clear and well known. We are resolved not to intervene in exchange markets except under extraordinary circumstances. We have come under criticism from some of our foreign friends—particularly in Europe—for pursuing what they call a policy of "benign neglect."
>
> By allowing the dollar to rise last year [1981] without any countervailing intervention, some believed we were forcing up interest rates in other countries and hurting their economies. And we have on occasion been branded as callous and insensitive to our economic trading partners.
>
> Now there are several problems with this view. First, it does not completely square with the facts. Occasionally, market participants have cited interest rate movements as the main factor in their assessment of exchange rates. But more often there has been no correlation between exchange rate movements and changes in interest rates differentials. Secondly—once again getting to basics—there is an inherent efficiency in free and open exchange market operations, and "concocted" government buying and selling of currencies inhibits that built-in efficiency.
>
> Exchange markets are large and complex, and the underlying relationships which determine exchange rates are not so clearly defined that any individual or government can tell you ahead of time what the exchange rate should be. And if they do tell you, they are almost certain to be wrong. When governments intervene in exchange markets they are just as likely to be guessing wrong on a very grand scale—throwing confusing

signals into the markets and wasting public funds. The facts show that despite the billions of dollars governments have spent to intervene in foreign exchange markets, they have never been able to affect the long-term equilibrium or direction of rates. So, fundamentally, we believe that intervention to fix or manage exchange rates is doomed to failure and will continue to be a waste of money.

The Fed and the Bond Dealers—A Cozy Club

It is clear that the withdrawal by the U.S. Treasury from all intervention in the foreign exchange markets has not resulted in a catastrophe. Rather, the dollar grew very much stronger in 1981, the first year of the operation of free markets. There may have been some disappointed people, notably the foreign exchange dealers who were previously often able to "stick it to the Fed," as the Fed was slower and generally frightened of making too sudden moves.

In the domestic open market operations of the Fed, the central bank has taken strong steps over the years to ensure that "stable market conditions" apply in the bond markets. Acting with its nose to the ground, the Fed has been unable to gain a perspective on the whole monetary scene. Preoccupied with a mass of day-to-day dealings, aimed at "stabilizing" securities markets, the Fed has failed to look to control of the monetary aggregates. Instead, there has been a crippling preoccupation with "moderating" movements in interest rates as typified by the federal funds rate. Over the years the Fed has always hit its interest rate targets but has hardly ever hit its money growth targets. This is because, as a monopolist, the Fed cannot control both the price of money (as represented by the level of interest rates) *and* the quantity of money (as represented by M1) *at the same time.* No monopolist can control both the price of sales and the quantity of sales *at the same time.* Think of the attempt by OPEC to control the world oil markets. It had to accept, as a condition of its attempt to control the *price* of oil, that it would have to restrict the *quantity* of oil it sold. Similarly, the Federal Reserve cannot control both interest rates (the price of money) *and* M1 (the quantity of money) at the same time.

Over the years—until October 6, 1979, at least—the Fed devoted its efforts primarily to controlling the rate of interest. Look at the charts below and on page 213.

Over the years, the Fed was trying to control the price of credit —the rate of interest—by changing the quantity of money. It necessarily ended up by controlling neither. It is possible for the Fed to peg the interest rate for brief periods of time, but this leads to subsequent changes in the quantity of money that undermine and

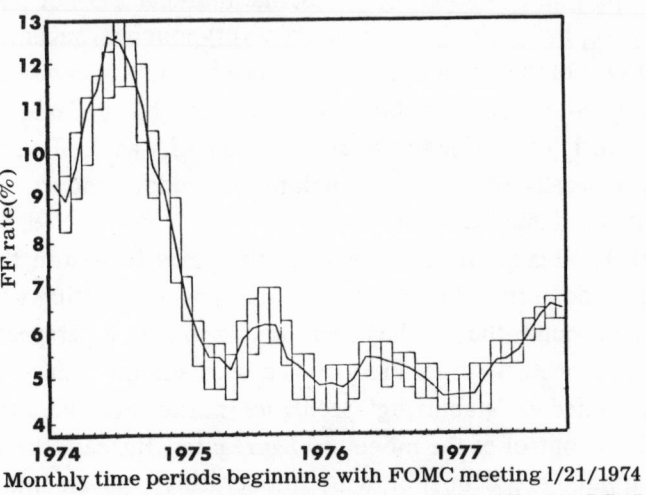

Monthly time periods beginning with FOMC meeting 1/21/1974

Source: Professor J.L. Pierce, "Congressional Supervision of Monetary Policy"

The vertical bars indicate the permitted range in which the federal funds rate was allowed to fluctuate between January 12, 1974, and the end of 1977.

The black line represents the average value of the federal funds rate for the month concerned.

As can be seen, the Federal Reserve had no trouble meeting its self-imposed "target" for the funds rate over these years. It even sharply narrowed the range of permitted variation in April 1976 and still hit its interest rate target.

Of course, hitting the interest rate target meant not hitting the money growth target, and this in turn meant massive excess growth of money and led to the inflation of 1976-1980, during which time the whole attempt to hold down the federal funds rate ended in collapse and disaster in October 1979, preceded by the departure of G. William Miller as chairman of the Fed in August 1979.

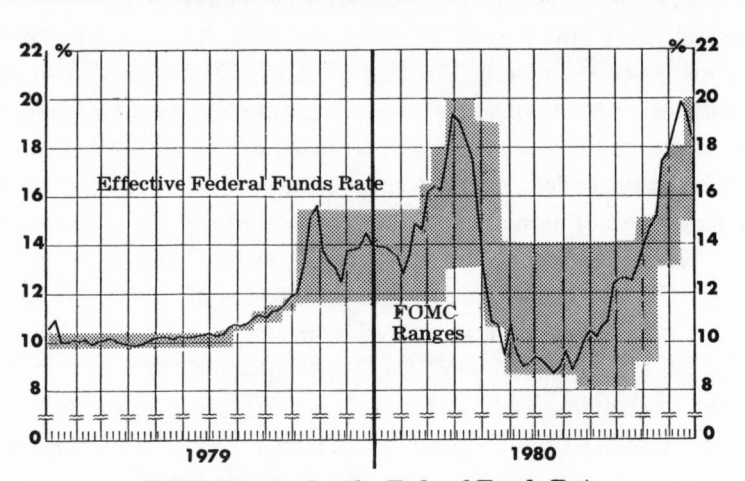

FOMC Ranges for the Federal Funds Rate

NOTE: Rates are calculated as weekly averages of effective daily rates. At each meeting the Committee specified a range for the federal funds rate. These ranges are indicated for the first full week during which they were in effect.   **Source: Federal Reserve Bank of St. Louis**

The chart shows the great widening of the "permitted range" of movement of the federal funds rate which was authorized by the Federal Open Market Committee of the Federal Reserve, following the collapse of October 1979 and the accompanying crisis of monetary policy.

Upon the widening of the permitted range of variation of the federal funds rate, all interest rates boomed upward. During the March quarter 1980 a further crisis occurred with the imposition of credit controls as a panicky measure to try to repair the damage of the previous four years of interest rate "narrow band" targeting and consequential inflationary money growth.

It was only with the collapse of inflationary expectations following the negative growth of money supply between November 1979 and April 1980 that interest rates also collapsed. They rose even more sharply during the second half of 1980, in tune with the rise in money supply of that period. Note that during the whole of the period shown, there was hardly an occasion in which the federal funds rate fell outside the "permitted band" laid down by the Federal Open Market Committee of the Federal Reserve.

The Federal Reserve still cannot make up its mind whether to target interest rates or money growth.

overturn the pegged interest rates. The greater the intervention, the greater the destabilization of interest rates and of the entire economy as well.

This attempt to control the rate of interest developed naturally from two factors. First, the Fed believed (and believes) that the level of interest rates "indicated" what the state of the money markets was. This is not surprising. The Fed Desk officer is deeply involved every day of his life in dealings in government securities. He is under orders from the FOMC as to the "permitted range" of interest rates. He is also riding orders, over the course of a month, quarter, or year, as to the growth of money that he is supposed to achieve. This target growth for money is specified in general terms. There is a range. Thus, for 1982, the target growth range for M1 is 2½ to 5½ percent; for M2 it is 6 to 9 percent, measured from the average of the fourth quarter 1981 to the average of the fourth quarter 1982.

As the Desk officer looks at his work each day, he necessarily gives top priority to meeting his interest rate target. That is something he *can do* on a day-to-day basis, and it is something that sticks out very clearly every day if it is *not* achieved. What is more, he is involved in an incessant pattern of communication with the big securities dealers (listed on page 203). If he starts allowing interest rates to fluctuate all over the place, there will be complaints as well as cries for help from the bond dealers. So he is always under pressure to "smooth out" interest rate fluctuations.

As can be seen from the charts on pages 212 and 213, the Desk officer over the years has been *very successful* in meeting the interest rate targets laid down by the FOMC. For years, up to October 1979, these targets were defined in *very narrow ranges.* This was an indication by the FOMC that it wanted to "stabilize" the money markets. The Federal Open Market Committee thought that by narrowly confining the movements in the rate of interest it was "moderating" the money markets. Of course, it was doing nothing of the sort. There was a missing element in its thinking. *That was the demand for money.*

There was another missing element. That was the growing fear of inflation, which gradually came to dominate thinking among the mass of participants in the financial markets of America.

Not only the United States, but the whole world economy is now paying a very high price for the failure of the Fed over the years up to October 6, 1979, to give *any sort of priority* to controlling the growth of money. Totally preoccupied with controlling the *price* of money, the Fed necessarily had to leave the *quantity* of money to be determined by other factors. In fact, the growth of money emerged as a sort of *random residual,* the result of the working out of the multitude of market forces operating against a *fixed price* for money.

The chart below shows the violence of the fluctuations in the growth of money in recent years. Compare this chart, with its wild swings, with the charts on pages 212 and 213, showing the much more controlled movements in the rate of interest. After October 6, 1979, by which time monetary control was fast collapsing entirely, Paul Volcker as chairman of the Fed announced there would be wider swings permitted in the rate of interest, as a means of bringing some measure of control to the growth in the quantity of money. Because interest rates would be allowed to fluctuate more freely, this would permit more concentration on the control of the supply of money. As the *price* of money could move more freely, its *quantity*

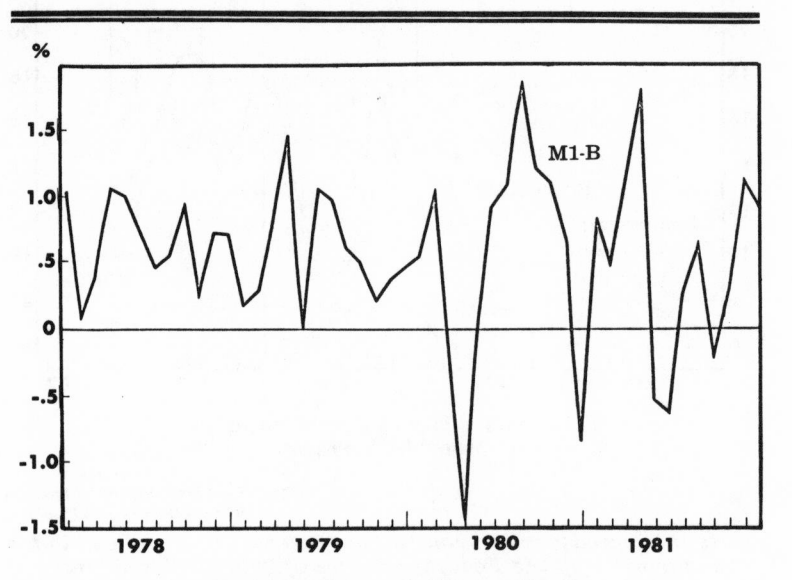

Monthly Change in Money Supply

There has been increasingly violent instability in the rate of growth of money in the last three years.

Although this provides a headache for those responsible for monetary and general economic policy, it also provides immense opportunities for profit for those who deal in the money markets. Profiting from instability is a major industry in American financial markets these days.

could be more closely controlled. Unfortunately the Federal Open Market Committee has undergone only a halfhearted conversion to the idea of giving control over the quantity of money pride of place. As a result, we have had the worst of both worlds. We have had violent fluctuations in the rate of interest *and* violent fluctuations in the growth of money. The consequence has been the destruction of the *raison d'être* of the Fed—namely, stability in the value of the dollar, in interest rates, and in money growth.

The Fed has been trying to do the impossible. It has been trying to control both the price and the quantity of money at the same time. It cannot be done.

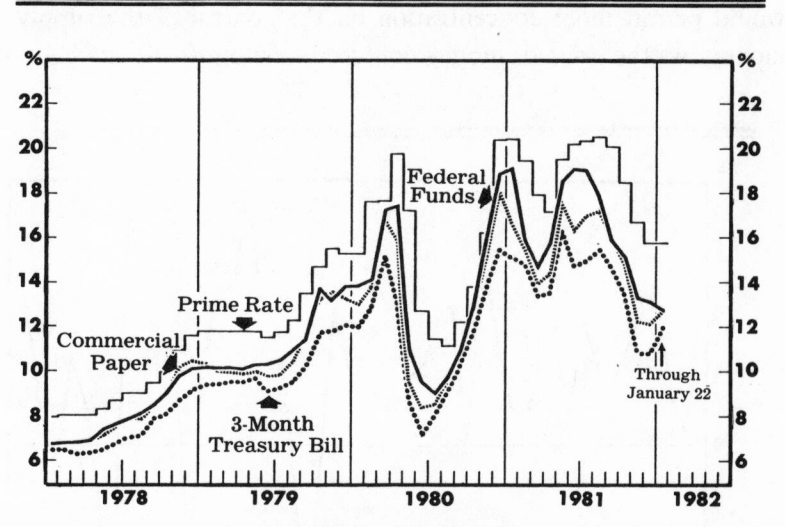

Short-Term Interest Rates
Monthly Averages

Source: U.S. Treasury
January 26, 1982-6
Office of the Secretary of the Treasury
Office of Government Financing

Note the increase in the volatility of interest rates following the abandonment by the Federal Reserve of "narrow band" interest rate targeting on the federal funds rate in October 1979. Note the big jump in all rates when the Fed took the lid off the federal funds rate at that time. The attempt to hold down the funds rate during 1976, 1977, 1978, and 1979 set off a huge inflationary boom.

Since October 1979, interest rates have been much more volatile, as the Fed has not known how to handle the new situation. It has failed to achieve control of either money or interest rates, thus giving us the worst of both worlds.

The chart on page 216 shows how wild the swings in interest rates have become. The Fed attempts from time to time to put a lock on interest rate movements. It tried this in the nine weeks ended January 25, 1982, when it strictly confined the federal funds rate into a range of 12½ percent plus or minus ½ of 1 percent. This attempt simply resulted in an explosion of money growth during December 1981 and January 1982.

Just as intervention in the foreign exchange markets finally was abandoned as a futile attempt to manipulate the markets in foreign currencies, so one must conclude that the attempt to intervene in the fixed interest securities markets of America (the markets for bonds —public and private—and bills) has been a terrible failure. The markets themselves are now in utter turmoil. And there is a complete loss of public confidence in the Federal Reserve as the manager of this market.

Volcker Gets His Chance

It was Paul Volcker's misfortune—but in the longer view also his great opportunity—that he came to power at the Fed in August 1979, at the very time when all the long-established theories and myths, practices and policies were under challenge. It was a time when the deep-seated conviction that inflation was to be a *permanent* factor of American life had finally caused a revolt by lenders. Real (inflation-adjusted) interest rates became positive under Volcker, and the consequences of this profound change were to bring about a reversal of attitudes by individuals and corporations to the allocation of their money.

Real assets—gold, real estate, antiques, commodities, houses— which had been the darlings of investors in the Age of Inflation, were progressively thrown into the discard. The price of gold fell from $700 an ounce in late 1980 to little more than $300 by March 1982. With the advent of positive real rates of interest, the attraction of real assets sharply declined and the attraction of financial assets—bonds, bills, certificates of deposit, and even some stocks—sharply increased.

Volcker came to power at the Fed about the time of the "second oil shock" in 1979, when OPEC raised the price of oil from $14 to

$28 a barrel virtually overnight, but by 1982 it was clear that this second oil shock was the last gasp of a massive revaluation of energy prices during the 1970's and would be succeeded in the 1980's by a worldwide energy glut. He came to power when the dollar was experiencing the last shakeout in its declining value, which had been taking place since Johnson first started the retreat from a gold limit on America's money in the mid-1960's.

By the second year of his term at the Fed, Volcker could look at a world in which the dollar was strong; in which energy prices were weakening drastically and the power of OPEC was fading fast; in which the "gold fever" of the 1970's was fast becoming passé, with the weakness of the world price of gold; in which the once-mighty De Beers diamond cartel had to fight for its life to prevent a total crash in diamond prices; in which American corporations, sated with debt, began to realize they would have to fight for their lives to remain solvent; in which major corporations would be able to survive only by making deals with employees and unions to backtrack on the outrageously generous wage contracts that had seemed so easy to finance in the early days of the inflationary boom, in the late 1960's and the early 1970's.

Volcker, in other words, was heir to the World of Disinflation. Nicocles Michas and Henry Wojtyla, the two brilliant economic strategists working for the Wall Street brokerage firm of Rosenkrantz, Ehrenkrantz, Lyon & Ross, characterized the sea change that occurred about 1980 as the downswing of the fifth "Kondratieff cycle," after the famous Russian economist Kondratieff, who identified and plotted long waves of economic activity in the advanced economies of the world. Michas and Wojtyla said that the current —fifth—Kondratieff wave began its upswing about 1965 and culminated in the inflationary boom of the 1970's. By 1980 the upswing had led to pervasive inflationary expectations and dislocations in the economy which complicated the transition to the downswing phase in the 1980's and aggravated the long contraction of economic activity that began about 1978 and was still in process during 1982—what I have called the Age of Recession.

To put the issue in perspective (see chart, page 219), the third Kondratieff wave began its upswing about 1900, reached its peak

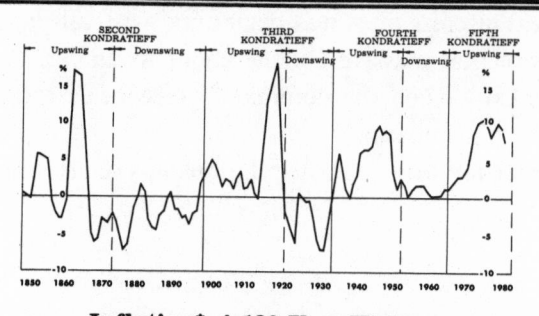

Inflation* A 130-Year History

*Producer Price Index; Five-year moving average.

Source: **Rosenkrantz, Ehrenkrantz,**
Lyon & Ross

This very evocative chart, prepared by Nicocles Michas and Henry Wojtyla (see text) plots the last three and a half Kondratieff cycles — the "long waves" of economic history. The chart shows the major inflationary booms in America in the Civil War (second Kondratieff), the First World War (third Kondratieff), and Second World War (fourth Kondratieff), and the Johnson-Nixon-Carter peacetime inflationary boom (the only peacetime inflation of significance in the last 130 years of U.S. history).

about 1920 and its bottom about 1930. The fourth Kondratieff wave began about 1930, reached its peak about 1946 and its bottom about 1965. Then the next upswing of the fifth Kondratieff cycle began to reach its peak about 1980.

Built into the upswing of this fifth Kondratieff cycle was a progressively stronger belief among the mass of the population in the pervasiveness and permanence of inflation. This attitude, reinforced by the events which occurred, notably the grossly excessive creation of money which fueled the inflationary boom, led to a commitment to real assets. Despite all the efforts of the major Western governments, gold could not be debased or dispensed with. On the contrary, the price of gold, which had been held at $35 per ounce since 1934 (it had been held at about $20 an ounce since 1914, before that), rose between 1970 and 1974 to $160 an ounce, fell back to about $125 by 1977, and then boomed up to over $700 an ounce in 1980 and then back down to about $450 an ounce in 1981, on average. By 1982 the gold price had really started to subside and interest in gold was evaporating, as the realization spread that a new World of Disinflation was on the way (under disinflation the rate of growth of prices declines; under deflation prices actually fall, on average).

Paul Volcker took over in August 1979 at the Fed as the transition to positive real interest rates was beginning, with all the portentous connotations of that massive change about to unfold. Positive real interest rates exist when the nominal or face value rate of interest exceeds the rate of inflation.

The following table sets out the relationships of prices and interest rates.

Period	Average Annual Increase in Consumer Prices	Average 90-day Treasury Bill Rate	Average 20-year Bond Rate
1960–1970	2.7%	4.6%	4.9%
1970–1980	8.6	6.8	8.0
1979	11.3	10.0	9.4
1980	13.5	11.5	11.5
1981	9.3	14.1	14.4
1982 (Three months ended January, seasonally adjusted annual rate)	5.0	11.5	14.1

During the 1960's, as the table shows, there was a positive real interest rate of about 2 percent. (The nominal rate—about 5 percent —excluded the rate of inflation of about 2½–3 percent.) During the 1970's there was a *negative* real rate of interest.

As the table above shows, in the three months to January 1982 the real rate of interest (meaning for all practical purposes the difference between the rate of price inflation and the nominal interest rates charged in the markets) had risen to a range of 6½ to 9 percent, rates unknown in the peacetime experience of the United States.

Corporate treasurers were slow to react to this enormous rise in the real cost of credit. During 1981, faced with recessionary conditions, declining profitability, excessive inventories, and a grave shortage of available long-term loans, they continued to amass a huge burden of short-term debt. There was, in fact, a stampede into short-term borrowing by American corporations during 1981. This was a very dangerous development that was accompanied by a rapid growth of business failures (and of personal bankruptcies). In the opening months of 1982 business failures were up almost 55 percent over a year earlier.

Corporations by the end of 1981 were paying an enormously enhanced proportion of their profits in interest. Between 1975 and 1981 corporate interest expense in America rose 45 percent while earnings before interest and taxes rose only 12 percent. Interest amounted to 46.6 percent of retained earnings plus interest in 1981, and if adjustments were made to retained earnings to account for inventory profits and underdepreciation of capital equipment, interest costs jumped to 65 percent of the return to capital. In the fourth quarter of 1981, earnings of American corporations before interest and taxes fell by 24 percent at an annual rate, as a consequence of the recession. At the same time, interest costs continued to climb by 10 percent at an annual rate. As a result, interest claimed over half of retained earnings plus interest in the fourth quarter of 1981 and nearly three quarters of adjusted earnings plus interest. These were very dangerous indicators of trouble for corporate America, the climax of the long period of declining faith in the value of money.

For individuals, the difficulties were no less daunting. The very high real rates of interest acted as a powerful deterrent to borrowing. Consequently, there was an evaporation of demand for consumer durable goods such as cars and for housing. Individuals took steps to cut back not only on their current rate of borrowing but also on their total outstanding loans, which started to decline in late 1981.

The failure of the ordinary family's biggest asset—its home—to continue to appreciate in value was another big shock for millions of American families. During the 1970's the price of existing homes in America had appreciated strongly; in many years the annual rate of appreciation in the current prices of existing homes was as high as 15 to 20 percent. This appreciation in the value of its home provided a big cushion of available borrowing power to the average American family. Many took advantage of this by taking out loans based on the inflationary appreciation of the value of the family home. This in turn provided millions of American families with a bonus of purchasing power during the 1970's. But with the arrival of high real interest rates it became clear this was not going to continue. During the closing months of 1981 the average price of existing homes in America was only about 4½ percent greater than a year previously, indicating a *decline* in the real (inflation-adjusted) value of the family home. What is more, the Reagan tax reforms had reduced the proportionate tax savings that could be made by deducting interest on borrowings. Hence, there was suddenly a total reversal of all the incentives to borrowing which applied during the 1970's and a very powerful stimulus to saving.

Volcker Inherits a Storm

Volcker became chairman of the Fed when these massive forces operating in the financial markets and in the American economy generally were beginning to make themselves felt. They were the effects of a sea change in the attitudes of Americans to the future value of money. And they resulted from a demand for *more than adequate* protection against inflation by the lenders who had been robbed in the decade of the 1970's.

Paul Volcker thus came to power at the Fed at a moment when many deep-seated convictions were under challenge. He began by instituting a series of alleged reforms of the Fed's operating procedures. These "reforms"—notably the decision to abandon tight interest rate targeting—did little to bring about the promised stability of money growth and of interest rates, as we have seen.

It was not hard to write Volcker off as yet another Fed official who would talk about reform but do nothing. Both publicly and privately he had played an important role in the international monetary crises that formed a constant backdrop to the Nixon economic policy. Volcker was associated with the "hard-line," tough nationalist U.S. policies typified by John Connally, Treasury secretary from February 1971 to May 1972. Volcker was a strong advocate of the emasculation of gold and the institution of the Special Drawing Rights of the International Monetary Fund. In 1971 he had been a strong defender of the status quo, arguing, in the face of the deteriorating American balance of payments position, that the situation could be met by limited mandatory capital controls and "an international open market operation" in the Eurodollar markets. He was obliged to accept the December 1971 collapse of all these efforts and the institution of a devaluation of the dollar through the so-called Smithsonian Agreements. But he continued as a strong opponent of gold and argued continually for the diminution of the role of gold as a reserve asset. Volcker was also right at the center of the next devaluation of the dollar which took place in February 1973. He had vigorously opposed floating exchange rates, having been a supporter of fixed exchange rates and the abolition of gold as a reserve.

But in March 1973 the system of fixed exchange rates which had been set up after the Second World War—the so-called Bretton Woods system—finally collapsed and was replaced with a system of floating currencies. In June 1973 Volcker stated his satisfaction with the new floating rates system before the Joint Economic Committee of Congress.

He had thus been a powerful advocate for a system of fixed exchange rates, for the abolition of gold as a reserve for international payments, and for controls on the international movement of capital. In domestic policy he was one of the important officials who helped in the preparation of Nixon's August 1971 New Economic Policy, which also abandoned many aspects of the free market in domestic policy. In other words, Volcker's whole background and experience were very unpromising.

"Volcker Could Be the Tiger"—Weintraub

Robert Weintraub was surprisingly optimistic about the possibility of Volcker's succeeding at the Fed. I say surprising because Volcker's record is not one that would have been expected to appeal to such a pioneer in monitoring and criticizing the Fed as Bob Weintraub. Nevertheless, when I interviewed him in October 1981, Weintraub said: "He could turn out to be the tiger [to force the Fed bureaucracy to change]. It's going to take a very strong chairman to bring them around. The bureaucracy's whole inertial movement is to continue what has been going on at the Fed for the past sixty-plus years. This is really the 'real bills' doctrine of John Stuart Mill dressed up in new clothing. That doctrine stated that banks should only make self-liquidating loans. That brings you later on to focus on 'free reserves.' And that brings you to focus on short-term interest rates. Winfield, Burgess, and Riefler established those doctrines. They were the high staff people of the Federal Reserve Board in the early days, back in the twenties. They set the tone for the whole of the Federal Reserve's technical apparatus, how it would move and so forth. If you were going to get along in the bureaucracy, you were going to have to go along with those fellows. They didn't promote people who had different ideas. That's true even today. Their successors have essentially brought up through the ranks those people who were prepared to think along the established lines. Now we have lots of them on the Board of Governors—Gramley, Partee, Nancy Teeters, Emmett Rice are all people with Federal Reserve experience.

"Now as to what should be done, there is no question about whether they can control money. They can do it better if they change from lagged reserves to contemporaneous reserves or to the system of advanced reserve accounting. But there is no question that you can do it, no matter how clumsily. But that is a second order question.

"Now you have to ask yourself, What about the chairman and about the attitude of the other governors and of the staff in terms of whether they are inclined to bring money growth down.

"And here I must say I am very suspect of everybody down there, but more of everybody excepting Wallich and Volcker. These boys may finally understand that you have to bring money under control. The others will tell you that you have to do it. But telling you doesn't mean anything.

"Volcker makes better noises in this direction than anybody. He says more often than most people that inflation is a monetary phenomenon and we've got to bring it down. He will also say, and rightfully, that it would help if we had a better fiscal policy.

"I think one reason for the attitude of Fed officials toward inflation —their attitude that it is not an important problem—is due to the effects over time on thinking of the terrible experience of the Great Depression of the 1930's. It colored a lot of thinking about what is right for the world. The Fed basically has a bureaucracy that is more terrified of unemployment than it is of inflation. And it has myopia. That is, it cannot look out beyond more than a year or so. This is because if you look out beyond a year or so, you cannot choose between unemployment and inflation. After a year or so, you're going to get unemployment *as a result* of inflation [my italics].

"So you might as well aim at zero inflation. And so we get this combination of people who are terrified of the short run and who are terrified of unemployment, who don't think there is any cost to inflation and who don't think in terms of the nation's history. This problem extends right up to the Federal Reserve Board, which is stacked with people who are either immersed in this sort of thinking, this sort of Federal Reserve philosophy, which is really a liberal philosophy; or else they are people who come to the Federal Reserve Board without any real competence to do the monetary policy job that has to be done and thence they become prisoners of the philosophy.

"Now to break that, you've got to get someone up there who simply says: 'Now what we have to do is to aim money growth towards the rate which will provide a long-run rate of inflation of zero. And we ought to get there as fast as possible and then stay there.' In the present situation, in my opinion, Volcker is the key person.

"This is because, although the President may have nerves of steel, these nerves of steel will turn to jelly if Volcker is telling him we can safely reverse course, or should reverse, because things are getting out of hand on the downside. So Volcker becomes a terribly important person, just as has been any Fed chairman, because they are going to have access to the President.

"There is also the problem that on the Federal Reserve Board there is unquestionably a majority of former Fed officials who would tend to direct policy away from the tough stance. That brings up the question of how these officials were appointed to the Fed. I would say that Partee was appointed because Burns wanted him appointed. He was appointed during the Ford administration. I would wager Gramley was appointed because Charlie Schultze [chairman of the Council of Economic Advisers under President Carter] wanted him appointed. Gramley did, too. He worked for Charlie Schultze over at the Council of Economic Advisers. I think Nancy Teeters was appointed because they were looking for a woman and she was very acceptable to them. Rice was appointed because they were looking for a black and he too fit the mold of someone the Federal Reserve

was very familiar with. Volcker got appointed because he was someone who was satisfactory to the foreign central banks and the banking community. And also he was not unacceptable to the Fed.

"I am not so pessimistic that I think he could fail. I think he could
turn out to be the tiger."

There are others who are less optimistic, seeing in Volcker really
the archetype of the Fed official, the lifelong bureaucrat who is more
a captive of the Federal Reserve System and its traditions than any
chairman since the Second World War. Professor David Meiselman,
professor of economics at Virginia Polytechnic Institute and a leading monetarist economist, worked with Volcker at the Treasury. He
has worked as a consultant to the U.S. Treasury under Beryl Sprinkel. Meiselman said in an interview with me: "Paul Volcker has been
loyal to the Fed throughout his career. He has been in and out of the
Fed for almost thirty years, alternating between the Fed and Chase
Manhattan and the Fed and the Treasury.

"He is a product of the Fed and, it seems to me, represents the kind
of person who devotes his career to the System and whom, in turn,
the System rewards and promotes.

"My impression of Volcker is that he essentially administers
rather than initiates policy. He is very good at carrying out orders.
He is an outstanding advocate, the consummate bureaucrat. I believe
that these administrative characteristics are the main features of his
years in the government, rather than any consistent set of policies
and goals or any systematic point of view of how the economy
operates.

"In fact, Volcker has been intimately involved on the opposite
sides of many important issues, usually representing the conven-
tional wisdom of the moment. He often shifted from promoting one
side of an issue to supporting the very opposite side—but he always
supports the Fed as an institution. When he first came to the Treasury in the early 1960's during the Kennedy administration, he was
a staunch supporter of the thirty-five-dollar price for gold and for the
system of fixed exchange rates, which were later abandoned.

"He was instrumental in the imposition of the interest equalization
tax, a crude and costly set of controls on capital movements intended
to support fixed exchange rates by restricting the flow of U.S. capital

abroad and increasing the cost to foreigners of borrowing in the U.S. capital markets. That, too, was a costly failure and was abandoned.

"When Volcker returned to the Treasury in 1969, after the election of Richard Nixon, after he had spent several years back at the Chase, he was appointed under secretary for monetary affairs. The U.S. was still fighting to hold on to the system of fixed exchange rates, which was then described as 'defending the dollar.' The U.S. finally gave up on fixed exchange rates, let the price of gold rise above the former thirty-five-dollar price, and went on to a dirty float of the dollar and the Smithsonian Agreements, and finally moved to a more or less clean float.

"He seems to have carried off all of these changes of policy with great aplomb, never being tarred with the responsibility for the flawed or failed policies.

"As far as I know, he was rarely out front on anything. Whatever the status quo happened to be, Volcker seemed to be defending it. It was only when existing policy was overwhelmed by events that policy would change. There was no anticipation of danger or appreciation of the flaws in existing arrangements and policies. There were few if any preparations for changes in a given set of arrangements.

"When I heard that Volcker was going to become chairman of the Fed, I thought of the Paul Volcker I had worked for in Washington and whose career I had followed.

"I knew little of what Volcker had done in the period he had been president of the New York Fed, so I phoned several people I knew at the New York Fed to inquire whether Volcker had changed. Every person I spoke to said that there was no change. Each person volunteered that Volcker still went along, that in his votes on the Open Market Committee he almost never voted against the majority and that he primarily acted as if he were carrying out orders.

"I came to the Treasury from the University of Chicago in 1962. At that time, Volcker was head of the Office of Financial Analysis, and he reported to or worked for Bob Roosa, who was then under secretary of the Treasury for monetary affairs. [Robert V. Roosa, under secretary of the Treasury for monetary affairs, 1961–1964.] I was an academic and I had come to the Treasury with the idea that I would, and could, apply my research skills to analyzing the technical issues that frequently, but not always, lie at the heart of many public policy issues. That was not how Volcker saw things or the role of rigorous analysis. Volcker seemed to feel that academics as a group were malleable and not particularly trustworthy and that they could easily come to just about any conclusion. He tended to be generally contemptuous of the professionalism and sense of objectivity and analytical integrity whereby serious economists would arrive at conclusions based on the evidence or the analytical merits of the case.

"In Volcker's way of thinking and doing, first there is a given position and then you find reasons to support it. For example, before I came to the Treasury, I had done some very important, pioneering work on the term structure of interest rates. The work was widely acclaimed and won a big prize. The research had very important implications for managing the national debt, but even though Volcker was sympathetic to my analysis he would not let me work on any debt management problems.

"The reason was that I had already reached some conclusions based on my research and that these findings had been published. In his view, therefore, I was not a free person. It was not safe for me to work on debt management in the Treasury because I had already come to a conclusion and was therefore committed. People who were working on debt management would come up to my office late in the day to discuss debt management issues. But Volcker would not let me work formally in the area, or have anything to do with it.

"In his eyes, I had already come to a conclusion about what should be done, based on the analysis I had done. In his way of thinking, you take a position on an issue for a number of reasons but usually for some political purpose. He may never have understood the alternative point of view then, and he may not understand it now. In his view you might also take a position because you are getting heat or because it's necessary for some other reason.

"Once you take a position, you marshal everything to defend it. This is precisely what a consummate bureaucrat, who is myopic, or a politician would do. And so that's why he has been on both sides of every important issue and that's why he slides from one side to the other. He would hardly ever vote against the chairman of the Fed or against the majority. He would go along.

"So my interpretation of Paul Volcker is that he will take orders. This is because he does not meet issues head-on. So if they put pressure on him I would predict he will cave [in]. I think that may be the major protection the public has right now. If the Reagan administration wants slow money, that will be his marching order.

"Under Jimmy Carter, when Volcker was chairman of the Fed, he also gave them what they wanted. The changes in policy procedures of October 6, 1979, were just a cover to permit a shift to another policy. By that time the Carter administration had become panicked because of double-digit inflation. Interest rates were soaring, and they didn't know what to do. The October 1979 changes were largely cosmetic. They did help, however, because they did permit some shift in attention away from interest rate targets. The Fed and the administration knew that the money supply mechanism was out of control, and so something had to be done. They knew in the last half of 1979 that the money supply was out of control and that they had to take measures which would inevitably lead to a big rise in interest rates.

"So they announced a change in their policy procedures and said, 'Well, we don't control interest rates. We don't have anything to do with interest rates. The market determines interest rates.' They used that bureaucratic fiction. But of course, they do have interest rate targets. This is in the directives of the Federal Open Market Committee. And they hit those targets. They don't miss the interest rate targets. They miss the money growth targets. If occasionally they do for some reason hit the money targets, it is an accident. If there is a conflict between the two, they will always choose the federal funds rate target. They can't control both."

Volcker's Term Has Seen Money Growth Decline—On Average

Under Volcker, there has been a decline in the *average* rate of growth of money. And Volcker keeps on *saying* he intends to reach the Federal Reserve's publicly announced targets. In 1980 he managed to get within shooting range of his annual target by suddenly restricting money growth in the closing few weeks of the year. That is, from the middle of the year to November there was an enormous splurge of money growth. Then in December 1980 there was a sharp restriction on money growth, and Volcker figuratively just ducked under the fence in time. In 1981 he overrestricted money growth for the long period in the middle of the year from April through October, and then in November and December he furiously stoked up money growth and avoided the embarrassment in that year of a major *under*shoot of his target growth for money.

In 1977 money (M1-B) had risen 7.7 percent; in 1978, 8.2 percent; and in 1979, 7.8 percent. Then in 1980, Volcker's first year, money rose 6.3 percent, in 1981 by a further 6.5 percent, and in the first seven months of 1982 at a rate of just over 4 percent. This was a substantial improvement; that cannot be denied. The deceleration in money growth contributed substantially to the movement to a much reduced rate of inflation in 1981 and on into 1982. But the great variability of the pattern of money growth under Volcker necessarily caused fears that the Fed was only managing to control money growth at all by a process of blind luck.

These fears were further underlined by the insistence of Volcker that the control of money growth was made much more difficult by the existence of the Reagan budget deficits. This totally unconvincing argument, lacking any basis in factual recording or analysis, necessarily aroused the suspicion that Volcker was looking for an excuse. The fears were further underlined by the evident reluctance of the Federal Reserve to change any of its traditional operating procedures.

Volcker had made a few halting steps in the direction of improving the control over money growth, *on average.* But his reign at the Fed had been noted for a major increase in violence of the movements in the money stock and in interest rates.

And in the background there was a growing fear among the participants in the financial markets that the overloaded debt structure of corporate America would, combined with the high real interest rates prevailing at the time, produce a form of financial collapse, involving the collapse of major corporations and a form of financial panic in the money markets of the nation. Volcker inherited the results of fifteen years of neglect and wrong policies in money management. Early in 1982 he looked as if he could still turn out to be the chairman of the Fed who would preside over the final disintegration of the Fed's "independence." He looked as if he could ultimately be overwhelmed by the force of the financial collapse that could occur as the denouement of the drama which had been played over the previous decade and a half.

9 Is the Desk Making Volcker the Fall Guy?

On Wednesday, February 17, 1982, I asked Walter Wriston, one of the most outstanding bankers in the United States and then chairman of Citibank, whether he thought that Paul Volcker was willfully failing to attempt to control the growth of money in America. Wriston replied that he thought the problem with monetary control in the United States was not that Volcker did not want to achieve it or was insincere, but rather that there was a basic failure of *execution* of monetary control through the Desk in New York.

Many excuses have been given for the failure of the Federal Reserve to provide slow, steady growth of money in the United States. One excuse is that the administration does not want it and cannot bear the cost of achieving it.

On February 18, 1982, President Reagan issued a statement preceding his press conference on that day in which he said:

> One of my major concerns today is high interest rates. They hurt everyone—people who must borrow, families who want to buy a new home, businesses struggling to get ahead. High interest rates represent the greatest single threat today to a healthy, lasting recovery. The high level of current interest rates reflects two concerns in the financial community—some fear that the Federal Reserve Board will revert to the inflationary monetary policies of the past; others worry that this administration will tolerate ever-widening budget deficits. Well, I want to make it clear today that neither this administration nor the Federal Reserve will allow a return to the fiscal and monetary policies of the past that have created current conditions.
>
> I have met with Chairman Volcker several times during the past year. We have met again earlier this week. I have confi-

232

dence in the announced policies of the Federal Reserve Board. The Administration and the Federal Reserve can help bring inflation and interest rates down faster by working together than by working at cross-purposes. This Administration will always support the political independence of the Federal Reserve Board. We also support the Federal Reserve's 1982 money growth targets which are fully consistent with the Administration's economic projections for the coming year.

Other excuses have been offered for the failure of the Fed to achieve stable money growth—particularly since October 1979, when targeting monetary aggregates was supposedly elevated to the top priority by the Fed. These include:

1. *Money Growth Should Attempt to Control Real Output.*

This is the argument that we should not confine ourselves simply to a broad control over money growth over a period of years but should attempt to "fine tune" economic fluctuations by the use of money growth variations. Experience shows, unfortunately, that economists do not have the knowledge about the relation between money and output over short periods to attempt to achieve such an ambitious goal. The best we could do would be to achieve a steady low rate of growth of money (which in my view would be a *zero* growth of money: as I pointed out earlier, this would then assure us that there would be no inflation).

2. *Money Growth Rate Reduction Will Cause Recession.*

"Okun's Law" (after the late Arthur Okun, who was chairman of the Council of Economic Advisers from November 16, 1964, to January 20, 1969) states that the cost in terms of lost output for each percentage point reduction in the inflation rate is 1 percent of a year's GNP. There are at least two major experiences that must cast doubt on that gloomy view. First, there was the great German hyperinflation. In the last months (August 1922–November 1923) of that disaster, the inflation rate averaged roughly 300,000 percent at an annual rate. But German inflation was virtually eliminated in early 1924, at the cost of virtually no transitional loss of output and employment. In other words, once a firm commitment to reduce money growth was made and convincing reforms in the money supply control process were put in place, inflation was brought under control almost immediately and with a relatively small downward shock in output and employment. Similarly, after World War II the rate of inflation in the United States was reduced, by determined monetary policies, from 14.47 percent in 1947 to 0.99 percent in 1949 and 1.06 percent in 1950 as a result of a cut in the rate of growth of money from 10.49 percent in 1947 to 3.05 percent in 1949 and 0.30 percent in 1950. There was a recession in 1949, but the largest four-quarter decline in real gross national product was 1.35 percent. That was a negligible cost to pay for the elimination of inflation and for the laying of the foundations for long-term noninflationary growth which followed the determined smashing of postwar inflation under President Truman.

Clearly it is most important that a strong anti-inflationary monetary policy be implemented in a convincing, determined, and consistent fashion. Otherwise, the process will be unduly prolonged and unduly costly.

3. *"New" Financial Instruments Make It Hard to Control Money.*

We are constantly being told—as often as not by officials of the Federal Reserve (it was one of Burns's big excuses)—that "financial innovation" makes it hard for the Federal Reserve to control money. Thus, the growth of money market funds is often given as an example of the problem that is said to arise when new financial instruments are invented which fall outside the control apparatus of the Federal Reserve System.

The argument is that these new financial instruments allow a given growth of money (defined, for example as M1, which does not include money market mutual funds) to support more inflation. This argument essentially comes down to stating that there is an increase in the velocity of money as a result of the invention of new financial instruments.

There are two answers to this excuse:

a. Experience shows that over a long period of time, the velocity of M1 or M1-B has grown steadily. It has grown about 3 percent a year over a period of twenty years. There have been changes in the rate of increase from year to year, but there has been nothing remarkable to suggest that on average the velocity of M1 will not continue to increase about 3 percent a year.

b. Even if the velocity of M1 did increase more quickly in the future than in the past, it would be quite feasible for the Federal Reserve to make an adjustment to its annual target rate of growth of M1 to make allowance for the increase in the rate of growth of M1 velocity.

4. *We Cannot Tell What Aggregate to Target.*

Experience shows that different measures of money grow at different rates. The relationship between the rate of growth of M1 and of M2, for example, is stable over time. It is up to the Fed to make the appropriate adjustment. In fact, it does this by providing for a substantially greater annual rate of growth of M2, as compared with M1. This is because experience shows the rate of growth of the velocity of M2 is less than that of M1. The important point is that the Fed should choose one aggregate and stick to it. In the past, the Fed has attempted to switch attention from one aggregate to another as a means of avoiding strict monetary control and of avoiding being held responsible for failures of monetary control.

5. *Budget Deficits Make It Much Harder to Achieve Monetary Control.*

This subject has been discussed at length. Suffice it to say there is no connection which can be measured between budget deficits and money growth, inflation or interest rates. The Fed does not have to monetize federal government budget deficits. Indeed, since the Federal Reserve–Treasury accord of 1951 the Fed has been under no formal obligation whatever to monetize the federal budget deficit, that is, to buy government debt in order to maintain a given level of interest rates. I may say that the Fed has often, over years at a time, acted as if it were trying to stabilize interest rates, which would be part of monetizing deficits. But any such actions have been taken by the Fed for its own internal reasons and have borne no consistent relationship whatever with the condition of the federal government's budget deficit.

There Is a Big Problem—The New York Desk Procedures

In looking at the failure of the Fed over time, we have observed a consistent pattern of an attempt by the Fed to control interest rates, notably the federal funds rate. We have seen that the attempt by the

Fed narrowly to control the movement of the federal funds rate has led to one disaster after another and has imparted a chronic inflationary bias to monetary policy. This inflationary bias became so pronounced by 1979 that the previous policy had to be formally abandoned and a supposedly new policy put in its place.

The question raised by the continuing failure of the Fed to provide stable, steadily declining monetary growth is this: the Fed has told us that it is not trying to target interest rates within a narrow band. It is concentrating on trying to control the growth of monetary aggregates. Is Volcker telling the truth about this? One would not be hard put, on the basis of the variability of money growth over the period since October 1979, to argue that he is telling lies when he informs us (and the president) that he is sincerely trying to achieve steadily declining money growth. But let us assume that he is not lying and let us look for another explanation. We find that there may be an explanation. It is that the Federal Reserve operating procedures, as carried out by the Desk in New York, still *amount in fact to interest rate targeting under another name.*

Despite all the cosmetic changes, the Fed is still, through the New York desk, attempting to manage monetary policy in a way which *gives the same results as if interest rate targeting were still fully in force.*

How the Desk in Effect Still Targets the Fed Funds Rate

To understand how the Fed has managed to make such an appalling mess of things, we have to try to get inside its thinking, and this is not easy. But let us try. We must try to find a rational basis for its apparently irrational and mulish, or, to put it differently, vicious and deceitful, behavior. We are not talking about some academic issue here. We are talking about the monetary stability of the economic system of the United States and hence about the monetary stability of the Western world.

I will give it to you first in the words of the man who is responsible for making this policy work, Peter D. Sternlight, manager of the Open Market Account in the Federal Reserve System. On June 15, 1981, at Ohio State University, he engaged in a debate with some of his critics, and this is what he said about how *he* controls America's monetary growth:

> Since October 1979, the Federal Reserve has sought to achieve its monetary growth objectives by aiming at associated reserve growth targets, while giving considerably less emphasis than previously to interest rates. The change in October 1979 was essentially a change in means, not ends. Both before and after that date, the Fed had sought to achieve growth rates for monetary aggregates chosen by the Federal Open Market Committee. The difference is that before October 1979, the Fed tried to bring about a desired monetary growth by aiming at a particular federal funds rate—that is, the overnight interest charge on bank reserves. Estimates were made of the degree of reserve pressure, as indicated by the federal funds rate, that would achieve desired monetary growth. Adjustments were then made in the funds rate objective as monetary growth was seen to be running above or below path.
>
> In theory, such an approach is quite feasible. There is a connection between pressure on reserve positions and monetary growth rates and the omniscient uninhibited application of the technique should be able to produce the desired results.
>
> In practice, the approach seemed to work reasonably well at times, but for significant periods, especially in the inflationary environment of recent years, *adjustments to the federal funds rate objective tended to lag behind* [my italics].

In other words, the system of trying to control money growth by varying the price of money failed because the price of money was held down for too long. But at least we have Sternlight admitting that the previous system failed because the federal funds rate was held down to unrealistic levels for too long. So far so good.

He went on:

> The change in October 1979 was to focus operations on a reserve target, instead of a funds rate target. The Open Market Committee still indicates a broad range for the federal funds rate but it has been a range of some 4 to 7 percentage points, in contrast to the one half of one percentage point employed previously. Moreover, and this is sometimes misunderstood, that broad funds range has not in practice been employed as an

237

absolute limitation. It has been more in the nature of a check point.

The relevant reserve targets are path levels of total and non-borrowed reserves (that is, other than those borrowed from the Fed) that are developed by the staff to be consistent with the monetary growth objectives selected by the FOMC—the Open Market Committee.

So the Fed officials work out what money growth they would like to see. Next they work out what total reserves would be generated by such a path (based on the proportion of the banks' deposits that have to be put into reserves). Then they work out what should be the path of nonborrowed reserves which will be applicable.

The path for nonborrowed reserves in turn is simply the total reserve path less the initially assumed level of borrowing to which the Open Market Committee has agreed. That level is usually placed close to the recently prevailing levels of borrowing, though it could be set higher or lower if it were desired to impart some initial thrust toward greater or less pressure on bank reserve positions.

A couple of figures will put this in perspective. In the week ended February 3, 1982, M1 was $449.4 billion; total bank reserves were $48.3 billion and borrowings from the Federal Reserve by the banks were $1.847 billion. Thus, nonborrowed reserves were $48.3 billion *less* $1.847 billion, or $46.453 billion.

Sternlight continued:

Under this approach, monetary growth in excess of path causes increases in borrowings from the Fed, which would be associated with higher interest rates and pressure on the banking system that would, over time, tend to return growth of money supply and reserves towards the desired paths. Shortfalls in growth would have the opposite effect, reducing the need for borrowings and thus encouraging lower interest rates and more vigorous monetary expansion.

Now let's get this clear. The Fed decides what its monetary growth target is going to be. In 1982 it has a formal target of 2½–5½ percent growth in M1 from the fourth quarter of 1981 to the fourth quarter of 1982. It then works out what level of bank reserves that money supply would normally be associated with. So it has an idea of what reserves the banks will be trying to get, as money grows. It then has a figure that is the figure of the amount the banks are *now* borrowing from the Fed, in order to reach the reserve target that exists at the moment. The week of February 3, 1982, this figure was $1.847 billion. This figure, which is the *borrowed* reserves figure (the amount the banks are "into" the Fed), turns out to be *the relevant policy variable.*

Sternlight went on to say:

These forces of greater or lesser borrowing can be augmented and accelerated by making adjustments in the nonborrowed reserve path; downward to enlarge borrowing and reinforce a restraining impact; or upward, to have the opposite effect, thus speeding the return of money growth rates to path. Discount rate moves can further augment these effects.

We are looking at the Fed trying to manipulate the money supply by, in effect, manipulating the tiny portion of total reserves which is *borrowed from the Fed.* In the week ended February 3, 1982, the critical element in the Fed's policy stance was the $1.847 billion that the banks had borrowed from it. Money supply was $449.4 billion, approximately *243 times* the amount of borrowed reserves. The tail wags the dog.

Sternlight mentioned the discount rate. Where does this come in? It comes in because it is the rate the Fed charges the banks when they borrow from it to make up the amount of reserves they have to have with the Fed.

Yet this apparently sane and detailed policy has in fact given us enormously violent fluctuations in money growth as well as violent fluctuations in interest rates and a general frantic scramble at the end of each year (1980 and 1981 being the first two years of this setup) to get back to the money growth path.

Sternlight said on this latter point:

To be sure, monthly or even quarterly growth rates deviated significantly from path growth rates, but there is little evidence that deviations over such short periods, if reversed subsequently, have significant consequences for the economy.

Rather, these variations testify to the substantial short-run variability in the relation between money and economic activity.

My comment would be that the extreme variability of money growth has contributed to the increasing lack of confidence in the Federal Reserve and has also contributed to the high level of interest rates generally, as these high rates contain a substantial element of "risk and uncertainty" premiums. So I would say that Sternlight brushes off a very major issue with a disregard for the destruction being caused and the costs being incurred by the extreme variability of both money growth and of interest rates that accompany this policy.

He also stated: "The weekly objective for nonborrowed reserves is by far the primary determinant of the Fed's day-to-day actions to add or absorb reserves." What this comes down to in practice is, of course, that the Fed has a weekly objective for *borrowed* reserves, as this is the variable that, as Sternlight said, "can be augmented and accelerated, . . . thus speeding the return of money growth rates to path."

One must find it almost incredible, to begin with, that such a tiny figure, $1.847 billion out of $449.4 billion, is supposed to be able to influence movements in money with any degree of precision at all. The whole idea is so outlandish as to strain credibility. We know it doesn't work because money supply does not respond smoothly and quickly to movements in borrowed reserves. We know, for example, that during the period from late April 1981 to late October 1981, money supply (M1) remained stationary. Over this period, borrowings from the Federal Reserve banks fell steadily, from about $2.5 billion to about $1 billion. From the end of November to the end of January, when the money supply skyrocketed (growing at an annual rate of about 20 percent), borrowings from the Federal Reserve banks rose very sharply, from almost zero to about $2.5 billion.

There are other reasons that the system could not be expected to work. In the first place, under existing law, the banks have to pay their reserve "entitlements" over to the Federal Reserve *two weeks after the period to which the reserve payments refer.* This is called lagged reserve accounting. Now what happens when the Fed makes a change in the reserves it intends to make the banks borrow, as part of its policy of tightening or loosening money growth?

The banks know the amount of reserves they are *required* to pay over to the Fed, with respect to their deposits of two weeks previously. They then adjust their operations to make sure they are well prepared for what they have to find in the way of cash to pay to the Fed. Where do they get the cash? They get it from the Fed. But the Fed is prepared to lend them the money they need—and which they have had ample notice they will have to find—by providing it at a concessional rate of interest through the so-called discount window. This is where the discount rate comes in.

The Fed keeps this rate stable for long periods of time. The rate is as often as not a cheap rate for money, available to the banks, to meet the reserves they know they have to pay to the Fed in respect to *two weeks' ago* deposits. Because the discount rate is usually well below market rates, the banks are quite happy to borrow from the Fed when they are short of cash. So the limitation that is supposed to apply does not work because the banks have ample time to prepare themselves and because the Fed will in any case lend them any money they need at a concessional rate of interest.

What this adds up to is that the only effective means the Fed has available to it, given its policy of lagged reserve accounting and a below-market discount rate, is the federal funds rate. Hence, by a very roundabout route, we find that the Fed is still effectively using the federal funds rate as its main policy control instrument.

The system of nominally "controlling" money growth through a "control" over the growth of nonborrowed reserves (which in effect comes down to a basically futile attempt to "control" money growth by "controlling" *borrowed* reserves) actually works out in a way which tends to exaggerate the tendency for the federal funds rate to fluctuate. This is because the banks always know what money they have to find to make up their required reserves, and they know that they can get this money cheaply from the Fed. So, as the Fed pushes the banks to some target of borrowing from itself, the banks are in a position to bid up the federal funds rate higher because they know that if they are pushed, they can get whatever additional money they need, from the Fed itself at the cheap discount rate.

This in turn makes the federal funds rate *tend* to fluctuate more violently. And these fluctuations in the funds rate in turn make the Fed very nervous. As a result, it will as often as not take steps to moderate the movements in the funds rate, by putting more cash into the system, thus increasing *total reserves* (and negating its own attempt to bring money growth under control).

Let me give you an assessment of the practices of the New York desk by Peter Canelo, a very perceptive vice-president and senior capital markets analyst at Merrill Lynch. In his *Weekly Money and Credit Summary* of February 16, Canelo said:

In spite of the announced policy of projecting a path for bank reserves as the intermediate technique of monetary control, the Federal Reserve continues to target a specific level of discount window borrowings and letting reserves and the monetary base change as they will. In recent weeks it has become apparent that the Fed has moved to raise the non-seasonal net-borrowed reserves in the banking system from about $0.5 billion in the first weeks of the year to about $1.0 billion currently. In so doing, the Fed has engendered extreme changes in bank reserves. In the last five weeks, bank reserves have moved down $0.4 billion, up $1.0 billion, down $0.5, up $0.0 and down $1.2 billion each week. In the last four weeks, nonborrowed reserves have moved up $1.0 billion, down $2.0, up $1.2 and down $1.0 billion.

It is important to note that targetting net borrowings is very much like targetting interest rates. There exists an excellent correlation between the level of net borrowings and the spread between the Federal Funds rate and the discount rate. At present, we estimate that a three to four percentage point spread between these two rates is consistent with borrowed reserves of $1.5 billion to $1.75 billion and net borrowings of approximately $1.0 to $1.25 billion. By apparently aiming for a net borrowed position of $1.0 billion, the Fed is thus attempting to maintain a Federal Funds rate of three percentage points above the discount rate, or 15 percent. Since loan growth continues to run at very rapid rates, if the banks attempt to increase their borrowings of cheap reserves at the discount window, the Fed will be either forced to raise the discount rate or to provide nonborrowed reserve credit more liberally to the banking system.

The net result of such an interest rate targetting procedure is, of course, that the Fed implicitly abandons control of the monetary base. In the last nine weeks, the monetary base of the St. Louis bank has increased from an annual rate of 6.0 percent to one of 8.1 percent.

I will summarize Peter Canelo's statement because it shows how the Fed has in effect lost control of money growth through its failure to raise the discount rate to a market level. As I said earlier, when the demand for loans increases, the banks draw down their reserves. They lend more, and their cash tends to decline as a proportion of their deposits. But their deposits are increasing. So they borrow money in the federal funds market. This tends to push up the federal funds rate. The Fed tries to increase the amount of reserves the banks have to pay over to it, by adopting a target for "borrowed reserves." The banks get around this because the Fed gives them the cash they need by lending it to them directly or indirectly by expanding the total amount of cash in the system. These loans to the banks are then included in the Fed's balance sheet as part of the monetary base. The expansion of the monetary base in effect amounts to a rise in the cash base of the system and provides a foundation for a further expansion of the money supply.

Not surprisingly, the Fed has, under the current system of supposedly targeting nonborrowed reserves, but in effect targeting borrowed reserves and the federal funds rate (which tends to move in a fixed relationship to the discount rate when the borrowed reserves target is stable), found that monetary conditions have become generally more volatile. And again not surprisingly, the critics of the Fed have not been slow to speak out.

For nearly twenty years Allan Meltzer, John M. Olin professor of political economy and public policy at the Carnegie-Mellon University in Pittsburgh, has been a student of the Fed and a founder, with Professor Karl Brunner of the University of Rochester, of the Shadow Open Market Committee, which has for the last ten years been a constant source of criticism of the Fed. Speaking at the same Ohio State University symposium as Sternlight on June 15, 1981, Professor Meltzer said:

We offer three main criticisms of the Fed's policies. First, they produce high and variable inflation; secondly they produce pro-cyclical monetary growth; third, their attempts to keep interest rates from rising in the past had exactly the opposite effect. Five or six years ago, the Federal Reserve took the first hesitant steps to set targets for money growth. These steps were not taken in recognition of failed policies. They were forced on the Federal Reserve by Congress, in response to complaints by many economists, including, I am pleased to say, the members of the Shadow Open Market Committee. What has been the record of their efforts to control monetary growth? The Chart [on page 245] shows no significant change in the rate of growth of the monetary base in the years during which they have set targets for money growth. The Table [on page 246] shows that in three of the five years the Fed missed the target for money growth. Each time it missed, money growth was too high, not too low. You see again in the Table [on page 246] what you saw in the Chart [on page 245].

There is no sign that the commitments to achieve slower money growth have been kept.

Late in 1979, the Federal Reserve abandoned efforts to control interest rates. Years of high inflation, slow growth, a devalued dollar, and a stagnating economy finally brought a response. But instead of adopting procedures to control money growth reliably, the Fed chose its own way of doing things. They didn't control the rate of growth of the monetary base, the assets of their own balance sheet. They didn't control the rate of growth of total reserves. They control nonborrowed reserves. What they usually say is that under prevailing institutional arrangements—that means under the rules they have fixed and which they could easily correct—total reserves are more difficult to control. Mr. Sternlight just made that argument to you. What he didn't say is that if they would eliminate the lagged reserve requirement rule and make the discount rate move with the market rates, they would be able to control total reserves more reliably.

Why are short-term policies so unstable? The Fed estimates bank borrowings from projections of interest rates and borrowing. Their procedures increase variability and reduce control. Our studies, and studies within the Federal Reserve by Peter Keir, reach the same conclusion. In Keir's words, a penalty discount rate would "make nonborrowed reserves virtually the same as total reserves and thus improve the desk's ability to hit its target for total reserves."

This is exactly the opposite of what you heard from Peter Sternlight a moment ago, but it has been recommended by the Shadow Open Market Committee for a very long time. It is our current recommendation.

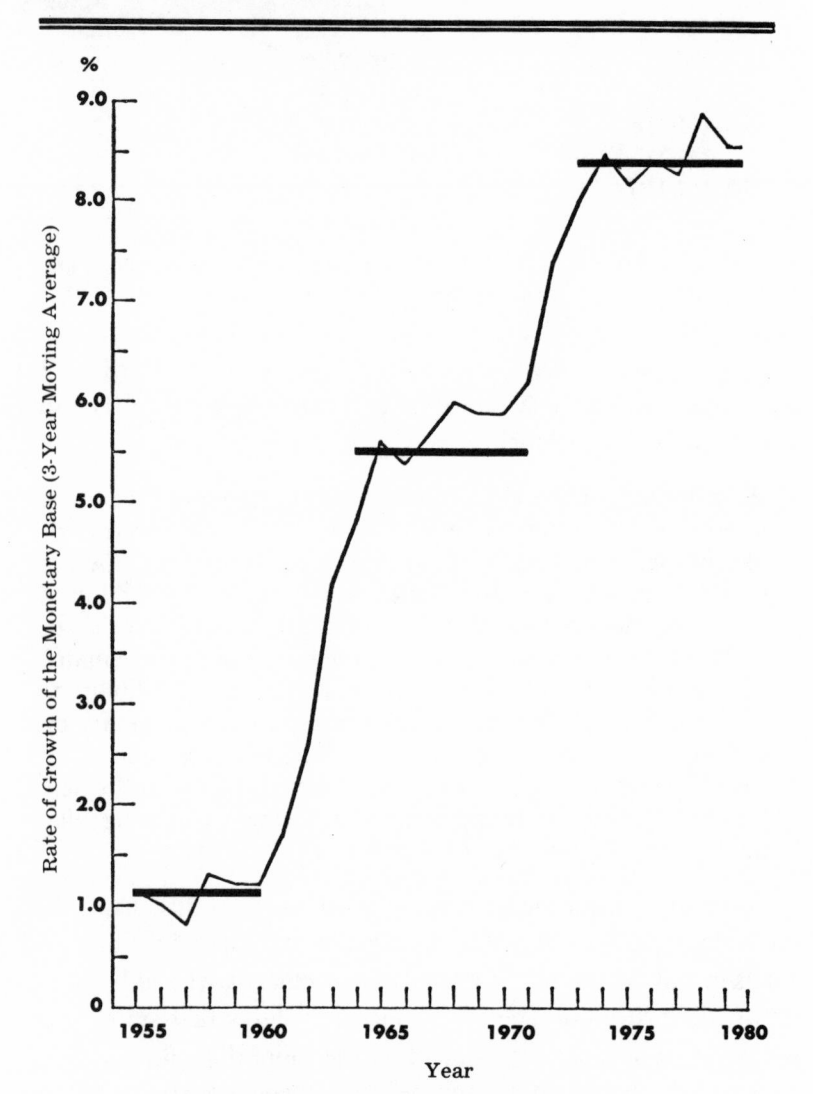

Rate of Growth of the Monetary Base
(3-Year Moving Average)

245

The Fed

Money Growth 1975–1980*

Period *Fourth Quarter*	*Percent Change from Fourth* *Quarter of Previous Year*	
	Target	Actual
1976 (M-1)	4.5%–7.5%	5.8%
1977 (M-1)	4.5 –6.5	7.9
1978 (M-1)	4.0 –6.5	7.2
1979 (M-1)	3.0 –6.0	5.5
1980 (M-1B)	4.0 –6.5	7.1

*The table shows the most frequently cited target for currency and checking deposits, formerly denoted M1 and now denoted M1-B.

Testifying before the Joint Economic Committee on April 8, 1981, Beryl Sprinkel, under secretary for monetary affairs in the Treasury, said of the Fed's technical procedures:

> We believe the Federal Reserve's control mechanism would be improved if the interest rate constraints were removed completely and efforts were concentrated on controlling the adjusted monetary base or adjusted bank reserves. Adoption of contemporaneous reserve accounting and a flexibly oriented discount rate policy would also help the Federal Reserve match their actions with their policy and thereby restore credibility to their anti-inflation efforts. Avoidance of extreme monetary instability is also necessary if policy direction is to be believed. A steady but persistent decline in monetary growth over the next four years will promote stable economic growth, declining inflation, and stable but lower interest rates.

To answer the question posed at the beginning of this chapter: yes, there does seem to be a big problem at the Desk in New York. Volcker may be the fall guy for his own officials who will not take steps to improve outdated operating procedures that simply make the problem of monetary control all the more difficult.

Why does change not take place? The reason is partly to be found in the reluctance of any big bureaucracy to change. It is also to be found in the close relationship between the Federal Reserve and its clients, the bond dealers and the major banks. And it is to be found partly in the destruction the Fed's own policies of regulating the banking system of America have wreaked on that banking system.

It is not surprising that with the American banks subject to massive attack from unregulated competitors, they are hardly willing to cooperate in any scheme proposed by the Fed—such as contemporaneous reserve accounting and penal discount rates—which would have the effect of making life still more difficult for them.

10 *How the Fed Has Helped Destroy the Banks–Its Charges*

Although most of us may think of the Federal Reserve as principally and overwhelmingly concerned with the administration of monetary policy, Milton Friedman has pointed out (in his July 1981 speech to the Western Economic Association) that the Federal Reserve governors devote 90 percent of their time not to monetary control, but to their regulatory functions, which include regulating the level of interest rates, the terms under which banks may borrow, the reserves they must hold, and so on.

Under the Monetary Control Act of 1980, the Board of Governors can require all depository institutions (commercial banks, savings banks, savings and loan associations, and credit unions) to submit directly or indirectly reports of assets and liabilities for monetary and credit control purposes. Each depository institution (there were about 22,000 of them subject to Federal Reserve requirements in 1981) must maintain reserves against transactions accounts in a ratio of 3 percent for amounts of $25 million or less and at 12 percent for amounts in excess of $25 million. The statutory range for amounts in excess of $25 million is 8 to 14 percent. No interest is payable on these statutory reserves.

The Depository Institutions Deregulation Act of 1980 provides for the phaseout of limitations on interest and dividend rates payable by depository institutions by extending the authority to impose such limitations for six years. During the six-year period, the ¼ percent interest rate differential paid on the deposits of thrift institutions, as compared with commercial banks, continues. A new Depository Institutions Deregulation Committee (DIDC) has assumed authority to prescribe rules for the payment of interest. Voting members of

DIDC are the secretary of the Treasury, the chairman of the Board of Governors of the Federal Reserve, the chairman of the Federal Deposit Insurance Corporation, the chairman of the Federal Home Loan Bank Board, and the chairman of the National Credit Union Association Board. The DIDC must exercise its authority to provide for the phaseout and ultimate elimination of interest and dividend rate ceilings as rapidly as permitted by economic conditions.

The existence of these acts, passed only in 1980, indicates the tangled mess into which the regulation of banks and other financial institutions has deteriorated under Federal Reserve control. Equipped with huge powers of regulation over depository institutions, the Federal Reserve has been able to impose a system of price controls on money. Like all controls, however, they generate incentives to evade them. It becomes profitable to work out ways of evading the controls. As a result, two sorts of financial institutions develop: those under Federal Reserve control and those that have managed to devise ways of evading it. Profitability for the institutions that have worked out ways to get out from under Fed controls results from their freedom to offer higher rates of interest on their borrowings and their freedom from the Federal Reserve requirements, which means a considerable addition to their profitability (as they do not lose money on noninterest-bearing reserves held with the Fed).

The principal sufferers from the Fed's price and profit control apparatus have been the banks, thrift institutions, and credit unions, which form the foundation of the "regulated" sector of the American financial system. Hence, the Federal Reserve System has presided over a major decline in the very institutions it was supposed to support and nurture—the banks of the United States. Largely as a result of the monetary and regulatory policies of the Fed, aided and abetted by technical changes such as the spread of computers and improved communications, the banks have declined rapidly as a force in the financial institutions of America. They have become more and more susceptible to the encroachment of new institutions and financial products. The thrift industry is collapsing as a viable force in American finance and is undergoing a major restructuring. It was destroyed by inflation, by the Fed's excessive creation of money, and by earlier attempts to freeze interest rates.

The reaction of Federal Reserve officials to the competitive weakening of their bank charges over the last fifteen years has been to demand more and more power to regulate and control. During the 1970's Burns was always complaining about the number of banks that were quitting the Federal Reserve System and about the growth of the savings and loan associations which in those days represented the sort of ogre that today is conjured up in the form of the money market mutual funds.

There is a good reason for the growth of new financial institutions and new financial products: the old ones have become corrupted by inflation and overregulation. The commercial paper market amounted to about $50 billion in outstandings six years ago. Today the outstanding total of commercial paper loans amounts to about $170 billion. In 1976 commercial paper amounted to about one quarter of the total of all commercial and industrial loans made by the American commercial banks. Today commercial paper outstandings represent about *one half* of all the commercial banks' commercial and industrial loans.

How did this come about? It came about in the same way as myriad other distortions in American banking and interest rates came about—through the operation of price controls on money, imposed by the Federal Reserve through the use of its so-called Regulation Q powers. Federal Reserve bank regulators received the legal authority to regulate interest rates that commercial banks may pay depositors in the Banking Acts of 1933 and 1935. The interest ceilings have been set under Regulation Q of the Federal Reserve and are therefore commonly referred to as Regulation Q. One of the primary reasons for imposing ceilings on deposit interest rates was to reduce the number of failing banks in the 1930's by reducing their interest cost. Another objective was to reduce the incentives for rural banks to hold large interest-earning balances with their correspondents in the financial centers.

Much of the concern in the early 1930's centered on interest payments on demand deposits. Interest payments on demand deposits were prohibited under the Banking Acts of 1933 and 1935. The maximum interest on all time and savings deposits was initially set at 3 percent, slightly *below* the average interest rate that commercial banks and thrift institutions had been paying on time and savings deposits, but *above* the then-existing market yields on high-grade short-term securities. The choice of the initial ceiling rate on time and savings deposits indicates that the purpose of these ceiling rates was not to keep them below yields on alternative investments but to reduce deposit rates slightly and thus lower the interest cost of depository institutions.

During the twenty years from the mid-1930's to the mid-1950's the ceiling rates on time and savings deposits were above market interest rates. In 1957 and 1962, when market interest rates rose near or above the ceiling rates on savings deposits, these ceilings were raised. Hence, the inherent tendency to distortion in the financial markets implied by the decision to allow the Federal Reserve to impose price control on credit—or on *certain forms* of credit I should more precisely say—was minimized. Inflation in the 1970's would bring about massive distortions, however.

In 1966 ceilings on interest rates were imposed on the deposits of thrift institutions. Sponsors of the enacting legislation asserted that interest rates were being driven up by competition for deposits among banks and thrifts and that ceiling interest rates on deposits at thrift institutions would stop this escalation. They assumed that by permitting slightly higher ceiling rates at thrift institutions specializing in residential mortgage lending, the supply of credit for residential mortgages at reasonable mortgage interest rates would be adequate. These controls in interest rates paid by thrift institutions were viewed initially as temporary measures to deal with "unusual" circumstances. Over time, however, thrift institutions have come to view the differentials between the ceiling interest rates on *their* deposits and those imposed on commercial banks as essential in attracting deposits to be used for residential mortgage lending.

As inflation gathered way during the 1970's, the distortions that were bound to be caused by the existence of Regulation Q ceilings on interest rates came out into the open. This was because the regulators at the Federal Reserve, like bureaucrats the world over, fail to adjust their policies to the realities of the marketplace. This is not surprising. The price controls which are being administered are *intended* to cause actual events to deviate from what would be the case if market forces were allowed to operate freely.

Booming Money Funds and Commercial Paper—Declining Thrifts

The restrictions on deposit rates payable by thrift institutions have had the effect of hobbling their growth and the flow of money into housing along with it. This in turn has been met by the creation of new government home loan agencies such as the Federal Home Loan Board, the Federal National Mortgage Association (Fannie Mae), and the Government National Mortgage Association (Ginnie Mae) to provide support to housing through government subsidies by means of buy-back of mortgages and of outright subsidies for home loans.

Regulation Q had the effect of stimulating the growth of a massive market in commercial paper as commercial banks were prohibited from paying interest on corporate deposits of under thirty days. And corporate treasurers, looking for shorter-term investments for their spare cash, soon came up with the idea of lending to each other, completely circumventing the shackled banks. The banks did, however, conspire in their own downfall to a degree because they provided backup lines of credit, without which many issuers of commercial paper would have been unable to access this enormous market. "The commercial paper market has no reserves, no capital and represents a massive overhang of uncertainty," said Harry Taylor, vice chairman of the Manufacturers Hanover Trust, "and one of those perverse effects of misguided regulations which, by emasculating the responsiveness of the banking system, also limits the effectiveness and efficiency of the central bank."

Another explosive growth of a new financial institution has been the development of the money market mutual funds. In 1977 the deposits at the money funds were $3.8 billion, in 1978 they were $10.3 billion, and at the close of 1981 they were $177 billion. At that time the combined total of money market funds and commercial paper represented an amount greater than the total of all demand deposits and all other checkable deposits in the commercial banks of America.

These money market funds boomed because they permitted ordinary individuals to gain a high market rate of interest on money they had previously held in banks or thrift institutions, where the allowable rates of interest were controlled by the Federal Reserve under Regulation Q. As short-term interest rates boomed in the 1970's (under the influence of the inflationary monetary policies of the Federal Reserve), there was an increasing gap between market rates of interest and the rates available to small depositors. This widening gap is shown on the chart on page 254. This chart shows the enormous gap between the ceiling rate payable on savings deposits at commercial banks (an indicator of the *general* ceiling rate available to small depositors) and the rate payable on three-month Treasury bills.

Individual investors were unable to tap the Treasury bill market because the minimum investment was $10,000 and they wanted a higher degree of availability for their deposits than was presented by a Treasury bill. The expansion of the money market mutual funds soon gave the individual investor (previously a bank depositor) a chance to benefit from the high rates available.

The growth of the money funds has thus been a product of regulation and inflation. These funds are not subject to regulation or to reserve requirements. They are bitterly resented by the Federal Reserve, and they are thoroughly disliked by both the commercial banks and the thrift institutions. At least the commercial banks get some of their money back in the form of money fund purchases of commercial banks' certificates of deposit.

As John F. McGillicuddy, chairman of the Manufacturers Hanover Trust, pointed out on October 13, 1981:

> A significant proportion of the $160 billion attracted by money market funds represents a conversion of once stable, long-term households savings into the hottest of hot money. Consumer surveys indicate that approximately $60 billion of the $160 billion now in money market funds came originally from depository institutions.

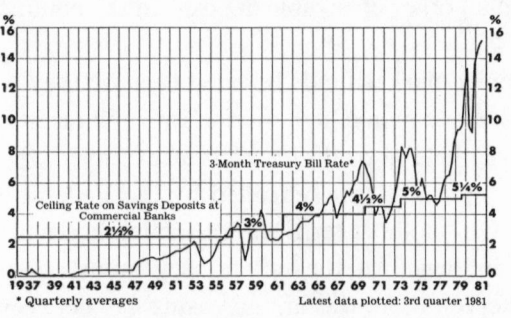

**3-Month Treasury Bill Rate and Ceiling Rate on
Savings Deposits at Commercial Banks**

*The rapid deterioration in the competitive position of banks,
savings banks, and savings and loan associations as a result of
inflation (leading to high interest rates) is shown in this chart
published by R. Anton Gilbert in the St. Louis Fed* Review *of
December 1981.*

To make up the deposit loss, banks have bought back approximately the same amount [by issuing certificates of deposit to the money funds]. But this conversion of core deposits
into money funds is costing the banking industry something
like $5 billion annually in additional interest expense. Obvi-
ously, this is an expense that banks must reflect in their pricing.

One other major effect of the combination of inflation and rising
interest rates was to undermine and for all practical purposes permanently to enfeeble the savings and loan and savings bank industry in the United States. These institutions found that they had to pay
more and more for their deposit money. They demanded, and got,
relief from interest rate controls on much of their deposit money and
were able to offer higher rates of interest as time went by. But their
assets, the mortgages in their balance sheets, were at rates of interest
fixed long in the past, at historically low interest rates. As a result,
they suffered huge losses, and many of them had to be merged to be
saved.

Anthony M. Solomon, chairman of the New York Fed, said on
January 28, 1982:

The thrifts are in a major dilemma, largely the product of
regulatory changes and interest rates levels. The great bulk of
their deposits is now in market sensitive instruments and so

their funding costs have risen. But what they are really suffering from is an asset problem that has defied simple solutions. The thrifts have not been able to restructure their assets. Well over half of them are in the form of long-term instruments, most with rates well below the market. And much of the cash flow from their assets has had to be committed to fund enormous deposit outflows, approaching $25 billion in 1981. [These outlays occurred because under Federal Reserve regulations the thrifts could not offer a rate of interest competitive with that offered by the money market mutual funds.] The result has been record losses—well over $6 billion on a nationwide basis, with a heavy share borne by New York savings institutions. The real problems are concentrated in a number of relatively large institutions. That has meant extensive action by the regulators to orchestrate a significant number of assisted mergers, at a cost to the insurance funds of about $2 billion. And the interstate combinations of savings and loans, unprecedented just a year ago, are rapidly becoming routine.

Harping on a traditional theme of ambitious regulators, Solomon went on to play on the sensitivities of bankers by trying to draw them into a demand for the money market mutual funds to be brought under regulatory controls, arguing in effect that "it isn't fair that they can compete with you while you are under regulatory controls." This tune has been played over and over again in America, with the result that financial markets have been subjected to incessant attempts by officials to extend their sway over markets as a solution to some problem that was in turn the result of the actions of the regulators themselves, in this case, the Federal Reserve.

This is how Solomon put it on January 28, 1982, to the New York State Bankers Association:

On the competitive side, your major concern has been the spectacular growth of nonbank financial institutions and their aggressive efforts to create integrated financial firms. Much of that growth has been in money market mutual funds, which have more than doubled, to over $180 billion in assets. To put that in some perspective, money funds are now one-fourth the size of the entire thrift industry. They have become a major link between individual investors and commercial paper issuers, the Federal Government and the banking industry itself. Bank obligations now make up about 40 percent of money fund investments. But while this means some of the money is flowing back to the banking system, the initial loss has been largely at the expense of core deposits, the return flow is at market rates and what's worse, the return flow is very uneven within the industry. Just as important, bankers are concerned about the loss of direct customer contacts which provide the basis for other service relationships. All in all, these concerns about the broadening penetration of the money funds are understandable and justified.

The money fund growth also raises difficult public policy issues. There is the question of the uneven regulatory treatment of competing institutions and the question of the size of consumer balances held outside the scope of deposit insurance and bank supervision.

The money funds have also introduced potential new complications for monetary control. *In my view, these concerns require a legislative response* [my italics]. Part of the answer is to expand the reach of regulatory instruments. But it would be a mistake to assume that any feasible degree of regulatory treatment would eliminate the underlying market forces to which the funds are responding. So another part of the answer will have to include providing the banks with the authority to offer more effective deposit alternatives.

In other words, Solomon is saying, "it's not fair" that the funds are not subject to price controls and, through the reserve requirements they are free of, profit controls. The answer is *not,* says Solomon, to abandon regulation entirely. No, the answer is to *expand* regulation. That is always the answer of the ambitious official who sees market developments leading to the undermining of his control. Yet the history of regulation shows how perverse and destructive its effects have been.

Changes in the Financial Structure of the U.S. Economy

1. We tend to think that commercial banks and thrift institutions dominate the nation's financial structure. But over the past thirty-five years, the role of these institutions has diminished significantly.

Financial Assets Owned by Sectors of the Financial Services Industry
Percent of Total

	1946	1972	1980
Commercial Banking	57.3%	37.9%	36.6%
Savings and Loans	4.4	14.0	16.9
Mutual Savings Banks	8.0	5.8	4.6
Credit Unions	0.2	1.4	1.9
Life Insurers	20.3	13.4	12.5
Private Pension Funds	1.5	9.0	7.7
State and Local Gov't. Retirement Funds	1.2	4.6	5.4
Other Insurance Cos.	3.0	3.9	5.0
Finance Companies	2.1	4.6	4.8
Open End Investment Cos.	0.6	3.4	1.5
Security Brokers and Dealers	1.5	1.3	0.9
Real Estate Investment Trusts	—	0.7	0.2
Money Market Funds	—	—	2.0
	100.0	100.0	100.0

Source: Board of Governors of the Federal Reserve System
Flow of Funds Accounts.

2. Tracking the share of assets held by various types of financial institutions tells only part of the story, since it doesn't include the financial activities of firms in nonfinancial industries.

Free of many of the regulations imposed on purely financial institutions, some large retail chains have accumulated larger portfolios of consumer receivables, have more credit cards outstanding, and derive more income from their consumer credit operations than even the nation's largest commercial banks.

Such companies have also established strong positions in insurance.

3. Moreover, while competition in traditional markets heats up, many companies are by-passing these markets. One way they do is by issuing IOUs directly to other nonfinancial corporations through the commercial paper market, which has expanded significantly in the past fifteen years.

Commercial Paper Outstanding
($ Billion, Rounded to Nearest Billion)

Year End	Financial		Non-Financial	Total	Percent Change	
	Direct	Dealer Issued			Total Paper	Bank Loans*
1965	$ 7 bil.	$ 1 bil.	$ 1 bil.	$ 9 bil.		
1969	21	6	6	33		
1970	21	5	8	34		
1973	27	5	9	42		
1976	33	7	13	53		
1977	40	9	16	65	22.6%	10.5%
1978	52	12	20	84	29.2	16.7
1979	65	18	30	113	34.5	17.9
1980	68	20	37	125	10.6	11.2

*Commercial and industrial loans
Source: Federal Flow of Funds Accounts

4. Another avenue for avoiding traditional markets is offered by the growth of the Eurodollar market—dollar denominated loans offered by institutions domiciled outside the United States. The markets have grown up rapidly because of highly regulated banking systems prevailing within national boundaries.

Net Size of Eurocurrency Markets
Net of Interbank Deposits, Billions of U.S. Dollars

	All Currencies	Eurodollars
1964	$ 12 billion	$ 9 billion
1965	13	10
1966	16	13
1967	21	17
1968	30	24
1969	44	36
1970	57	44
1971	71	51
1972	92	67
1973	132	90
1974	177	125
1975	205	150
1976	247	183
1977	300	211

	All Currencies	Eurodollars
1978	377	255
1979	475	318
1980	557*	370*

*Third quarter

Sources: Bank for International Settlements, Citibank estimates

5. Foreign banks are suppliers of many of the Eurodollar loans. They also are competing directly in the U.S. market for financial services. Because they were not formerly subject to the same branching restrictions as U.S. banks, many of these foreign banks operate banks in two or more states.

Activities of Foreign Banks in the United States

	November 1972	November 1974	May 1977	November 1979	March 1981
Number of foreign parents	52	69	96	151	165
Foreign parents operating in only one state	29	37	46	74	N.A.
Foreign parents operating in two states	20	17	27	38	N.A.
Foreign parents operating in three or more states	3	15	23	39	N.A.
Number of foreign parents operating banking facilities over $500 million in two or more states	2	9	8	16	N.A.

N.A.—Not Available

Source: Board of Governors of The Federal Reserve System

6. Foreign banks have been acquiring U.S. banks. This leads to the anomalous situation that foreign banks are free to acquire banks in any state while U.S. banks can only acquire institutions in their own one state, and sometimes not even then.

Foreign-Owned U.S. Commercial Banks
Ranked in Top 100 at Yearend 1980

	Deposits ($ Billion)	Deposit Rank
1. Marine Midland Bank N.A., Buffalo Hong Kong & Shanghai Banking Corp.	$14.2 bil.	13
2. Union Bank, Los Angeles Standard Chartered Bank Ltd., London	5.0	25
3. Republic National Bank, N.Y. Trade Devel. Bank Holding, Luxembourg	4.5	29
4. National Bank of North America, N.Y. National Westminister Bank Ltd., London	4.45	30
5. Bank of Tokyo Trust Co., N.Y. Bank of Tokyo Ltd.	3.3	44
6. European American Bank & Trust Co., N.Y. Owned by six banks		
7. California First Bank, San Francisco Bank of Tokyo Ltd.	3.1	47
8. Lloyds Bank California, Los Angeles Lloyds Bank Ltd., London	2.3	60
9. Bank Leumi Trust Co., N.Y. Bank Leumi le-Israel, Tel Aviv	1.74	84
10. Sumitomo Bank of California, S.F. Sumitomo Bank Ltd., Osaka	1.72	85
11. J. Henry Schroder Bank & Trust Co., N.Y. Schroders Ltd., London	1.6	94

Source: The American Banker

The Commercial Banks Have Lost Market Share

Inflation and regulation have combined to bring about a sharp decline in the commercial banks' share of the financial assets owned by the financial services industry. The tables on page 257–260, drawn from material prepared by Citibank, show that the commercial banks' share has fallen from 57.3 percent in 1946 through 37.9 percent in 1972 to 36.6 percent in 1980. The big gainers to the 1970's were the savings and loan associations, which were able to exploit their regulatory advantage over the commercial banks in being free to offer higher deposit rates. The future of the whole savings and loan industry is now under a cloud, and the growth of this industry may take years to recover from the shattering setback caused by the boom in interest rates during the 1970's.

While the banks have been under the control of federal regulations on their offering and lending rates, they have been under attack not only by the commercial paper market and the money market mutual funds but also, of course, by a whole range of major new financial institutions that have grown up in the free air outside the stifling atmosphere of Federal Reserve control. The most outstanding example of the development of a nonbank financial institution which carries out virtually all the functions of a bank is Merrill Lynch.

Merrill Lynch—The Bank of the Future, Today

As Walter Wriston said on January 21, 1981, in an address to the New York Securities Association:

> Merrill Lynch is not resting on its laurels. The heights they've already reached so impressed the "New York Times" that it headlined a story "Merrill Lynch and Company, Bankers." The lead sentence nailed down the point precisely: "It sponsors a major credit card, holds billions of dollars in accounts subject to demand checking, and generates two thirds of its profits from interest." In the 1960's, Merrill Lynch didn't even sell mutual funds. Now, less than 30 percent of their income derives from commissions on listed stocks. The rest of their revenue comes from such diverse sources as option trading, government bond trading, investment banking, insurance sales, money market funds, interest income, and real estate sales—sales made by Merrill Lynch's own force of 4,000 realtors—and still growing —who operate throughout the country. As some of you may remember, I have frequently applauded Merrill Lynch for offering the public, right now, the financial services of the bank of the future. Merrill Lynch accurately reflects the financial world as it really is and offers a package of services that no U.S. bank can match.
>
> The actual events of the financial world are confused with the image of what used to be. The image is that the banks are places

261

to deposit money and get loans; that brokerage firms are places where securities are bought and sold and distributed; that thrifts are places to maintain savings and obtain mortgages.

Yet the reality of the actual events taking place is that computers, satellites, electronic funds transfer mechanisms, microcircuitry and high-speed optical telephone lines are eliminating the constraints of time, geography, and volume in financial transactions. A man in Texas takes his money out of a savings and loan, calls a toll-free telephone number in Arizona and his money ends up in a money market fund in Boston—or anywhere else on the globe.

There are other vast new corporations being created to take advantage of the new world of financial services. Recently Prudential Insurance took over the New York securities firm of Bache; American Express took over Shearson Loeb Rhoades, another major New York securities firm; Philipp Brothers, a huge international commodities trading firm, took over the powerful investment banking and brokerage firm of Salomon Brothers.

Every Financial Institution Rushing to the Same Market

As the forces breaking down barriers within the financial services grow in strength, there is a challenge to the regulatory authority of the Federal Reserve. Talking to the California Bankers' Association on January 8, 1982, Deputy Secretary of the U.S. Treasury R. T. McNamar said:

Changes in technology are making banking as we knew it obsolete. You are all familiar with automatic teller machines and cash dispensers in airports. Many of you consider ATM's the wave of the future. With 25,000 presently installed nationwide, they are the "wave of the present."

In the future, thanks to cable television, satellites and the telephone, the consumer will not even have to go to the bank, to an airport or to an ATM. He will do his banking from his home or from his place of business. Indeed, not just his banking, but all of his financial business, including stocks, bonds and insurance.

And this is not the distant future: Touch-tone billpayer services are already with us and I recently read of a Midwest grocery store which directly debits customers' checking accounts from the check-out line. A Warner Communications-American Express joint venture already offers an "inter-active" two-way cable system [the Qube system in Columbus, Ohio] and this subsidiary was awarded franchises covering more than two-thirds of the homes for which franchises were offered in 1980. One communications industry consultant has predicted that some form of in-home banking will be available to a fifth of American households in the next five years.

The average consumer uses over 30 financial services a year and goes to more than a dozen financial institutions to obtain them. We are witnessing today a change in this environment and the emergence of supermarkets in the financial services industry.

Many of you are undoubtedly aware of who your competitors are and of the range of services that they offer but let me review them briefly:

Your competitors *the money center banks* offer credit cards, check cashing, consumer finance and travel planning nationwide, loans in most states and mortgages in some locations.

Your competitor *Manufacturers Hanover of New York* recently bought a string of 67 consumer finance offices in California, Oregon and Washington. [MHT is also the owner of one of the biggest leasing organizations in the country.]

Your competitor *Merrill Lynch* offers mortgages, checkwriting, trust and estate planning and money management.

Four of your competitors—*savings and loans, including one here in California*—are seeking to operate a securities brokerage subsidiary and to offer investment advice and portfolio analysis. An additional 150 to 200 S and L's have indicated an active interest in becoming associated with this subsidiary.

Two of your competitors—*both banks*—have already taken similar steps. And these are just the "regulated" institutions.

Your "unregulated" competitors have greater flexibility. Your competitor *Sears* has long offered insurance and consumer credit. It has recently acquired the nation's fourth largest brokerage firm [Dean Witter], decided to establish a money market fund and purchase the nation's largest real estate brokerage firm [Coldwell Banker]. It is also the largest savings and loan holding company in the United States. Sears President recently announced it is their intention to become "*The* largest consumer oriented financial services entity."

Your competitor *American Express* offers credit cards, cable television, securities brokerage, commercial real estate financing, mortgage insurance and leverage leasing.

Your competitor *National Steel*—yes National Steel—owns three savings and loans.

Your competitor *Baldwin United,* formerly best known for its pianos, has also acquired a savings and loan.

Your competitor *General Electric* is involved in real estate loans, second mortgages, commercial real estate financing, mortgage insurance and leverage leasing.

The End of Geographic Limitations on Banking?

Along with the proliferation of diverse product offerings, there is a vigorous expansion of financial services across state lines. Donald T. Regan, former chief executive of Merrill Lynch and now secretary of the U.S. Treasury, said on November 5, 1981:

Just as the market for financial services has transcended institutional distinctions, so too it has rendered geographical barriers to banking absurd. The largest banks now compete nationally —and legally—for "wholesale" and retail business. They do so through surrogates for full service branch facilities.

For example, there are at least 350 loan production offices operating in about 20 states. The latest data indicate that 35 of the largest 100 "non-captive" finance companies are subsidiaries of bank holding companies—for example, Finance America and B of A. Likewise, banks and bank holding companies control 47 of the largest 100 mortgage banking firms. In fact, one bank holding company operates 13 subsidiaries, including a finance company with 370 offices scattered through 39 states. Foreign banks have achieved a unique presence in the American market. Thirty foreign banking organizations—"grandfathered" under the International Banking Act of 1978—conduct operations in more than one state. Six of the ten largest banks in California have their home offices in foreign countries. Today, a foreign bank can cross the Atlantic or the Pacific far more readily than a Utah bank can cross the Rockies. If it is not already doing business here, that foreign bank could simply acquire an existing bank in Colorado—something a bank based in Utah couldn't do. I suggest that this is ludicrous. For some of your other major domestic "banking" competitors, state lines have never existed. Merrill Lynch has 442 offices nationwide; Shearson Loeb Rhoades—recently acquired by American

Express—has 246 offices and American Express has 1100 offices; E. F. Hutton has 269 offices; Dean Witter (acquired by Sears) has 283 offices; and Paine Webber has 229 offices.

These are just a few examples of the market's having out-stripped the regulations. But perhaps the most dramatic market changes are attributable to technological innovation [through the use of computers, cable television, electronic funds trans-fers, and the telephone].

These Innovations Frighten the Fed—Needlessly

The growth of new types of financial institutions, outside its con-trol, frightens Fed officials. They have responded by demanding more and more powers, to impose profit and price controls.

Under the 1980 Monetary Control Act, the number of institutions required to report to the Fed was increased from 5,422 to more than 22,000. Yet monetary control was not improved. By virtue of their powers of regulation, Fed officials have the power of life and death over thousands of depository institutions under their control. This power to *regulate* has not added to the Fed's skill in monetary control. There is no reason to believe that it would. Yet time and again we hear Fed officials like Anthony Solomon, president of the New York Fed, suggesting that *more regulatory power* is needed in order to improve monetary control. There is a very serious confusion here in thinking inside the Fed.

Another technical issue arises because of the pace of financial innovation, which is described in this chapter. Fed officials argue, as did Solomon (page 256), that monetary policy control will be im-proved if the Fed is given still more regulatory power—particularly the power to impose noninterest-bearing reserve requirements on the money market mutual funds. This demand for more regulatory power is supported by the theory that the pace of financial innovation is making it more difficult to control the quantity of money.

Yet no evidence supports this contention. If there were a founda-tion for the complaint made by Solomon, we would find it more difficult to predict the level of M1, or M2, by reference to the mone-tary base. The so-called money multiplier would start going awry. Yet meticulous analysis carried out by, among others, Robert Ras-che of the University of Michigan (on behalf of the Shadow Open

Market Committee) and by Anatole Balbach at the St. Louis Fed (published in the April 1981 issue of the St. Louis Fed *Review*) shows that the money multiplier relationships between the adjusted monetary base and M1 and M2 have remained very constant.

Subjected to this sort of rigorous analysis, the complaints of Fed officials like Solomon seem to come down to a general complaint that they want more regulatory power because they want more regulatory power. This same sort of complaint by Fed officials relates to the alleged inappropriateness of M1 for monetary control purposes. It has been argued that the existence of money market mutual funds, Eurodollar accounts, repurchase agreements, and other innovations in recent years have negated the long-standing relationship between M1 and the nominal gross national product—the velocity of M1. Yet thorough analysis shows that the relationship between M1 and GNP has remained highly stable.

The tables on page 267 are taken from the March 1982 report of the Joint Economic Committee. They show that M1 velocity (the ratio of nominal gross national product to M1) has moved with great stability during the period of twenty-five years shown. Robert Weintraub, who wrote this section of the JEC report, states on page 239 of the report:

> It is clear that M1 growth has been and remains a reliable and useful gauge of the thrust of monetary policy and that it is a better measure of this policy than M2 growth. When M1 accelerates, it is a good bet that within two or three years, nominal GNP growth will also accelerate and it will do so percentage point for percentage point. Vice versa, when M1 growth slowed, it is a good bet that nominal GNP growth will soon slow commensurately.

In trying to get the people of America to concede it still more regulatory power, to meet a need which does not exist (the need to widen its ambit of control to take in money instruments included in M2 but not in M1—such as money market mutual funds), the Fed is not being honest. Its deeper intention is no doubt the usual desire by all officials for more power. Yet the exercise of its regulatory power has already served to confuse and weaken the existing financial institutions.

Gross National Product, Money Supply, and Velocity Measures

[Year-to-year percent changes]

Year	Dollars minus GNP	M1	M1 velocity	M2 velocity
1956	5.42	1.17	4.20	
1957	5.29	.54	4.71	
1958	1.28	1.17	.11	
1959	8.49	2.23	6.12	
1960	3.82	.06	3.76	.07
1961	3.57	2.06	1.48	-2.97
1962	7.74	2.46	5.15	.03
1963	5.58	3.09	2.42	-2.62
1964	6.88	3.92	2.85	-.90
1965	8.35	4.27	3.92	.23
1966	9.39	4.58	4.60	2.63
1967	5.78	3.98	1.73	-1.12
1968	9.22	7.00	2.07	.76
1969	8.08	5.93	2.03	1.76
1970	5.18	3.78	1.35	1.24
1971	8.55	6.81	1.63	-3.20
1972	10.06	7.19	2.68	-2.18
1973	11.85	7.30	4.24	1.69
1974	8.12	5.01	2.96	1.78
1975	8.03	4.69	3.19	-1.35
1976	10.89	5.71	4.90	-2.05
1977	11.64	7.64	3.72	-1.18
1978	12.41	8.22	3.87	3.22
1979	11.96	7.77	3.89	2.83
1980	8.79	6.26	2.38	-.08
1981	11.28	6.92	4.08	1.45
Using shift-adjusted M1: 1981	11.28	4.62	6.36	

Yearly Percentage Change in GNP, M1, and M1 Velocity

[2- and 3-year nonoverlapping periods, 1956 to 1981]

	Dollars minus GNP	M1	M1 velocity
2-year period:			
1956 to 1957	5.35	0.86	4.46
1958 to 1959	4.88	1.70	3.12
1960 to 1961	3.69	1.06	2.62
1962 to 1963	6.66	2.78	3.79
1964 to 1965	7.62	4.10	3.39
1966 to 1967	7.59	4.28	3.17
1968 to 1969	8.65	6.47	2.05
1970 to 1971	6.87	5.30	1.49
1972 to 1973	10.96	7.25	3.46
1974 to 1975	8.08	4.85	3.08
1976 to 1977	11.27	6.68	4.31
1978 to 1979	12.19	8.00	3.88
1980 to 1981	10.04	6.59	3.23
3-year period:			
1956 to 1958	4.00	.96	3.01
1959 to 1961	5.29	1.45	3.79
1962 to 1964	6.73	3.16	3.47
1965 to 1967	.84	4.28	3.42
1968 to 1970	7.49	5.57	1.82
1971 to 1973	10.15	7.10	2.85
1974 to 1976	9.01	5.14	3.68
1977 to 1979	12.00	7.88	3.83
1980 to 1981	10.04	6.59	3.23

The Stability of M1 Velocity

Source: Joint Economics Committee Report, March 1982

267

The fear of financial innovation by Fed officials is not new. The explosion of financial innovation in the 1970's was a source of deep concern to the Federal Reserve, and Arthur Burns was incessant in his complaint that the innovations would undermine the execution of monetary policy. In his long personal apologia—"The Anguish of Central Banking," of September 30, 1979—he said:

There are other effects that raise doubts about the meaning of particular growth rates of the monetary aggregates. I have in mind changes in financial practices that evolved in the United States during the 1960's and that culminated in an explosion of financial innovations in the 1970's.

Many of these changes were facilitated by regulatory actions or the development of new computer technology. But the driving force behind them was the incentive that sharply rising market interest rates gave to financial institutions and their customers to change their ways of doing business. Commercial banks responded to rising rates by economizing on noninterest-bearing reserves and their customers responded by economizing on noninterest-bearing demand deposits. Both banks and large corporations developed new sources of funds in the Eurodollar market and the domestic commercial paper market. Banks developed new techniques of liability management by exploiting these sources as well as the vast potential of the federal funds market and the market for negotiable certificates of deposit. Other financial institutions—including savings banks, savings and loan associations, credit unions, and money market funds—developed new transactions services in connection with customer accounts on which they paid interest. Banks fought this competition for transactions balances by offering large depositors special services that reduced the average level of balance they had to carry and by employing various ingenious means to pay interest on balances that were held in large part for transactions purposes.

Developments of this kind have profound consequences for the environment in which American monetary policy operates. As a result . . . central banking has not only lost its moorings in interest rates; that has happened to a large extent also in the case of the monetary aggregates.

In 1980, in response to complaints like this from officials and regulators who felt their power was being diminished, the Carter administration passed the misnamed Depository Institutions Deregulation and Monetary Control Act. In fact, this vicious piece of legislation had the effect of vastly expanding the regulatory power of the Federal Reserve to cover *every depository institution* in the country. There was a huge extension of the power of Federal Reserve officials to interfere in the pricing and allocation of credit.

Here are some of the provisions of this abominable piece of legislation:

> The Board of Governors can require all depository institutions [commercial banks, savings banks, savings and loan associations, and credit unions] to submit directly or indirectly reports of assets and liabilities for monetary and credit control purposes.
>
> Each depository institution must maintain reserves against transaction accounts [demand, negotiable order of withdrawal, share draft, deposits subject to automatic and telephone transfers].
>
> If five Board members find extraordinary circumstances exist, the Board may, after consultation with Congressional banking committees, alter reserve rations from the statutory ranges for renewable 180-day periods.
>
> Depository institutions with transaction accounts or nonpersonal time deposits are entitled to the same discount window privileges as member banks.

This was the answer devised by the Carter administration to the financial innovations of the 1970's—*innovations that were in large part the response of a beleaguered financial services industry to the inflation and regulations imposed by the Federal Reserve in the first place.*

There is no doubt that the Federal Reserve is seeking to impose still more restrictions on the financial services industry, particularly on the money market funds. It will be able to play on the divisions within the financial services; it will be able to appeal to those already under the yoke of its regulations with the argument that "it's not fair" that others have escaped its controls.

Walter Wriston warned of this trap in January 1981:

> Unequal laws are a transient phenomenon, as by its nature government has to strive for equity. Modern parlance talks

about level playing fields. The poet John Donne wrote: "Never send to know for whom the bell tolls. It tolls for thee." It tolled for the banks when the Monetary Control Act of 1980 gave the Federal Reserve vast new powers over the whole banking industry. It tolled for the money market funds in 1980 when President Carter invoked the Credit Control Act to impose reserve requirements on them. It tolled for Merrill Lynch when the Oregon attorney general ruled that their Cash Management Account was unlicensed banking and barred it from the state.

A History of More and More Regulation

When the Federal Reserve was created in 1913, it was intended purely as a simple insurance scheme for the member banks. It was intended to be not a central bank, but a means of helping member banks out of trouble from time to time.

Any loans made to member commercial banks had to be backed by "eligible" paper, such as advances, bills, and discounts arising from private production and marketing of real goods. Federal Reserve bank managers were to decide if applications for loans satisfied the eligibility requirements. The discount rate charged by the Federal Reserve banks to commercial banks was to be a penalty rate, to prevent the discounting privilege from becoming a subsidy. The Federal Reserve banks themselves had to fulfill statutory gold reserve requirements, so that they were constrained by the principle of gold redemption for the money they issued.

In the Great Depression of the 1930's the Federal Reserve was a failure. Its actions made the depression far worse than it already was. This disaster was accomplished by the Fed's action in restricting credit as interest rates fell (because declining interest rates "meant" credit was easy). President Hoover found the Fed to be a very weak reed in his time of trouble. Consequently, the Federal Reserve's powers were expanded through the Federal Reserve Acts of 1933 and 1935, which gave it the power to purchase government securities, specify reserve requirements for "member" commercial banks, and impose ceilings on interest rates. Contemporary legislation prohibited all monetary transactions in gold and all private gold holdings beyond a certain minimal amount. The basis for full-scale central banking, free of any significant limit, and directed toward a pervasive control over the detailed structure of the financial services industry in America, was thus established.

Donald Regan and Ronald Reagan Attempt a Reform

The Reagan administration has set about attempting to roll back the tide of regulatory power accruing to the Federal Reserve. In September 1981, Donald Regan, secretary of the Treasury, said:

The regulatory structure has several distinct problems.

The *first* problem is *interest rate restrictions.* In the mid-1960's thrift institutions became subject to such restrictions to protect them from the effect of rising interest rates and excessive competition from the banks for funds.

Another problem fostered by regulation is *specialization.* The financial markets today change rapidly as one innovation follows another. Institutions have to be able to adjust and the more specialized an institution, the less capable it is of adjusting.

The *third problem* area is regulation of *geographic markets.*

Geographic limitations stemmed from a historic context characterized by fear of financial power concentrated in the hands of banking institutions. The result was a statutory framework that separates one class of depository institution from another, that proscribes bank mergers and acquisitions across certain geographic boundaries and that has Balkanized our financial system into 42,000 depository institutions including 15,000 commercial banks.

Such artificial geographic constraints run counter to the nature of a modern financial services industry, which is inherently an interest business and in which wholesale banking activities are already being conducted on an interstate basis.

The *fourth* problem involves the *growth of the regulatory agencies themselves.*

Traditionally, there have been five Federal regulatory agencies supervising the Federally chartered and/or insured institutions: the Board of Governors of the Federal Reserve System, the Federal Deposit Insurance Corporation, the Federal Home Loan Bank Board, the National Credit Union Administration Board, and the Comptroller of the Currency. In addition, state regulatory agencies are responsible for supervising state-chartered institutions. More recently, the Depository Institutions Deregulation Committee and the Federal Financial Institutions Examination Council have been added. There is a growing

belief that the existing regulatory structure is inefficient, that it
lacks flexibility needed to accommodate market changes and
that a substantial reorganization and rationalization of the system is overdue.

If we can let this heavily regulated industry compete, the
chief beneficiary will be the individual consumer of financial
services—the small, retail consumer who must go from door to
door trying to satisfy his financial needs.

Just in case you got the idea from that rousing statement by
Donald Regan that there is an irresistible force for reform of the
American financial system afoot, may I make it clear that the Depository Institutions Deregulation Committee, established as part of the
1980 Monetary Control Act to reduce the regulation of interest rates,
is proceeding at a snail's pace, caught up in a maze of conflicting
attempts by members of the financial services industry to protect
their own special positions.

More important, the Federal Reserve is looking to still more ambitious ways of imposing controls on *every single financial transaction* carried out in this country. Anthony Solomon, president of the
New York Federal Reserve, said in that institution's 1981 annual
report:

> At some point, the process of innovation and deregulation may
> move us to a new situation in which a more fundamental
> reevaluation of our use of monetary targets may be necessary.
> I do not know how far we may be from such a situation but the
> time is probably less than a decade and may possibly be sub-
> stantially less than that. If, for example, the sweep accounts
> [typified by the cash management–type of account where the
> account is swept clean daily] should spread as rapidly as the use
> of the money funds has in the past couple of years, the need for
> a basic new look at our procedures could come on with uncom-
> fortable speed.
>
> As I have already suggested, in this new world the bulk of
> all transactions balances will be paying market-related rates.
> Thus, all meaningful definitions of money might exhibit the
> kinds of control problems that the broad definitions are already
> beginning to show. One possible means of remedying such a
> situation would be to develop legislation defining a "transac-
> tions" aggregate very broadly, perhaps to include all instru-

ments payable at "par" within a few business days and then to impose reserve requirements on such instruments.

The regulators never give up. Their permanent complaint always is: we could do a lot better if you gave us more power; if you gave up yet some more of your freedom. There would be more sympathy with any such response were there the slightest reason to believe that the vast expansion of the powers of the Federal Reserve in regulation since 1913 have been accompanied by a major increase in monetary stability and economic growth in the United States. On the contrary, monetary instability has increased seemingly without limit and we are now in the middle of the biggest economic contraction in fifty years.

11 *A Ray of Hope*

By early 1982 it was possible to believe that if the Federal Reserve did not lose control of the growth of money, the United States was on the verge of an extraordinary breakthrough into a new world of disinflation, unknown since the early 1960's. Beginning in May 1981, when the Fed first made a beginning on the mid-1981 money growth freeze, there was a sudden and sustained fall in the rate of growth of producer (wholesale) prices in America.

In the first half of 1981 producer prices rose about 10 percent a

The Collapse of the Inflation of Producer Prices United States Year-on-Year or Seasonally Adjusted Annual Growth Rates

Year	Percent Increase
1973	11.8%
1974	18.3
1975	6.6
1976	3.7
1977	6.9
1978	9.2
1979	12.8
1980	11.8
1981	7.0
I	12.8
II	6.8
III	2.8
IV	5.6

year and in the second half of the year by about 4 percent, on average. This reduction in the rate of growth of producer prices was a reflection of the reduction in the rate of growth of M1-B that had taken place in the preceding four years.

M1-B Percentage Increase—Fourth Quarter to Fourth Quarter

1978	8.3%
1979	7.5
1980	6.6
1981	5.0

These fourth-quarter to fourth-quarter figures dramatically point up the slowdown in monetary growth during 1981. Annual average figures also show a similar story.

M1-B Annual Average to Annual Average—Percentage Growth

1978	8.2%
1979	7.7
1980	5.9
1981	4.7

Slower monetary growth was a fundamental element in breaking the trend of inflation in the United States in 1981.

World Energy Markets Collapse

Another important element in breaking this trend was the particular effect of the collapse of oil markets in 1981. Following the ill-advised move by the OPEC cartel in 1979 to make a second huge increase in crude oil prices, world energy markets experienced a fundamental change, soon reflected in an emerging world oil glut in 1981, which carried over in even more extreme form into 1982. The overall effect of this change, accelerated by the decision of President Reagan in early 1981 to deregulate oil prices in the United States, was to smash the dominance of the OPEC oil cartel and bring about a surplus in world energy markets accompanied by declining nominal oil prices and even more rapidly declining real oil prices.

275

The world energy balance outlook is summarized in the following table, prepared by Nicocles Michas and Henry Wojtyla of the New York brokerage firm of Rosenkrantz, Ehrenkrantz, Lyon & Ross. These two economists were foremost in the world in forecasting the 1981 and 1982 oil glut.

As can be seen from the table, there was a very modest 0.3 percent annual rate of increase in world energy demand from 1973 to 1982, reflecting the depressing effects of the fifteen- to sixteenfold increase in nominal oil prices which took place. Between 1982 and 1987 a

World Energy
(Millions of Barrels a Day, Oil Equivalent)

	1973	1981	1982	% Increase Annual 73–82	1987	% Increase Annual 82–87
World Energy*						
Demand	87.0	92.1	91.0	0.5%	101	2.1%
Real World						
GNP (1978 $)	6510	8545	8720	3.3	10610	4.0
'000 BTU/GNP	28.29	22.82	22.09	−2.7	20.15	−1.8
Supply						
Nonoil Energy						
Output	39.1	48.0	50.0	2.8	61	4.1
Oil Production	48.3	43.1	40.0	−2.1	40	0
Stock Change,						
etc.	−0.4	1.0	1.0	—	0	—
Non-OPEC Oil						
Production	16.5	20.7	22.0	3.2	28	4.9
OPEC Oil†						
Production	31.8	22.4	18.0	−6.1	12	−7.8
OPEC Exports	30.1	20.0	15.3	−7.2	9	−10.0
To: U.S.	3.0	3.0	1.5		0	
Europe	15.4	8.0	6.5		5	
Japan	5.0	3.5	3.0		2	
Other	6.7	5.5	4.3		2	

*Excludes communist countries
†Includes total Gulf

more rapid 2.1 percent annual rate of growth is forecast, based on the fact that real energy prices are expected to decline over this period.

A powerful trend toward conservation of energy is evident in the fact that the number of BTU's (British thermal units, a measure of energy) per unit of world (noncommunist) gross national product fell 2.7 percent a year between 1973 and 1982 and is slated to fall by a further 1.8 percent a year between 1982 and 1987.

The essential ingredients of the table on page 276 are:

1. A continuing steady decline in the number of BTU's per unit of gross national product, indicating the impact of energy conservation in the last decade.

2. The growth of nonoil energy output, stimulated by the 1972–73 and the 1979 "oil shocks." Output of coal, notably, has been greatly stimulated.

3. The growth of non-OPEC-oil output, as higher cost producers, previously unable to produce oil profitably, were brought into production following the stimulus to oil and gas production worldwide provided by the rise in nominal crude oil prices in the last decade.

4. The decline in OPEC oil production, as OPEC nations attempted to hold prices by cutting their own output.

5. The even more rapid decline in OPEC exports, for the same reasons.

Within two years of the 1979 second oil price shock there was a large and pervasive world oil glut and indeed a glut in *all* world energy markets. By the end of 1981 nominal prices of oil had started to fall. By the summer of 1983, it could be postulated, the nominal "marker" price of oil, set by the OPEC group at a minimum of $34 per barrel (Saudi Light basis) in 1981, would have fallen farther.

The Payoff for Tougher Money Policies

The Federal Reserve's monetary policy over the three years ended 1982 was very patchy in its execution, in that it generated highly variable trends in money growth. But there was at least, overall, a reduction in the average rate of money growth. The initial impact of slower money in slowing down the growth of real gross national product after 1978 put pressure on all markets, including commodity markets and labor markets. Falling demand for commodities assisted in bringing about the major reversal of world commodity markets in 1982. Among these commodity markets, the world oil market was a very important part.

As progress in reducing the rate of price growth in America occurred, following the gradual reduction in money growth, a self-reinforcing effect came into play. Declining prices for commodities helped cause a change in inflationary expectations, and further falls in prices of commodities occurred, as evidenced by the continuing collapse in the market for gold, the spot price of which fell from $500 an ounce in mid-1981 to little more than $300 an ounce in March 1982. The Commodity Research Bureau Index of Future Commodity Prices crashed from a peak of nearly 340 in 1981 to 230 in mid-1982, a drop of one-third.

Changes in the attitude of the American public to future prices was an important factor in the growing weakness in house prices, which spread rapidly during 1981, culminating in early 1982 in the situation in which home prices were actually lower than a year previously—as compared with the average annual increases of 15 to 20 percent to which homeowners have become accustomed in the 1970's.

These all were examples of the "virtuous cycle" of disinflation set in train by the degree of monetary restraint achieved after 1979. The key issue in early 1982 was: Would the Fed follow through? Or would there be another failure as occurred in 1970 and 1976?

The Strong Dollar

During 1981 the dollar appreciated substantially in value, compared with other major currencies. The nominal appreciation of the dollar, on a trade-weighted basis, was 15.6 percent, a very substantial improvement that had the general effect of restoring the external relative value of the dollar to where it was ten years previously. During 1978, 1979, and 1980 the external value of the dollar had fallen, reflecting the failure of monetary policy in the United States to provide a stable price level, compared with what was occurring in other major countries.

There was a substantial improvement in the United States current account balance of payments with the rest of the world in 1981. From a current account deficit of $14 billion in 1977 and 1978, there was a change to a surplus of $1.4 billion in 1979 and on through a surplus of $3.7 billion in 1980 to a surplus of $6.5 billion in the first three quarters of 1981.

The improvement in the strength of the dollar reflected in part the stabilization of oil import costs in 1981, which actually declined toward the end of that year. It also reflected major increases in the surplus of the United States on "services," which includes all the returns from past American overseas investment. Another factor was a shift to dollar-denominated assets, which may well have been a consequence of the evident improvement in the inflation situation in America during 1981. This improvement, of course, reflected itself, as we know, in huge increases in real interest rates in America during 1981. Large sales of dollar assets by foreign central banks were initiated during 1981 in an attempt by those nations to inhibit the rise in the value of the dollar relative to their own currencies. But this did little to prevent the dollar from rising. The growing preference for dollar-denominated assets relative to other assets no doubt reflected a positive response by overseas investors to the improvement in the control of inflation in America, as well as a general endorsement of the "free market" policies espoused by President Reagan, compared with the growing trend to socialist policies in major European countries, notably France and Germany.

In this context, it is important to examine how the "hands off" policies of the U.S. Treasury, under Beryl Sprinkel and Donald Regan, worked out during 1981. In the *Economic Report of the President, February 1982* (the annual report of the Council of Economic Advisers, the membership of which is described later), the trend of official intervention in foreign exchange markets is explained as follows:

> There is a long tradition among monetary authorities of intervention in the foreign exchange markets to prevent what is known as overshooting, undershooting, or more generally, disorderly market conditions. But there is no conclusive evidence that official intervention in the past has achieved its purpose. The large purchases of dollar-denominated assets by foreign

279

central banks in 1977–78 did not prevent the dollar from depreciating and their large sales of dollar assets in 1980–81 did not prevent the dollar from appreciating. Moreover, intervention may have been counterproductive. Market participants did not know whether it signaled a change in monetary policy, thereby leading to increased uncertainty on their part.

There was no doubt about the commitment of the U.S. Treasury under President Reagan never to return to the practices of the past, when the Federal Reserve had carried out huge daily intervention in the foreign exchange markets. This constant "churning" in the foreign exchange markets was analogous to the constant "churning" of billions and billions of dollars in the domestic bond markets by the Federal Reserve.

The success of nonintervention in foreign exchange would be used as a justification for abandoning all the domestic market intervention by Fed officials. The *Economic Report of the President* spelled out the criticism of past Fed policies further:

> When the previous [Carter] Administration left office, intervention by the United States was being conducted at a relatively high volume, virtually on a day-to-day basis, with the objective of using the periods of dollar strength first to cover outstanding foreign currency liabilities and later to build foreign currency reserves. This was the first time, at least in recent history, that the United States had embarked on a deliberate policy of acquiring substantial foreign currency reserves.
>
> Early in 1981 the new Administration scaled back U.S. intervention in foreign exchange markets. In conjunction with a strong emphasis on economic fundamentals, this Administration has returned to the policy of intervening only when necessary to counter conditions of severe disorder in the market.
>
> As in the past, no attempt has been made to define disorderly conditions in advance.
>
> With the President's economic program firmly in place and with the Federal Reserve following a policy of gradually reducing the rate of monetary growth to a non-inflationary level, the occurrence of disorderly conditions is likely to be significantly less in the future than in the past.

Thus, following the persistent excessive increase in money supply in America over the decade of the 1970's, compared with what was happening in other major countries, the real exchange rate of the dollar (that is, the result of adjusting the nominal index of the U.S. exchange rate by relative movements in consumer prices to give a measure of the dollar's foreign purchasing power) had fallen to about 80 percent of the March 1973 level. By mid-1981 this index had risen to over 110 and at the end of the year was still in excess of 100. The

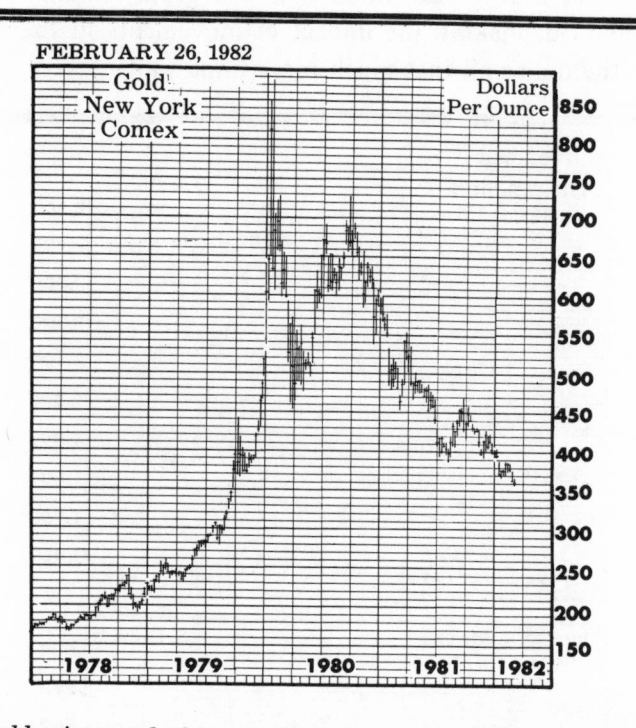

FEBRUARY 26, 1982

Gold
New York
Comex

Dollars Per Ounce

850
800
750
700
650
600
550
500
450
400
350
300
250
200
150

1978   1979   1980   1981   1982

The gold price reached its zenith in the early months of 1980, the culmination of the inflationary upward ratcheting process of the previous fifteen years. In October 1979 Volcker dashed back to the United States to announce the abandonment of the attempt to hold down interest rates. It was this attempt which had precipitated the final monetary explosion of 1979. The gold price made a recovery of sorts in the second half of 1980, when the Fed instituted the "elect Carter" money growth boom. With the election of President Reagan, the move to a tighter monetary policy, the freeing of the dollar, and the rise in real interest rates, the fate of gold was sealed.

The next charts show the collapse of non-dollar currencies — the pound and the Deutsche Mark are the two examples given — following the initiation of disinflationary economic policies in America combined with the abandonment of official intervention in the foreign exchange markets.

purchasing power of the dollar in terms of other major currencies improved and assisted in putting a lid on price increases in the United States.

The effect of an appreciating dollar was thus added to the effect of declining money growth rates in 1981 in reducing the rate of growth of inflation in America. Moreover, during the 1970's the proportion of exports and imports to the gross national product nearly doubled, making the impact of movements in the relative value of the dollar all that much more important.

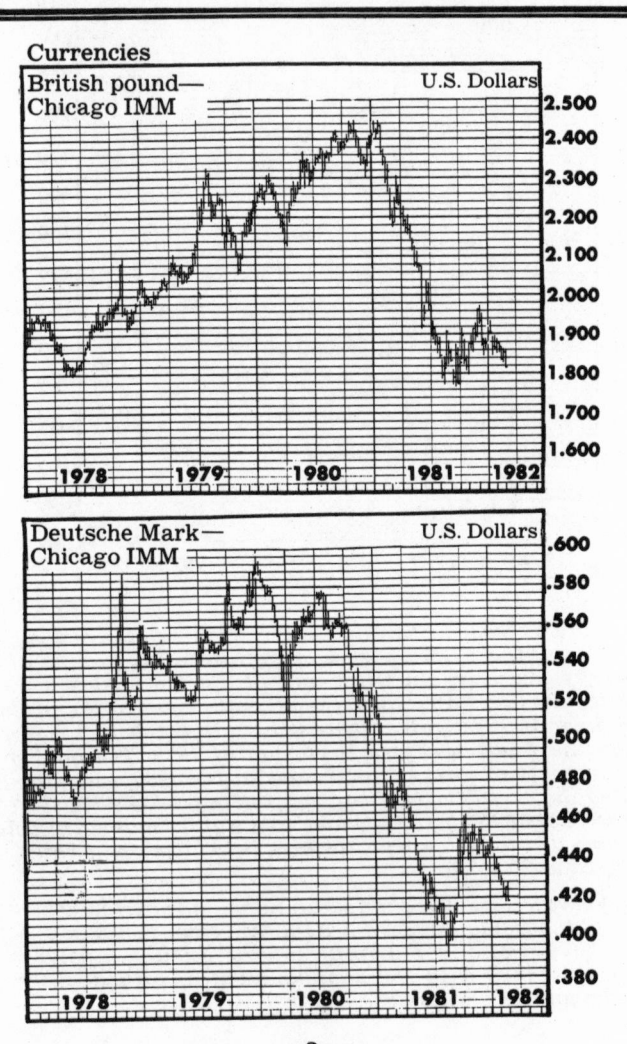

All told, the strength of the dollar in 1981, which was a result of improved monetary control and of the general "free market" attraction of the U.S. economy, provided a further bonus toward disinflation in America. The deregulation of oil in America and the improved monetary policy in 1981 (on average) were important elements. The overall success of the United States in the world economy in 1981 was accomplished, let us underline, without any significant direct official intervention at all in foreign exchange markets. The Federal Reserve was kept out of these markets virtually completely.

Real Interest Rates Actually Rose Despite Disinflation

In spite of the crash of inflation rates during the last half of 1981, nominal interest rates declined only moderately. Accordingly there was a very sharp *increase* in real interest rates. This boom in real interest rates during 1981 at the time represented, as we have seen, a crucial threat to the continued financial stability of the whole economic system, being a very sharp, even extreme increase in the real burden of current indebtedness. Combined with the continuing boom in short-term borrowing by corporations during 1981 and 1982, the rise in real interest rates came to represent a threat to the continuing stability of the financial system.

The Federal Reserve has argued, through its chairman, Paul Volcker, that the rise in real interest rates during 1981 and into the early months of 1982 was the result of fears among investors of prospective large budget deficits by the federal government.

In testimony to the House Banking Committee on February 10, 1982, Volcker said of the future of interest rates:

Experience during 1981 illustrates the variety of forces impinging on interest rates and credit market conditions. Over long periods of time there should be a relationship between interest rates and inflationary expectations—that is, both lenders and borrowers might reasonably expect a small positive return on loanable funds in "real" terms, after allowing for inflation. When economic conditions were relatively stable in the postwar period and inflation low, that relationship with respect to long-term interest rates was fairly steady. But history is replete with deviations for a time in either direction and high levels of income taxation distort the comparison. Before taxes, "real" interest rates (measured on the base of actual inflation) were negative during part of the 1970's but recently have been extraordinarily high. One factor, particularly in long-term markets, appears to be concern about whether public policy will, in fact, "carry through" the fight on inflation.

Even with inflation subsiding, the threat of prolonged large Federal deficits as the economy recovers points to a more imminent concern—direct government competition for a limited supply of savings and loanable funds. The clear implication is greater pressure on interest rates than otherwise, with those interest rates serving to "crowd out" other borrowers.

It may have been that part of the reason for the persistence of high real rates of interest in 1981–82 was the fear of future budget deficits. There was great publicity on the subject and many prominent business organizations, such as the prestigious Business Roundtable group, comprising the chief executives of about 300 major corporations, called on the president to take action to close the budget deficits that seemed to be looming. I find it difficult to take very seriously the impact of anything as nebulous as a future budget deficit due in two years on the movement of interest rates today. Much more likely in its impact would be the fear of future inflation, based on bitter past experience.

Boom in Real Interest Rates: 1981 and Early 1982

	Prime Rate	% Increase Consumer Price Index	Real Interest Rate	Federal Budget Deficit $ Billion
1976	6.84%	4.8%	+2.04%	−$66.4 bil.
1977	6.83	6.8	+0.03	−45.0
1978	9.06	9.0	+0.06	−48.8
1979	12.67	13.3	−0.33	−27.7
1980	15.27	12.4	+2.87	−59.5
1981	18.87	8.9	+9.97	−57.9
1982 IQr.*	15	4	+11	−70.

*Estimated Annual Rates

Volcker did show some awareness of the need for continued monetary restraint when he told the House Banking Committee: "To accept inflationary increases in the money supply in an attempt to lower interest rates would ultimately be self-defeating; even in the short run, market sensitivities might well give the opposite result."

The following points in the table above stand out:

1. The very sharp rise in real interest rates in 1981 and 1982 was due to the failure of nominal interest rates to fall, despite a very sharp reduction of inflation. Continuing fears about inflation were responsible for the failure of rates to decline more sharply as inflation came down.

2. The emergence of high real rates of interest was not accompanied by any sudden massive increase in the actual rate of budget deficits. In 1980, 1981, and the first quarter of 1982 the rate of budget deficits was very similar.

In early 1982 differing viewpoints were clearly expressed by the Treasury and the Federal Reserve on the issue of the relative importance of inflationary expectations on the one hand and of huge federal budget deficits "crowding out" the limited capital available to the private sector on the other.

Sprinkel Nails His Flag to the Mast—Deficits Don't Matter to Interest Rate Moves

The Treasury view of what was likely to happen was expressed by Beryl Sprinkel on February 1, 1982, when speaking about the same general time as Volcker was addressing the House Banking Committee. Sprinkel metaphorically nailed his flag to the mast, denying that deficits would cause higher real interest rates.

Interest rates have moved up in recent weeks, but I am confident that they will return to their previous downward trend. It is baffling that many economic analysts do not even agree on the *direction* that interest rates will head. Now why is this? I think there are a number of reasons. First, there is a difference of opinion over the relative power of market forces.

The bearish fellows believe, I *think,* that the level of interest rates will be forced up by a forthcoming expansion of credit demand colliding with an alleged restriction of supply by the

Federal Reserve. Big borrowing by the Government puts upward pressure on interest rates. Economic growth produces corporate demand for loans for business expansion, which also puts upward pressure on interest rates. If you have big government deficits *and* economic expansion—as we will have this year—then you will supposedly get a double whammy effect on credit demand. If you add to this the popular notion that the Fed is keeping *credit* tight, you can see why some believe interest rates will go through the roof.

This argument appears to be saying that it is the law of supply and demand that is controlling. A greater demand to borrow money—especially when its supply is being held in check—will supposedly result in a higher price for the money.

All that sounds very compelling, doesn't it? And it sounds as if it came right out of Adam Smith's *Wealth of Nations.* Let me say that there is *some* truth to this view. The law of supply and demand is alive and well in the marketplace and increased demand for credit does exert pressures—on interest rates.

But our case, it turns out, is also based on Adam Smith—the part in his book where he says people would rather make money than lose money.

If you are in the business of lending money, and you are trying to anticipate your future profit margin, you begin to think about future risks: possible default, future tax liabilities, and future inflation. Even if that borrower is the most creditworthy sort, you are going to charge him higher interest rates if you think he will be paying you back in inflated—and therefore less valuable—dollars.

If you think that the rate of inflation will be low in the future, you can reduce your rates and still expect to make a profit. And if you don't lower your rates accordingly, you can bet your competitor will.

In a nutshell, therefore, we have one view that says an increase in demand for credit puts upward pressure on interest rates. The other view says that declining inflation—due to responsible monetary policy—puts downward pressure on interest rates. In fact, there is pressure pushing rates both ways. But the downward pressure is *much* stronger than upward pressure.

Now if the argument in the abstract leaves you cold, let's forget theory for a moment and look at history. In the fall of 1975, as post-recession real economic growth was gaining speed, interest rates moved up for a few weeks. However, the Fed maintained a steady hand on the tiller. And what happened? As the economy continued to grow that fall, and into the following year, inflation continued to go down.

This was a period, please remember, of massive Federal deficits: $66 billion in Fiscal year 1976. A deficit which, as a percentage of GNP, is larger than the deficit projected for this year. And yet there was solid economic growth. And as inflation was declining to under 5 percent, interest rates *continued* their downward trend. Not until late 1976 did rates move up. Because not until late 1976 was money growth increased sharply.

Now the second reason why there is disagreement over the future direction of interest rates has to do with a fundamental —and therefore critical—misunderstanding of what money is not. Money is money. It is a device which is used to facilitate economic transactions. It is *not* credit. And credit is *not* money.

If someone believes that inflation is caused by excessive money *and credit,* he would also believe that an effective anti-inflationary policy would have to restrict the supply of money *and credit.*

Unfortunately, many people view our monetary policy as an attempt to do just that. And, of course, they see a conflict; the Fed is seen as restricting the supply of credit while the budget deficit represents an increase in credit demand. When supply declines and demand increases, the result is obvious—prices rise.

But you see, the argument ends up wrong because it starts out wrong. The Fed is dealing with the supply of money. Unless the budget deficit is monetized—which we do not intend to do —it affects only the demand for credit. Money is not credit. Growth in credit is not inflationary. Growth in money is inflationary.

And the price of credit rises and falls depending on—what? In large part, depending on what people think will be the future purchasing power of money.

There is a rather subtle shift taking place in America. And failure to perceive this shift is, perhaps, a third reason for the differing views.

In periods of accelerating inflation—which is what we had until the last year—real assets tend to have a greater real rate of return than financial assets. As a result, over the last several years, savvy investors have tended to move out of such things as stocks and bonds and into such things as houses, land and antiques.

Conversely, in periods of decelerating inflation, there is a tendency for investors—institutions and individual households —to shift their portfolios somewhat from real assets to financial assets. The reason for the shift, of course, is that investors see a shift in the rate of return of one category of assets relative to the other category. I am not saying that everyone is selling rugs and condominiums and buying stock. But there is some of that going on.

And in a $4 trillion economy—which we are on the verge of having—a shift of one or two percentage points puts tens of billions of dollars into the system in the form of expanded potential credit. Thanks to declining inflation, that phenomenon is already happening and additional credit needed for economic expansion is forming rapidly.

Finally, there is a fourth explanation of the differing "upstairs downstairs" ideas on interest rates.

Some who say interest rates are going higher actually are saying: "The Fed is going to blow it . . . again." When economic recovery really picks up steam later this year, there may be some temporary upward movement of interest rates. And there is fear that, if this happens, the Fed could overreact and send a gusher of new money out. Now if that were to happen, I heartily agree, we would be in for high interest rates. Fortunately I am confident that that will *not* happen.

Sprinkel was arguing that as long as a tight monetary policy remained in place, the problem of high interest rates would cure itself. Volcker, along with a great number of business individuals, prominent spokesmen for Wall Street (notably Henry Kaufman, the economist for Salomon Brothers, and Al Wojnilower, the economist for First Boston Corporation), and the Democratic party, was arguing that interest rates would fail to decline and might even rise even higher should the federal government fail to bring the prospective deficits under control.

Sprinkel was just as strongly opposed to deficits as anyone else. But he did not believe they were a material factor in holding up interest rates, as long as a tight money policy was pursued.

The outcome of this divergent assessment by Volcker and Sprinkel on the movement of interest rates in 1982 would affect the power and prestige of the Fed very materially. If Sprinkel were proved to be

right and interest rates did collapse during 1982, the ground would
be laid for another attack on the independence of the Fed as set out
in the *Economic Report of the President, February 1982.*

1982 Economic Report of the President—Powerful Criticism of the Fed

As of February 1982 there was no doubt that the monetarist critics
of the Federal Reserve were very influential in the administration.
The *Economic Report of the President, February 1982* contains major
criticism of past Federal Reserve policies and in effect suggests a
reform that would remove discretionary power from the Fed to a
very large extent.

The report was signed by President Reagan and included a fore-
word by him, endorsing the views expressed. It was the policy statement of the President's Council of Economic Advisers, who in February 1982 were:

*Chairman Murray L. Weidenbaum, an economist who had spent
the preceding years of his professional career at Washington University, St. Louis, in the study of government regulation.

*Jerry L. Jordan, former dean of the Anderson School of Manage-
ment at the University of New Mexico and a former member of the
influential monetarist Shadow Open Market Committee.

*William Niskanen, former professor of Graduate School of Pub-
lic Policy, UCLA, at Berkeley, 1972 to 1975, and before that an
economist with the Ford Motor Company, which he left following
disputes with that company.

These three economists had deep-seated commitments to free market policies, tough money policies, and the reduction of government
intervention in the economic life of the nation. Later, both Weidenbaum and Jordan resigned, only to be replaced by two equally committed "free market" economists:

*Martin Feldstein, then director of the National Bureau of Eco-
nomic Research.

*William Poole, professor of economics at Brown University, a
former Fed official, and a fierce monetarist critic of the Fed. Not
surprisingly, the Council of Economic Advisers' *Economic Report*

was powerfully critical of the Federal Reserve's past policies. Among the fundamental criticisms of the Fed's policy and policy attitudes are:

1. *A strong distinction between "money" and "credit."*
Says the *Economic Report:*

Money is an asset that people generally accept as payment for goods and services. It consists of coins, currency and checkable deposits. Credit, in contrast, is one party's claim against another party, which is to be settled by a future payment of money. Confusion about the difference between money and credit arises because people can increase their spending either by reducing their money balances or obtaining credit.

Monetary expansion leads to an expansion in nominal income and activity, which in turn generates an increased demand for credit, thus reversing the initial decline in interest rates. In addition, a sustained higher rate of monetary growth will soon produce higher nominal interest rates to compensate lenders for the expected decline in the real value of their wealth.

When interest rates are high, credit is often said to be "tight," meaning that it is expensive. This does not necessarily mean that money is tight in the sense that its quantity is restricted. Indeed, quite the opposite is likely to be the case. "Easy" money, in the sense of a rapid growth in the stock of money, may very well be the underlying reason for a tight credit market. Conversely, tight money, in the sense of slow growth in the stock of money, is likely to lead eventually to a fall in nominal interest rates as inflation expectations subside. But it is credit, not money, that is easy.

This line of argument, of course, negates the complaint of the Fed and indeed the vast majority of business and media pundits that budget deficits cause high interest rates. It is the biggest single misconception dominating today's thinking and discussion about inflation.

2. *A strong support for M1 as an appropriate target for monetary control,* thus undermining another Fed complaint that financial innovations, such as money market funds, undermine the conduct of monetary policy.
Says the *Economic Report:*

Statistical support for this assertion is dubious. What would have to be demonstrated is that financial innovation—which is to a large extent the result of policy-imposed constraints on the financial system in an inflationary environment—has made it more difficult to achieve a given monetary target, and that the link between changes in nominal GNP and changes in the monetary aggregates—that is, changes in velocity—had become less predictable. The evidence does not seem to support either proposition. A study recently published by the Federal Reserve suggests that the authorities have the ability to control the measure of transactions balances known as M1 with a reasonable degree of precision. Furthermore, changes in velocity do not appear to be any more volatile than they have in the past. Indeed, changes in the trend of the growth rate of nominal GNP over the period 1960 to 1981 are almost entirely attributable to changes in the trend of the growth rate of the money stock (M1), as opposed to changes in the trend of the growth rate of velocity.

3. *A demand for a market-oriented penalty discount rate.*

Says the *Economic Report:* "The volatility of borrowed reserves could be reduced by tying the discount rate to market rates so as to reduce variability in the incentive to borrow. To keep such variability to an absolute minimum, the Federal Reserve would also have to set its discount rate somewhat above market rates—that is, to act as a penalty."

As we know, the Fed has in recent years, with the exception of 1979–80, tended to keep the discount rate *below* market rates, thus vitiating its intended use as a means of monetary control. In 1981 the discount rate was persistently below the federal funds rate. In mid-year the discount rate was only 14 percent while the federal funds rate was up around 19 percent. This sort of gap made the discount rate quite useless as an instrument of monetary policy because it was invariably cheaper for the banks to borrow from the Fed than through the ordinary open market. In raising this issue of the level of the discount rate, the *Economic Report* goes right into the very heart of the Fed's operating policies and, of course, presents a very fundamental criticism of the Fed, one that is strongly resented by senior Fed officials. Anthony Solomon, president of the New York Fed, strongly criticized such reforming ideas in December 1981, in a speech, "Financial Innovation and Monetary Policy"—a defense of the Fed's attitudes on "innovation as an excuse for monetary policy failure" and an attack on demands for market-oriented discount rates and contemporaneous reserve accounting. His speech, showing hardly a mite of recognition of the mountain of criticism of the Fed's procedures which has grown up in the community, was subsequently further honored by being converted into the *Annual Report, 1981, of the Federal Reserve Bank of New York*.

4. *A demand for contemporaneous reserve accounting,* another reform that has been long and successfully resisted by the Fed.

Says the *Economic Report of the President:* "An even more successful operation of a penalty rate would require a switch from the Federal Reserve's lagged reserve requirement rule to a system of contemporaneous reserve requirements."

Under existing rules, instituted in 1968, the banks have to pay the Federal Reserve the money due as reserves, based on the level of their deposits, two weeks previously. This change was introduced in 1968 as a means of attracting more smaller banks to join the Federal Reserve System. Until that time the banks had to pay the Fed for the reserves based on the level of deposits in the week in which the reserves payment was due.

Although many monetarists would like to see a return to contemporaneous reserve accounting (basing reserves payable on the current week's deposits), the banks and the Federal Reserve have resisted the change until very recently, when the Fed agreed to introduce contemporaneous reserve accounting during 1983.

The *Economic Report* continues:

The Federal Reserve Board has requested public comment on its proposal for a return to a system of contemporaneous reserve accounting [as practiced before 1968]. An important reason for going back to contemporaneous reserve accounting would be to permit greater flexibility in the discount rate, at a penalty level or otherwise, which in turn would provide more precise short-run control over total reserves by reducing the volatility of borrowings. Even in the absence of a penalty discount rate, however, contemporaneous reserve accounting would allow open market operations to have a more immediate effect on total bank reserves.

5. *The enactment of a monetary control rule, to which the Fed would have to conform.*

There could hardly be more powerful evidence of the extent to which the administration had lost faith in the Federal Reserve than the decision to raise this extremely sensitive issue in the *Economic Report of the President.* In effect, the *Economic Report* raised the whole question of the future independence of the Fed by exploring this inflammatory issue.

The report says: "Enactment of a statute or constitutional amendment requiring the monetary authorities to abide by a rule regarding monetary growth or inflation is another method that has been suggested for dealing with the problem of maintaining long-run price stability."

It is an indication of the mistrust which pervades the attitudes of the Treasury and the Council of Economic Advisers that it would be thought necessary to enact a *constitutional amendment* to tie the Fed's hands permanently. This radical suggestion reflects in turn the disillusion over Federal Reserve policy in the past—particularly the failure in both 1970 and 1976 to capitalize on the reduction of inflation that had then been achieved by persisting with a tight money policy thereafter.

The demand for a constitutional amendment also reflects the disillusion with the failure of acts of Congress as means of restraining the Fed. The passage of HCR 133 in March 1975 and the confirming legislation of PL 95-188 in November 1977, requiring the Fed to publish targets for money growth, were seen at the time as hopeful means of ensuring a permanent commitment to low, stable money growth. The manner in which the Fed evaded the intention of that legislation has clearly left a legacy of bitterness, which has welled up into demands for a permanent, constitutional lock on the Fed's discretion.

This issue had in fact been raised by the archcritics of the Fed in the Shadow Open Market Committee, the group of economists under the tutelage of Professors Allan Meltzer and Karl Brunner who have done so much over the years to bring to the fore criticism of the Fed's execution of monetary policy. Professor Brunner personally initiated and developed the idea of a constitutional amendment that would oblige the Fed by *constitutional fiat* to restrict its activities to bringing about a steady and stable, predetermined rate of increase in the monetary base. So in raising this issue so openly in the *Economic Report,* the administration was in effect waving a red flag at a bull.

The *Economic Report* discusses two possibilities:

a. *A rule on inflation.*

The advantage of formulating a [constitutional amendment] rule on the final outcome for inflation is that the monetary authorities would be free to devise the best monetary strategy to achieve the mandated outcome. That is, a rule would be laid down that inflation must not exceed, say, 2 percent a year and it would be up to the Fed to work out how to do that. The disadvantage would be the rule's flexibility. Temporary changes in the price level can be caused by a variety of shocks for which the monetary authorities cannot be held accountable. One approach would be to state the final outcome in terms of the average rate of growth of the consumer price index or nominal Gross National Product over a period of several years.

b. *A rule on monetary growth.*

The alternative of a target rule for monetary growth would have to be specified in such a way as to be consistent with price-level stability, again, over a period of several years. The rule could be revised from time to time in the light of any changes in the ratio of money growth to inflation. Such calibration would be the job of the central bank. Of course, the mere institution of a rule would not ensure its successful implementation.

Implementing a Fixed Rule over the Fed's Actions—How It Would Work

How would this system of a fixed and virtually inflexible rule be implemented? The *Economic Report,* in its discussion of ways and means to hogtie the Fed, says:

Each year, the monetary authorities [the Fed] would announce the rate of growth of the money supply that is consistent with achieving their medium-term objectives for nominal (GNP) income and inflation. Over the longer run, the rate of growth of the money supply must be consistent with the achievement of the rate of growth of nominal income implied by the inflation objective. To implement this procedure, the Federal Reserve would determine the rate of growth of total bank reserves that was consistent with the targeted growth of the deposit component of M1. Open market operations by the Federal Reserve would expand the monetary base by a sufficient amount to provide total bank reserves and the currency component of targeted M1 growth.

This is not very different from what the Fed already does now. The monetary target would be published, as is now the case. Thus, in 1982 the Fed published a target for the growth of M1 of 2½ to 5½ percent over the average of the fourth-quarter 1981 value for M1. That target of money is then "translated" by the Fed into a target for the growth of bank reserves (which target is worked out by studying the past relationships between bank reserves and M1). In turn, there is a well-known historical relationship between the monetary base (the total of bank reserves and currency) and the money supply, M1. This is called the money multiplier. Hence, by adjusting the monetary base, which the Fed can manipulate by buying or selling securities in the open market, the Fed can over time achieve a predetermined level of the money stock, M1. There has been important work done on the subject of monetary control by means of manipulating the size of the monetary base. Robert Rasche and James Johannes have done much of this work for the Shadow Open Market Committee, in which they have confirmed the predictability of the money multiplier. Similarly, Anatole Balbach, in the April 1981 issue of the St. Louis Fed *Review,* has given rigorous analysis of how this can be done.

Such a rule, says the *Economic Report of the President,* would free the Federal Reserve from having to interpret either the "social welfare function" of the country or, more practically, the objectives of current elected officials. The rule could be stated either in terms of an ultimate objective for inflation, as it is in some industrial countries, or in terms of a monetary growth target that would be consistent with the maintenance of price-level stability.

Bear in mind that what is being proposed here is a *constitutional amendment* which would remove a great deal of—perhaps all—

discretion from the president in the establishment of a growth target for money. This would in turn remove the president's power to influence the rate of growth of money and at the same time would drastically reduce his power to influence the rate of growth of the economy. A revolutionary proposal is thus raised in the *Economic Report* of 1982. It is an indication of the appalling loss of confidence in the Federal Reserve which has permeated the highest reaches of government in America.

The *Economic Report* continues:

> Ultimately the Federal Reserve would set a reserve growth path consistent with the desired price-level performance on the basis of estimates of several parameters:
> These would include:
> * The trend path of real output;
> * The trend of M1 velocity;
> * The trend of the ratio of M1 to the monetary base.
> As these changed, the targets for nominal income, M1 growth and the growth of the monetary base would be altered to maintain a stable price level. Unexpected changes in any of these parameters could be offset to maintain long-run price stability.

Milton Friedman's Proposal for Tying the Fed Down

A very similar proposal for reform of monetary policy was advanced by Milton Friedman in his July 1981 speech to the Western Economic Association in San Francisco. He called for the replacement of lagged reserve accounting by contemporaneous reserve accounting; for the setting of a target path several years ahead for a single aggregate, such as M2 or the monetary base; for the mechanical, predetermined feeding out by the Fed of a weekly amount of reserves, by a predetermined mechanical system of weekly purchases of securities; for the announcement of the scheduled purchases in advance and sticking to it; and for making the discount rate a penalty rate, tied to a market rate so that it moves automatically. Friedman said:

> Such a policy would assure control over the monetary aggregates—not from day to day but over the longer period the Fed now insists is all that matters. It would remove uncertainty

about Fed policy and establish credibility for that policy. It would leave to the market the day-to-day and seasonal adjustments that the market is well qualified to handle—and could do so far more effectively if it knew precisely what the Federal Reserve intended to do, than in the present state of uncertainty, with the weekly guessing game about Fed intentions that follows each Friday's release of the figures on money supply.

But it would have other effects as well. The open market desk could be replaced by the part-time activity of one employee to make the designated purchases. He would be buying roughly $100 million a week, not as now $184 hundred million or more than $18 billion [a week]. The Federal Open Market Committee could meet once every three or six months instead of monthly. The research staff at the Federal Reserve and at the twelve regional banks could be cut drastically. A large fraction of those research staffs—for the most part, highly trained and competent economists—have as their main function preparing their presidents for the monthly open market meetings.

"The Future Challenge"

Having delivered itself of a tremendous broadside against the officials of the Federal Reserve, the *Economic Report* goes on to outline the way it thinks policy could work out:

The whole process of renewed economic growth without inflation can be speeded up if the policy of monetary restraint is believed by the public, since it is an unanticipated decrease in money growth that significantly affects output and employment in the short run.

If the decrease is generally anticipated, wages and prices will begin to rise more slowly and the adverse short-run effects on output and employment will be minimized. That is why it is so important for the public to be convinced that an anti-inflationary monetary policy has finally been adopted. The Federal Reserve can maximize the credibility of its monetary policy and hence reduce the transition costs of eliminating inflation by announcing a specific target for the rate of money growth and by minimizing short-run deviations from that target.

The monetary system is evolving toward one in which the Federal Reserve will have very close control over M1, suitably redefined from time to time, through control of reserves. With uniform reserve requirements on transaction accounts (as spe-

297

cified by the 1980 Monetary Control Act), there will be relatively little variability in the ratio of M1 to the monetary base.

Longer-term movements in this ratio can be offset by open market operations. Monetary aggregates other than M1 may serve as useful indicators of the effects of policy actions, but they will not be directly controllable by the Federal Reserve and therefore will not be useful as short-run targets.

What can be avoided are the procyclical changes in the growth of the money supply that have occurred in the past.

This comes down to a very fundamental criticism of the Fed along the following lines:

1. The Fed has failed to control money growth, which has often been procyclical.

2. The Fed cannot be left alone to go on as it has. There have to be major changes, including the establishment of a market-oriented discount rate, contemporaneous reserve accounting, and the adoption of a predetermined rate of growth of the monetary base.

3. The Fed is to stop meddling in the money markets on a day-to-day basis, as it has been obliged to stop meddling in the foreign exchange markets.

4. All attempts to control interest rates must be abandoned.

You will not be surprised to learn that the criticisms of the Federal Reserve made in the *Economic Report of the President* are very similar, if not actually identical, to those of the Shadow Open Market Committee, of which Beryl Sprinkel was a member for nearly ten years before he went to the Treasury.

Nor will you be surprised to learn that on April 8, 1981, ten months before the report was published, Sprinkel enunciated the very same criticisms in his long attack on the Federal Reserve in evidence to the Joint Economic Committee. That evidence concluded as follows:

1. Sprinkel demanded the abandonment of multiple aggregate targeting such as the Fed had carried on for the preceding years, as part of its attempt to cover its tracks and avoid congressional criticism.

2. "It is our belief," he said, "that a meaningful reduction in inflationary pressures requires that the rate of growth of the adjusted

monetary base be reduced smoothly and persistently by about one half between 1980 and 1984."

"If that pattern is followed we are quite confident that: (a) the systematic deviations of money growth from the trend will be reduced; (b) the trend of money growth will fall; (c) the level and variability of interest rates will decline; and (d) inflation will abate significantly."

3. "We hope that the Federal Reserve will decide to move to a flexible market-oriented administration of discount policy and we applaud its consideration of restoring contemporaneous reserve accounting."

4. "I would add that I am pleased by the increased emphasis on reserves and relaxation of the Fed Funds restraint [meaning the Fed has allowed the federal funds rate to move in a wider band] since October 1979."

Has Anything Been Done?

Despite all the words from the Treasury, Beryl Sprinkel, the president, the Council of Economic Advisers, the Shadow Open Market Committee, and its own research staff, the Federal Reserve has adopted only one of these recommendations—that relating to contemporaneous reserve accounting. As I have already pointed out, it has not adopted a market discount rate policy; it has persistently reverted to targeting the federal funds rate; it has a system of trying to manipulate the financial system of the largest economy in the world by a laughable policy of fooling around with a billion or two of borrowed reserves.

12 *Deficit Myths*

By early 1982 the president's economic policy was under very sharp attack and the principal point of concentration of this attack was the prospective large deficits of the federal budget. Many different groups participated in this assault, and although individual motivations differed, the end result of the criticism launched against the president was that the big budget deficits would cause interest rates to remain high. As things turned out, the whole case for high interest rates resulting from high budget deficits fell to the ground with the collapse of interest rates after June 1982.

Even before the collapse of rates—forecast so correctly by Beryl Sprinkel—it was difficult to find any factual basis for this criticism. Among those who have made the criticism are:

1. The Democratic party. This attack has come down to a demand for a sharp deceleration in the growth of defense spending proposed by the president and to a demand for abandoning proposed reductions in tax rates.

2. The New York bond dealers, typified by Henry Kaufman of Salomon Brothers. These have argued that the budget deficits will cause the bond markets to be flooded with government loan issues, which will keep interest rates up. Much of this argument sounds like special pleading from the bond dealers, who are concerned that the value of their inventory will be undermined.

3. The business community, through some of its leading associations, such as the Business Roundtable. There is a belief that reduction of the budget deficits will lead to lower interest rates.

Let me say at the outset that the problem of mounting government deficits has to be tackled because it amounts to a diversion of the nation's savings into the hands of government. Government deficits enrich current taxpayers by robbing future taxpayers (that is why deficits are so hard to cure; no one is around to speak for future taxpayers). So deficits are bad. They must be dealt with. The way to deal with them is further to restrict the growth of federal spending, which has risen to ever higher proportions of the national income of America [from 17 percent of gross national product in 1965 to 23 percent in 1982].

That having been said, let us address the allegation that rising deficits, or high deficits, or both, will somehow bring about a substantial increase, or indeed any significant increase, in the rate of interest.

This is the argument used by Volcker and by Burns to attempt to justify their failure to achieve monetary control and to bring about a reduction of interest rates. They allege that they suffer from the "burden" imposed on the Federal Reserve to finance federal government deficits and that this "burden" undermines their ability to control the growth of money.

This argument is wrong. Hence, it cannot be used by the Fed to justify its failures; nor can it be used by the critics of the administration to allege that interest rates are high, at any particular point of time, because of the size of the federal budget deficit.

Why is the argument wrong?

1. *Interest rates rise when inflation rises and when money growth rises.* Look at the first chart on page 302. This chart shows that since 1963, a period of nineteen years, the inflation rate and interest rates have moved together. That is the long-term picture.

In the short term, we know that this experience has been translated into a reaction where interest rates rise on news of increased money supply. Why? Because an increase in money supply means a threat of more inflation. Interest rates jump on news of a rise in money. They fall on news of a decline in money.

In 1981 we had sharply rising money (pointing to rising inflation) between December 1980 through April 1981. Interest rates rose. From April to October money was static; interest rates fell. From October 1981 to January 1982 money rose sharply, and so did interest rates.

2. *Interest rates rise with inflation for a very good reason. Lenders want their money back in real dollars, not in depreciated dollars.*

For years, during the 1970's, lenders lost money because they were not awake to the fact that they were being robbed by borrowers, who were giving them back inflation-depreciated dollars for the good

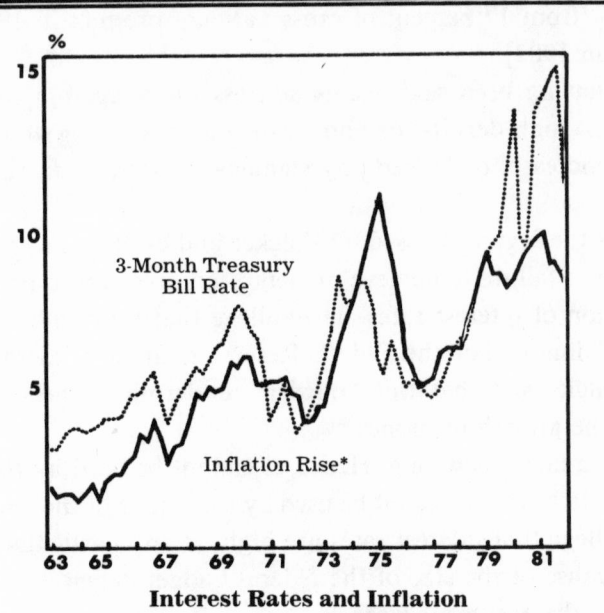

Interest Rates and Inflation

*Growth from year earlier in GNP deflator
Plotted quarterly

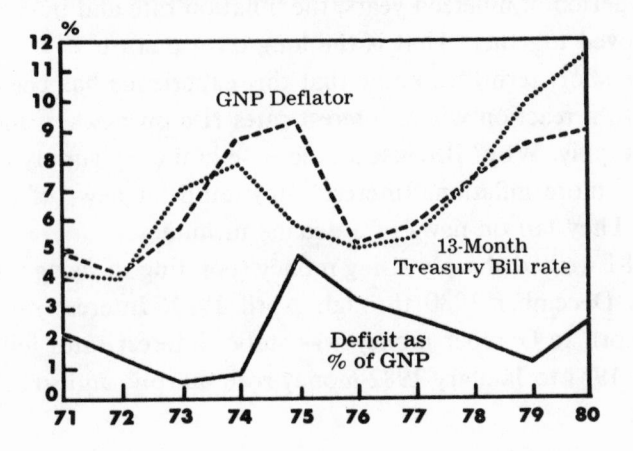

dollars they had lent. Nowadays everyone on Wall Street and in the financial markets across the nation knows that inflation is caused by excessive money growth. So every Friday night, when the money figures come out and show a rise, bond prices drop (meaning interest rates rise).

Sometimes, there will be a lag between a fall in inflation and one in interest rates. That is more typically so nowadays than was the case in the 1970's. The reason is that today's participants in the financial markets have had their confidence in the future value of money smashed and undermined by the record of failure in monetary control over the previous fifteen years.

3. *There is no relationship which can be identified between the budget deficit and the growth of money, inflation, or interest rates.*

Look at the second chart on page 302. It relates inflation (the GNP deflator—the price index of the gross national product), the Treasury bill rate, and the federal deficit. From 1971 through 1980, the deficit moved in the *opposite direction* from inflation and interest rates.

4. *The Federal Reserve is not in fact "burdened" with the need to finance deficits.*

The table on page 304 shows that the Fed has not had any consistent policy of purchasing government debt. In the last three years of really roaring inflation (1979–81 inclusive) the Fed has hardly purchased any government debt (bonds, Treasury bills) at all. In other words, it has not monetized any significant proportion of the budget deficit in recent years. Over the whole period of eleven years shown in the table, there has hardly been any year in which the Federal Reserve's purchases of federal debt have amounted to a row of beans. They have been tiny in relation to the deficit or the money supply.

Because the Fed has not thus monetized any significant amount of the government debt, that has not been a factor in inflation. The real problem has been that the Federal Reserve *itself* has been creating excessive amounts of money.

5. *The Federal deficit has been very small in relation to GNP and will remain so.*

Look again at the table on page 304. The third column shows that the "unified" budget deficit in relation to gross national product has exceeded 2.9 percent in only two years, 1975 and 1976. The "total"

	Unified budget deficit* $ billions	Federal debt purchased by Federal Reserve $ billions	Unified deficit as percentage of GNP	Total federal budget deficit* as percentage of GNP
1971	− $23.0 billion	$7.8 billion	2.1%	2.2%
1972	− 23.4	5.8	2.0	2.1
1973	− 14.9	3.7	1.1	1.2
1974	− 4.7	5.5	0.3	0.4
1975	− 45.2	4.3	2.9	3.6
1976	− 66.4	9.7	3.9	4.5
1977	− 57.9	10.3	2.3	2.9
1978	− 48.8	10.1	2.3	2.8
1979	− 27.7	0.7	1.1	1.7
1980	− 59.6	5.3	2.3	2.9
1981	− 57.9	3.6	1.4	2.8
1982				3.8
1983				3.1
1984				2.6
1985				2.0
1986				1.7
1987				1.3

Source: Harris Bank and *Economic Report of the President, February 1982*, p. 98.

*"Unified" budget deficit includes all items passed by Congress. The "total" federal budget deficit also includes so-called off-budget expenditures such as federal government loans and guarantees.

budget deficit exceeded 3 percent in only two of the last ten years— also 1975 and 1976. And they were years of the worst recession since the 1930's up to that time. They were also years in which interest rates *fell* sharply.

One powerful driving force for the future growth of the country is the tax cuts that are included in President Reagan's Economic Recovery Act. These tax reductions have not yet had any significant effect because their more positive results have still been overwhelmed by the effects of past inflation and built-in tax increases. It will not be until fiscal 1984 that "bracket creep" will finally be arrested.

The problem of high interest rates is not the result of the federal budget deficits; the problem is and always has been the failure of monetary control by the Federal Reserve. Built-in inflationary expectations and the cynicism about the Federal Reserve which has grown up are the source of the high interest rates.

6. *The deficit will be a worse problem if the president's tax cuts are rescinded.*

In 1982 the American economy is going through an agonizing adjustment to a drop in inflation. That inflation was caused by the inflationary policies of Nixon, Burns, Ford, Carter, Miller, and Volcker. The problem of America is not Reaganomics but Nixonomics, Burnsonomics, Fordonomics, and Carternomics. They were the instigators of today's crippling inflation and today's high interest rates. Volcker has given us more financial instability than the United States has ever known in peacetime.

Between 1945 and 1965, a period of twenty years, total federal government outlays (spending) rose from $92.7 billion to $118 billion. This was an increase of 27 percent over twenty years, or less than 1 percent a year. In the next five years—the years of Johnson's sway over federal spending—there was a rise of 66 percent, something like five times the rate of increase in the previous twenty years. Under Nixon-Ford, federal spending rose by 150 percent, or about twice as fast as in the already hectic Johnson spending surge. Nixon-Ford was followed by a rise of more than 60 percent again in Carter's four years. Nixon-Ford and Carter were the big spenders since World War II. They made Johnson and Kennedy look like amateurs.

The Vindication Of Monetarism—Interest Rates Collapse

In the September quarter 1982, beginning in early July, interest rates in the United States collapsed—just as the critics of the Fed in the U.S. Treasury and in the Shadow Open Market Committee had said they would.

Persistence with a policy of gradual restraint on money growth culminated in an extraordinary decline in interest rates between June and September, accompanied by the huge bull market in the stock exchanges during August, September, and October of 1982.

This collapse of interest rates was not accompanied by any decline in the rate of the federal budget deficit; if anything the deficit widened.

What happened was a total vindication of the monetarist theory which had stated all along that if the Fed persisted in reducing the rate of money growth this would lead to a reduction of inflation and this in turn would lead to a wholesale reassessment of the relative desirability of investing in financial assets, as compared with "real" assets.

By early October 1982, interest rates generally were lower than when President Reagan came to power in January 1981. The prime rate was about 21 percent in January 1981; it was 13 percent in early October 1982. The yield on long-term Treasury bonds was about 14 percent in January 1981; it was 11 percent in early October 1982. The yield on 90-day Treasury bills was nearly 15 percent in January 1981; it was 7.5 percent in early October 1982.

This amazing collapse of interest rates and the accompanying huge bull market in stocks, which pushed the Dow Jones industrial average up from just over 800 in June to over 1000 in early October, were the complete answer to those who had argued there would be no substantial reduction in interest rates until the federal budget deficit was eliminated.

 *What Should We Do with the Fed?*

I have been through the Fed's actions for the last fifteen years in detail. There is one compelling and in my view unanswerable conclusion: the Fed has exercised a malign influence on the economy of this country. It has failed to indicate any serious intention of mending its way. Its intervention in the financial markets of America over the last decade and a half has resulted in:

1. Persistently excessive money growth.

2. This has led to persistent accelerating inflation. The peak of every inflationary cycle has been higher than the peak of the previous cycle, and the trough of each cycle has been higher than the previous trough.

3. Major elements in the American financial system have been destroyed by controls over interest rates. The whole thrift industry has been gravely undermined by interest rate controls under Regulation Q. The commercial banks have suffered large inroads into their business because of their inability to offer competitive products. The result has been the explosive growth of commercial paper and the money market mutual funds.

4. The financial strength of American private corporations has been seriously undermined, owing to the combination of inflation and excessive rates of taxation, which have led to a bleeding of the profitability of corporate America. In turn, American corporations have become ever more deeply indebted and their debt has become ever shorter in term. A very seriously unstable financial situation has thus developed.

These are the major consequences of the Federal Reserve's activities in monetary control and in regulation of the financial services industry.

Critical Weakness of American Corporations

Erich Heinemann and Charles Lieberman, the economists at the Morgan Stanley Bank, said of the crisis in the finances of corporate America on February 26, 1982, in the bank's weekly review *Money and the Economy:*

> Three years of negligible real economic growth and high interest rates have significantly undermined corporate balance sheets. [As is evident in figures 1 and 2 below and on page 309] profit margins have declined dramatically from a recent peak of 6.0 percent in the third quarter of 1979 and about 5 percent through the mid-1970's to just 3.7 percent in the most recent quarter for which data are available.
>
> The level of profits [in 1981–82] is virtually unchanged, in nominal dollars, from 1978 levels and therefore is down sharply in real terms. Thus, the entire growth of corporate cash flow since 1978 has come from depreciation.
>
> Corporate cash flow, as a percentage of fixed business investment, also included in Figure 1, measures the ability of firms to finance internally their capital needs. After hovering near

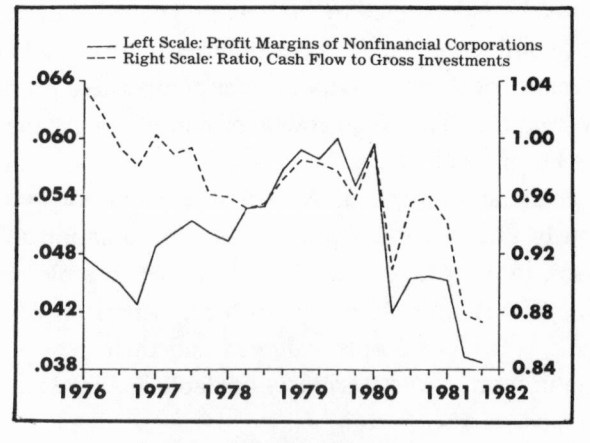

Profitability Has Declined...

Sources: Federal Reserve Board; Econalyst Data Base; Morgan-Stanley Research

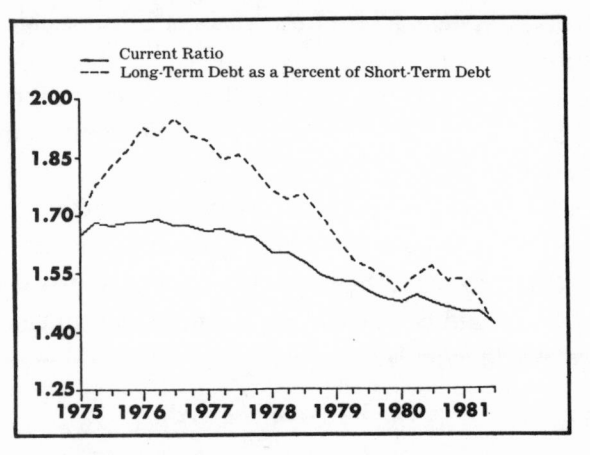

...and Balance Sheets Have Deteriorated Accordingly

Source: Federal Reserve Board; Econalyst Data Base; Morgan-Stanley Research

100 percent in the mid-1970's, this measure has since deteriorated with a sudden, rapid erosion appearing in the most recently available data. In the third quarter of 1981, corporations managed to fund only 87 percent of their investment needs internally from cash flow, the lowest level in almost a decade. The impact of the reduction in corporation profitability is captured in Figure 2, which provides measures of balance sheet deterioration. The current ratio, the ratio of current assets to current liabilities, and a useful proxy for working capital, has declined almost continuously since 1976. Some improvement occurred after the 1974 recession, but the erosion since then has been dramatic, particularly in the most recent quarters.

The composition of the corporate sector's liability structure also provides clear evidence of deterioration. The ratio of long-term debt to short-term debt declined throughout the past decade, achieving a new low in the most recent period. In the early 1970's, long-term debt was just over twice as large as short-term debt. Today, this ratio is down to 1.42. Thus, not only are corporations less liquid today and more highly leveraged, they are also more exposed to fluctuations in interest rates, since a more significant portion of their liabilities are short-term.

The result has been an increase in the vulnerability of corporations to failure and an increased vulnerability of the whole corporate sector to major collapse. Among the indicators of the extraordinary weakness of the system, after fifteen years of irresponsible monetary policy, were:

1. The number of commercial and industrial bankruptcies, as measured by Dun and Bradstreet, was up 50 percent from the comparable period of 1981.

2. Failures of going business concerns by the middle of 1981 had risen to over 60 per 10,000 commercial and industrial firms listed by Dun and Bradstreet, the highest ratio in nearly two decades. By March 1982 it could be judged that the ratio was up to the highest level since World War II.

Do We Need the Fed?

By its actions, the Fed has, over the last fifteen years, undermined confidence in money and undermined confidence in the conduct of monetary policy. Its actions were a dominant, if not *the* dominant, factor in the high level of real interest rates which applied early in 1982.

It could be argued we need some institution to provide a lender of last-resort facility, a sort of insurance policy for the financial services industry. But that function can be carried out by any number of institutions. We do not need a central bank for that. The Federal Deposit Insurance Corporation (FDIC) or the Federal Savings and Loan Insurance Corporation (FSLIC) are insurance institutions that were set up to provide insurance to depositors. Unfortunately in the case of the FSLIC, it is evident that its reserves may not be equal to the task of refinancing the collapse of the American thrift industry under the weight of interest rate escalation caused by the policies of the Federal Reserve. The federal government may have to provide substantial sums from its general revenues to add to the insurance reserves that have been built up over the years to protect the depositors in the thrifts. In the event of a similar disaster overtaking American commercial banks, similar federal government intervention would be needed.

It may be that there is no realistic prospect of a collapse of a series of major commercial banks. That is certainly the most likely outcome—they will survive. But the commercial banks have given many hostages to fortune in the form of major loans to communist and Third World countries. In recognition of this fact, among others, Moody's on March 22, 1982, issued a long and damning report on the financial condition of America's banks, pointing to the damage inflicted on the banks by the previous twenty years of regulation and inflation, the very matters reported on at length in Chapter 9. As a result of the review made by Moody's, the rating service downgraded the rating on the senior long-term debt of the following banks from Aaa to Aa: BankAmerica Corporation, Chase Manhattan Corporation, Chemical New York Corporation, Continental Illinois Corporation, First Bank System, Inc., Manufacturers Hanover Corp., Mellon National Corporation, National City Corporation, and Northwest Bancorporation.

That Moody's survey of the state of American banking was a pointer to a real danger to the financial stability of America which existed in early 1982. Evidently major banks were not as sound as they might appear to the untutored eye. Some form of insurance might be needed to prevent a collapse of one or more of these banks from creating undue destruction.

But there is no need for a central bank to exist in order to carry out this narrow function of insurance. It can be carried out separately. The insurance premiums can be paid over to an institution like the FDIC, and the issue can be left there. Without the inflation that the Fed has caused over the last fifteen years there would be no need for the massive bailout of the American thrift industry which is taking place.

Do we need the central bank for any other purpose? The Federal Reserve has financed a small part of the federal government's debt needs over the years, but this, as we have seen, has been a small proportion of the total debt issued by the federal government, and consequently, a small adjustment of federal borrowing programs would end the need for any such accommodation. So we don't need the Fed to finance the federal government. Indeed, given the extreme difficulty experienced in controlling the growth of government spending, it would be most desirable to remove from the hands of ambitious politicians the temptation to be able to get some easy money quickly.

So we don't need a central bank to provide "lender of last resort" facilities to the banks or to any other financial institution. Those facilities can be provided separately. The trend in America today is in any case toward the avoidance of all such involvement in "lender of last resort" stunts. The money market mutual funds have no insurance at all. They are insured simply by virtue of the fact that they lend very short and match their lending and borrowing very closely. The commercial banks are perennially trying to devise ways of getting out of becoming involved in giving reserves to the central bank (see below). The commercial paper market has no "lender of last resort" facility. Nor do the huge Eurodollar markets. It may be desirable to oblige these various markets, through their participants, to pay some sort of insurance premium in the event that one or more of their number behave so stupidly as to go bankrupt. But we certainly do not need a central bank to carry out this function.

One of the most dynamic banks in the country is Merrill Lynch. Where does it fit into the mold of the Federal Reserve's pattern of controls? The answer is it does not fit in. Nor does Shearson–Amex, nor Bache–Prudential, nor Sears, and so on. Maybe these big financial institutions will go broke. So be it. They will not drag the nation down with them. There have always been business failures.

The Banks Are Constantly Trying to Get Out of the Fed's Grip

Not only have Federal Reserve controls over interest rates undermined the whole thrift industry, but the existence of Federal Reserve powers to demand the payment of reserves on certain types of deposits has also encouraged an explosive growth of "nonreservable" transactions, such as Eurodollars, overnight repurchase agreements, money market mutual funds, and commercial paper. These transactions have been devised primarily to escape the Fed's profit, price, and reserve controls.

One reason for the constant search by banks for new means of evading the Fed's reserve requirements is that the banks are paid no interest on their reserves. That is the reason, in turn, why the Fed makes such fantastic profits, 90 percent of which are turned over to the U.S. Treasury. In fiscal year 1981 the Fed made a profit of $14.1

billion. That is a very big profit. It is not a profit in the sense of a return on business capital or enterprise but is rather a discriminatory tax on the members of the Federal Reserve System. It is a very big tax and a solid source of revenue to the federal government.

Naturally the banks constantly try to evade payment of the tax. And that is why they are constantly inventing new financial instruments which will fall outside the reserve requirement.

This constant search for new ways of evading the Federal Reserve power of taxation through nonpayment of interest on mandatory reserves introduces yet more distortions into the financial system. Thus, the money market mutual funds pay no reserves tax because they are not obliged to hold reserves with the Fed. No reserves tax is payable on Eurodollars, an immense market which has escaped the taxing power of the Fed because the Eurodollar deposits are lodged with foreign banks or overseas branches of U.S. banks.

Lately another avenue for escape has developed. Under the new CHIPS system (clearinghouse interbank payments system) a customer can make a payment from an offshore account (an account in an overseas branch of a U.S. bank, for example) and assure the recipient that "good funds" will be available that day. This means that offshore accounts have all the flexibility and liquidity of domestic accounts. And dollar accounts held anywhere in the world can be used as money in the United States, with the same ease and speedy clearance facilities as if they were in a domestic U.S. bank branch.

This development has the same effect as repurchase agreements. Banks save reserve requirements, and their customers escape interest rate ceilings. Under the repurchase agreement, the bank will sell a security overnight to a customer. This means the customer is getting some return on overnight money. It also means that his balance at the bank is wiped out for that night, and consequently, the bank's required reserves payment to the Fed is reduced. Banks are actively seeking to expand their business in repurchase agreements into "retail" RP's, whereby smaller customers can be drawn into the system. This allows the banks to compete in the rate they can offer customers for what is in effect demand money, in competition with the likes of the money market mutual funds that have been able to offer far higher rates than the banks are legally permitted to offer.

What I am describing here is the reality of U.S. finance—namely, that a variety of expedients have been created to escape any control by the Fed and to make it difficult, if not impossible eventually, for the Fed to force the banks to hold the reserves they would otherwise be obliged to hold. A concerted effort is being made by the banks to counterattack the controls they have suffered from, while money market funds and new megabanks like Merrill Lynch, Sears, Shearson–Amex, and others get off free and clear, paying none of the hidden taxes that have been levied on the banks.

Have you ever heard of such a mess?

Now look at the table on page 315 to see how the banks and money market mutual funds have expanded to get out from under the stifling impact of Federal Reserve interest rate and other regulations.

Between 1975 and 1981 there has been a drastic change in the rate of growth of "traditional" deposit forms and the "new wave" forms. Over this six-year period, total demand deposits and "other checkable" deposits at the banks have risen by only 22 percent; total savings deposits and small and large time deposits have risen by only 20 percent. All these categories are subject to Federal Reserve regulatory controls. Now look at the tremendous expansion of overnight repurchase agreements, Eurodollar accounts, commercial paper, and money market mutual funds. This group of transactions, all designed to get around Federal Reserve controls, has risen by 446 percent in five years. With the advent of electronic funds transfers, through computer links and satellites, this category of transactions will expand even more rapidly.

It is a largely unregulated sector, with no reserve requirements. It represents a vote of "no confidence" in the Fed's controls and interest rate ceilings.

Is there an answer? The answer is clearly to abandon all Federal Reserve price controls, for that is what they are. The Fed has attempted to put controls on the price of money—to split the market for money into myriad parts, with fixed prices for different types of money. The institutions that are subject to the controls and can get out of them will do so. This is obviously the route being taken by the major commercial banks of America. Those that cannot get out of the controls and are hopelessly stuck in the morass of unprofitability

The Boom in "Nonreservables"
$ Million

	1975	1981	% Increase
1. Demand Deposits and Other Checkable Deposits	$208.3 mil.	$254.2 mil.	22%
2. Savings Deposits, Small Time and Large Time Deposits	1,237.5	1,482.9	20
3. Overnight Repurchase Agreements (RP's); Money Market Mutual Funds; Euro-dollars; Commercial Paper	68.9	375.9	446

NOTE:

The first two categories are subject to reserve requirements by the Federal Reserve and are also in most cases subject to interest rate controls by the Federal Reserve.

The growth of these two categories has been stunted. The effects have been to deprive the banks of previously cheap sources of deposits and at the same time to frustrate the availability of cheap loans based on such deposits.

In the place of the growth of these "reservable" and controlled deposit sources, the banks have gone to other sources, including overnight repurchase agreements and Eurodollars. Outside the banking system, money market mutual funds and commercial paper have boomed as sources of corporate finance and as repositories for deposits.

Under President Reagan, the process of increasing regulation has been temporarily and perhaps permanently blocked. As a result, we must expect that there will be a still more explosive growth of "nonreservable" and uncontrolled deposits and loans.

However, this development does not mean that the Fed's ability to control the growth of the money supply has been materially weakened. This is because the link between the monetary base and the money stock remains very strong—through the money multiplier. The link between the money stock and the gross national product also remains very strong—through the velocity of money.

and even pending bankruptcy—like the thrifts (savings banks and savings and loan associations)—are fighting against freedom for the commercial banks. But this is a losing battle. Bankruptcy will overtake the institutions that cannot compete.

What is the Fed's answer to this problem? As I indicated in Chapter 10, quoting from Anthony Solomon, president of the New York Fed, its answer is: "Give us still more power to put the institutions outside our ambit of control under our control." That is always the answer of bureaucrats who find their controls not working. They want more controls.

What effect would this have on the ordinary American? Today the ordinary American can put his money into a money market mutual fund and get a return not much worse than that which is available to a very rich man who can afford to put $100,000 or so at a time into the funds. In the past the man with $100,000 could get a high return on his money, but the small man had to be content with no interest or a very tiny rate of interest. Today the small man has a chance to get a big return on his money—or at least a competitive return. Interest rate controls on savings banks and savings and loan associations meant that small depositors were putting their money in and wealthy depositors were able to borrow from these institutions, at rates of interest which were, after inflation, very often *negative.*

Seen in this light, the development of the new financial institutions like the mutual funds represents a heartening example of what the free market system can do to ensure a more equitable and vital society.

Abandon All Fed Interest Rate Controls and Other Regulations

The pace of technical change in banking is such that the system will not permit Fed interest rate controls and other regulations to work without further grave distortions and inefficiencies in the nation's finances. At present there are barriers on the interstate movement of big banks. They may not take deposits from outside their base geographical area. Yet these banks today are decreasingly dependent on ordinary deposits as they used to be thought of. Major

New York banks today *buy* about 85 percent of the money they subsequently lend out. Because of the breakdown of the whole apparatus of noninterest-bearing deposits, through inflation and the growth of alternative outlets such as the money funds, the commercial banks have to *buy* the overwhelming share of their deposits. These deposits no longer come in the door through the traditional apparatus of branch banking. Millions of Americans throughout the country today put their money into money funds or other financial instruments such as certificates of deposit and hardly visit "the bank" at all. They make their deposits to an institution that may be thousands of miles away. They may never see its office. They have a checkbook that they get through the mail. If they want cash, they can go to an automatic teller machine operated by a bank or by a credit card company.

I detect a rapid decline of interest among New York commercial banks in the idea of buying interstate banks, even if they were allowed to. Events have passed by the small bank with a few branches, protected by geographically restrictive laws against the intrusion of "out-of-state" banks.

The major money center banks have already set the pattern of future development by their diversifications out of traditional banking through the bank holding company medium, using worldwide new communications networks and the establishment of "quasi banking" operations throughout the United States. Undoubtedly, major money center banks will look for acquisitions should the government ever get around to permitting formal legal movement of banks across interstate boundaries, for the purpose of gathering deposits. But the major banks seem to be leaping right over this barrier, toward a new world of national and international financial services, linked with computer and communications facilities, which permit rapid clearance of millions and millions of transactions across state, national, and international boundaries. The small local, state, or county banks that have proliferated in thousands across America may simply be passed by in the move toward a completely new national and international financial services industry, in which the credit card, in one form or another, is the basis for the consumer's actions and where the gathering of deposits is carried out by national and international advertising and soliciting, not through the medium of the local brick and mortar branch bank system.

The money funds have taught Americans that no matter where they live they can obtain a top rate of interest on their money and at the same time have the freedom of writing checks or getting cash. The Merrill Lynch Cash Management Account (their trademark) has shown Americans across the nation that they can have someone look after every free cent of cash they possess, ensuring that they get a top return, while through the use of a nationwide checkbook (and a Merrill Lynch computer system) and a nationwide credit card, cash is always instantly available.

In all this, where is the Federal Reserve? The answer is that it has been left far behind. Despite the attempt, in the 1980 Monetary Control Act, to expand the power of the Fed over thousands upon thousands of depository institutions not previously under its direct control, its leverage over the financial services industry is necessarily declining. The controls that it maintains over interest rates and reserve requirements must necessarily decline, as the nonbank financial services companies (Merrill Lynch, Shearson–Amex, Sears, National Steel) and money center banks' subsidiaries (Manufacturers Hanover Leasing, Manufacturers Hanover Mortgage Company, Manufacturers Hanover Commercial Corporation, and Manufacturers Hanover Consumer Services) simply walk around the central bank's attempts at control.

The retention of interest rate controls, of controls over interstate banking and over the diversification of banks into the securities industry simply means that the more feeble elements in the banking industry as it presently exists will die on the vine while the more energetic elements work out ways of moving around the Fed controls into a new world of massive new growth.

This process makes Fed bureaucrats very nervous, as they can see their power being reduced. Consider the following quotation from Anthony Solomon, president of the New York Federal Reserve, in the 1981 annual report of the New York Fed:

There is a question as to whether any legislation would be desirable to deal with the effects of innovation on monetary policy. The Federal Reserve Board's proposal to impose reserve requirements on checkable money fund accounts can be accepted on competitive equity grounds alone. But to be effective from a monetary targeting point of view, reserve requirements would probably also have to be extended to the sweep accounts [the Merrill Lynch Cash Management Account type of account] and perhaps to other instruments. Imposition of reserve requirements on sweep accounts could prove to be a complicated and contentious matter.

In any case, incrementalism in regulation often seems to result in a chase, in which the markets seek to keep ahead of the regulators. This was true in the 1960's, when the regulators had to apply Regulations D and Q to new types of instruments successively, in an earlier effort to protect monetary policy from the eroding effects of financial innovation.

Perhaps for the present, the clearest point that emerges is simply the need for us to be aware of the problems that innovations are creating for the coherence of the monetary targeting approach. *The issues raised by this process are, I submit, of substantially more fundamental importance than the relatively technical matters that have been receiving much attention recently, such as contemporaneous reserve accounting and the design of our approach to adjustment borrowing at the discount window* [my italics].

The answer is not to give the Fed more powers of regulation. The answer is for the Fed to face the fact that its operating procedures are obsolete.

It is also unfortunately very clear that the Fed has failed since the so-called watershed of October 6, 1979, to undertake changes in its operating procedures which would permit monetary policy to work more effectively. Experience shows that fundamental failures in its management of monetary policy have been the cause for the Fed's failure in that field—not a lack of control over the financial institutions of America. There, the Fed's actions over the years have laid waste vast areas of those very institutions it was supposed to nurture and protect.

The experience of monetary policy administration in America since October 6, 1979, has led to an utter lack of faith in the Federal Reserve in the financial markets.

The Fed's scope for monetary policy change is limited. There is little chance of its being able to revert to the practices of the past—the long period up to October 6, 1979, when very narrow control over the federal funds rate was the dominant aim of policy. All the stated public intentions of the Fed to meet monetary growth targets in the period preceding October 6, 1979, were mere camouflage. After telling lies about its intentions for so long, it is hardly surprising that the Fed finds it difficult to get the financial markets to believe in the purity of its intentions in the world of 1982.

The fundamental admission made on October 6, 1979, was that during the preceding thirty or forty years the Fed had *not* been attempting to control the growth of money but had been trying to stabilize the rate of interest on federal funds.

There has been *some* reform since October 6, 1979. The federal funds rate is nowadays usually allowed to fluctuate within a range of four or five percentage points instead of being locked down to a range of one half of one percentage point, as was the case in the long years of failure preceding October 1979.

But there has been only a very *limited* reform of the Fed's operations. The Fed refuses to embrace other important reforms.

Over the last fifteen years we have seen time and again the tangled thread of manipulation of money for blatant political ends. We have seen the "pumping up" of the money supply in 1968, 1972, 1976, and 1980. We have seen Burns and Martin and Miller and Volcker abandoning stable policy for short-term electoral advantage. We have seen the Federal Reserve's powerful and successful counter-attack against the imposition of money growth targets by the Congress. We have read the reports of the House Banking Committee's Subcommittee on Domestic Monetary Policy in which bitter disillusion was expressed about the Fed's failure to follow what seemed then—and what certainly is today—the logical path of ensuring a stable, steady declining growth path for money. We have read all the explanations and justifications by the Fed for its persistent failures to control money growth. We have seen the Fed exposed in October 1979 in the mammoth deception it had perpetrated—that the Fed was, in fact, giving top priority to the control of the monetary aggregates. Under the force of an inflationary and foreign exchange crisis in October 1979, a new Fed chairman, Paul Volcker, had to find an excuse for jettisoning interest rate targets, because those targets had been pushed to the limit by the Fed and had become an embarrassment *to the Fed*—not to America. We have read the many statements by the Fed since that time asserting its commitment to concentrate all its energies on the task of bringing about stable growth of money. But we have observed how in practice things have not worked out. There has been a high degree of latent interest rate targeting still taking place. Both interest rates and money growth have become more variable.

In 1974 William Poole (now a member of the Council of Economic Advisers) was the senior economist in the Division of Research and Statistics at the Federal Reserve Board in Washington. In July of that year he resigned from the central bank and took a teaching position at Brown University, where he is professor of economics.

Poole is a leading analyst of the Federal Reserve. In his February 4 paper to the American Enterprise Institute Conference on "Current Issues in the Conduct of U.S. Monetary Policy," he strongly criticized the Federal Reserve's record since October 1979.

Among the key points he made were:

1. The Fed has failed to deliver the stability of money growth promised in October 1979.

2. The Fed has not made any changes in its operating procedures (apart from the greater willingness to allow the federal funds rate to fluctuate more widely) which would lead the financial community to believe in its sincerity.

3. The Fed has failed to institute contemporaneous reserve accounting or a market discount rate.

4. Such reforms would greatly enhance the credibility of Fed policy and would be a demonstration of sincerity. But they have not been attempted. In their absence, the Fed has to operate its policy on a day-to-day "hands on" basis. Were reforms of procedures carried out, the Fed could go on to a system which might be described as "adjustable autopilot."

5. As a result, many people do not believe the Fed has even embraced the elements of "practical monetarism," as outlined in this book, and this lack of belief is apparent in the neurotic behavior of

the money markets as they react to every scrap of information about money growth.

Here is the answer to the question Why will the Fed not change? The answer is: Fed officials, from the chairman down to the operators on the Desk in New York, have *too much to lose.*

A Monetary Rule—Anathema to the Fed

It is not surprising that the Fed would fight against the imposition of an "adjustable auto pilot" system. This would be analogous to a system like the gold standard or the constitutional monetary rule as advocated in the *Economic Report of the President, February 1982.* Such a system would remove most of the Fed's discretionary power. It would amount to a tremendous reduction in the power of Fed officials. Why would they want to commit hara-kiri?

There is absolutely no evidence of any desire on the part of Fed officials to abandon the "hands on" approach to monetary "control." They have clung to this policy through years of bitter criticism from outside the Fed and through years of abysmal failure.

There is nothing surprising in this. The principal aim of the bureaucracies, their overriding need, is the maintenance of their own power. That is why government spending is so hard to cut. It is also why bureaucratic systems plunge relentlessly on to their own doom, as is currently the case with the worldwide communist economic system.

Do We Need a Central Bank?

Experience over the last fifteen years has shown that inflation has been made *much worse* by the policies initiated by the Federal Reserve. The Fed is feared as an unpredictable, undependable factor in the financial markets.

We would be far better off without it. Insurance of deposits in the financial services sector could, as I have already said, be carried by a separate insurance system, with an expanded FDIC or FSLIC. The Fed is already out of all foreign exchange dealings. It is only a small purchaser of government securities and should in any case buy no such securities, as part of any program of restoring fiscal responsibility in America. The ideal arrangement in America would be for a *zero growth of money* to be the rule, leaving any expansion in the transactions needs of the economy to be provided by the normal growth of velocity of money.

We would then return to a situation that existed during the first century and a half after independence in the United States: there would be no central bank. The absence of a central bank did not prevent the United States from enjoying amazing economic growth during that period. There have been long periods in other countries when they have not had a central bank and have prospered. The expansion of Hong Kong since the Second World War was carried out without a central bank. Two local banks issued their own bank-notes and were kept honest by mutual competition. The same went for Scotland during the eighteenth century.

Our experience in America in the last fifteen years has shown the central bank, the Fed, to have been a willing participant in the inflationary excesses that occurred. Fed officials were easily drawn into the pattern of monetary profligacy that played a leading role in the emergence of stagflation. The Fed did not demonstrate that resistance to political spendthrifts expected at the time it was established and for which it was granted such remarkable freedom from any external control.

The fundamental reason for this failure is that the Fed was never under any automatic external control. Its chairman is not subject to dismissal for his failures or to the limitation imposed by elections on the power of presidents. He does not have any financial limits on his actions. He is totally free from significant external controls on his actions. Not surprisingly, the Fed chairmen have taken the easy way out over the last fifteen years.

Some form of limitation must be imposed. The simplest of these would be to make the Fed a subdepartment of the U.S. Treasury. In that way, monetary policy would be integrated with the other economic policies of the administration, joining with tax, spending, import, tariff, export, and energy policies.

There is no sign that short of such reforms the Fed will ever grow into anything better than the impediment to harmonious inflation-free economic growth which it has become. It is incorrigible—end it.

Index